John Carroll

Past and Present

a description of persons and events connected with Canadian Methodism for the

last forty years

John Carroll

Past and Present
a description of persons and events connected with Canadian Methodism for the last forty years

ISBN/EAN: 9783337105198

Printed in Europe, USA, Canada, Australia, Japan

Cover: Foto ©ninafisch / pixelio.de

More available books at **www.hansebooks.com**

PAST AND PRESENT,

OR A

DESCRIPTION OF PERSONS AND EVENTS

CONNECTED WITH

CANADIAN METHODISM

FOR THE LAST FORTY YEARS.

BY A

SPECTATOR OF THE SCENES.

> "Come, let my Carper to his life now look,
> And find there darker lines than in my book.
> He findeth any—yea, and let him know,
> That in his best things there are worse things too!"
> — JOHN BUNYAN.

TORONTO:
PUBLISHED BY ALFRED DREDGE,
88 YONGE STREET.

1860.

TO THE

REVEREND ENOCH WOOD,

SUPERINTENDENT OF CANADIAN WESLEYAN MISSIONS

FOR THE LAST THIRTEEN YEARS;

AND

PRESIDENT OF THE CANADA CONFERENCE DURING THE LONG PERIOD
OF SEVEN YEARS,—FROM EIGHTEEN HUNDRED AND FIFTY-ONE TO EIGHTEEN
HUNDRED AND FIFTY-EIGHT,—WHOSE BROTHERLY AND INFLUENTIAL
PATRONAGE HAS ENCOURAGED HIM IN A BOLD AND UNTRIED
UNDERTAKING; AND WHOSE CARE AND
OVERSIGHT HAVE DIMINISHED ITS DEFECTS AND BLEMISHES,—THIS
LITTLE VOLUME IS RESPECTFULLY
INSCRIBED
BY THE APPRECIATING THOUGH HUMBLE
AUTHOR.

OTTAWA, April 3, 1860.

PREFACE.

About twelve years ago I was in the receipt, monthly, of the LADIES' REPOSITORY AND GATHERINGS OF THE WEST; and felt myself much interested in the *sketchy* and *memorial* part of it. I naturally thought, "Why should not similar memorials be preserved of what God has done by the instrumentality of Methodism in Canada?" During that year, at several intervals of leisure, mostly at night, after being wearied out with severe studies, a few of the following sketches, substantially, were thrown off—although without any definite decision about publication in any form. My occupation of an invalid station, about eight years later, afforded me leisure to add a few more; when all of those which related to *deceased* persons in my reminiscences, to the number of *twenty-six*, were given to the public in the columns of the CHRISTIAN GUARDIAN, over the signature of "A VOICE FROM THE PAST"—to test what reception matter of that description would receive. So far as I learned any thing about them, they were regarded with some favor. Relief from the full amount of *pulpit* work, about a year after, by the presence and labors, in my next station, of the REV. JAMES CAUGHEY, gave me time to retouch them; the rest I had by me; and I then arranged them pretty much in the order they now assume, with the persuasion that some day they might see the light. Mr. C—— encouraged me to have them published; still I hesitated, mostly because I thought they would scarcely make a sizable book. There the matter slumbered till the late Conference, when I fell in with WATSON'S TALES AND TAKINGS, and the notion possessed itself of my mind—more fully expounded in another place—of adding some sketches of *living* Ministers, and thus make out a medium volume. I was now pretty much decided to publish, if it met the approval of disinterested and judicious friends. This course was followed. The rest is known from my Circulars.

By those who can think of nothing being worthy of perusal but what relates to far distant times and scenes—aye, and those described too by some writer far away—such a volume about *Canadian* Methodism will be likely to be spurned. Still it has recurred to the writer:—What is literature, but a picture of manners? If we have pictures of other things, why not a picture of them? If a picture of manners in general, why not of Canadian manners? Or, why not have Canadian literature? If a picture of Canadian manners in general, why not that particular phase of them found in its *religious* society? And religious society within the pale of *Methodism;* or within the circle of its influence? Such a description would not necessarily ignore, much less disparage, what has been enacted within the operations of other evangelical communities (whom the Lord in mercy bless!) while it simply portrays what the writer happened to have witnessed.

Some of these incidents may seem very simple, if not trivial, to some minds. Still, are they not natural? And when nature is addressed, she will always respond. The arts of the *literatuer* the unpretending author knows nothing of; but he found by frequent recitation of parts of these incidents by the fire-side, that they always interested. He therefore concluded that what interested *the few* might also interest *the many* · and probably some outside of Methodism. For, "as in water face answereth to face, so the heart of man to man." "But you wrote the sketches merely to amuse people!" a serious brother exclaims. Not wholly so; but if I had, I would have done a good work in furnishing a book that was mirthful without being harmful, which, alas! cannot be said of all books of amusement. But I further aspired to the production of a work, which, while it was adapted to amuse the young people of our Methodist families, would reveal to them something of its heroic *animus*, and attach them more fully to its institutions; and aggressive, onward efforts. Was that wrong? And will our favored land and Church furnish no materials for such a book? Shame on the Canadian Methodist who says "NO"!

As to what relates to "matters personal," I refer the reader to the article "THE CONFERENCE AND THE CRAYONS." Some will have prejudged the writer's ability to accomplish creditably the task undertaken: to such our only answer is, the work must testify; it will give us pleasure if those who thus object will write a better.

Having written most of the articles at different periods and under the difficulties of interruptions, and some of them after the previous ones were sent to the press, there may be a want of congruity between some of its parts, as well as some repetitions; if so, we promise to correct and reduce them to greater conformity in a second edition, if a generous public buy up the present.

Such are some of the reasons for our presumption in attempting this piece of authorship. We have yet another, not before revealed. We hoped the avails of our publication might furnish us the means of educating liberally our two children, which we find our ministerial salary wholly unequal to. With this frank disclosure of our position and views, we shall patiently await the ordeal of criticism.

TO THE READER.

Every one has observed in reading, occasional mistakes of the Printer; such as a letter, a word, or a point misplaced. The wonder is, that such inaccuracies do not more frequently occur, considering the care which is necessary to procure perfect correctness, and the haste with which printing is often executed. The following ingenious and eloquent apology for faults of this kind is given in Peter Martyr's "Common-Places," a book which was published in the year 1574. The original spelling is preserved :—

"There is no garden so well trimmed but hath some weeds; no silver so well tried but hath some drosse; no wine so well fined but hath some leeze; no honie so well clarified but hath some dregs; finallie, no human action, but hath some defect: mervell not then, (good readers,) that this volume, consisting of so manie leaves, lines, and letters oftentimes varied, both in forme and matter, a fault or two doo escape; were the corrector's care never so great, his diligence never so earnest, his labour never so continual, his eies never so quick, his judgment never so sound, his memorie never so firm; brieflie, all his senses never so active and livelie. Such faults, therefore, as are passed, being but few in number, if it please you, in reading favourablie to amend."

CONTENTS.

PART I.

	PAGE.
Preliminary Annals,	9
The Old Framed Meeting House,	37
My Spiritual Father,	40
An Early Classmate,	44
An "Elect Lady,"	47
Sammy Richardson; or the Zealous Irishman,	50
One of my first Pastors,	55
A Nation Born in a Day,	56
A Canadian Camp-Meeting Thirty-five years ago,	62
"Father" Youmans,	66
One of our Supplies	68
"The Venerable Thomas Whitehead,"	73
The Two Soldier Preachers,	79
The Rev. Thomas Madden,	86
The Rev. James Wilson,	90
Rev. Franklin Metcalf,	95
Ezra Healy,	99
The Rev. Alexander Irvine,	103
The Outset,	106
"My First Circuit,"	110
My First Colleague,	114
An Estimate of Prindel,	121
An Old Fashioned Quarterly Meeting,	123
The Last Night of a Youthful Homicide,	127
Rev. William Smith,	134
Lorenzo Dow,	139
"Father Magraw,"	147
Bread Cast on the Waters,	152
Scene in a Ferry-Boat	157
Admonitory End of an Early Colleague,	160
My Fellow Candidates,	162

CONTENTS.

Traditionary Recollections,	169
Revival Coincidence,	180
Experiences of a Self-Taught Minister,	182
Genius in Poverty and Obscurity,	197
The Big Snow Storm,	203
Remarkable Answers to Prayer,	206
Though Reprehended, Still Remembered,	213
The Father of Canadian Missions,	220

PART II.

The Conference and the Crayons,	235
Father Corson,	242
Rev. Enoch Wood,	244
Rev. Samuel Rose,	246
Rev S. D. Rice,	247
Doctor Stinson,	248
Rev. H. Hurlburt,	250
Rev. James Brock,	252
Rev. S. Waldron,	254
"Father Wright,"	256
Rev. Henry Wilkinson,	258
Rev. Richard Jones,	260
Rev. William Tomlin,	261
Rev. James Masson,	263
Rev. Robert Robinson,	264
Rev. Edmund Sweet,	264
Rev. L. Warner,	265
Rev. E. B. Harper,	267
Rev. Wm. Pollard,	268
Rev. William Ryerson,	270
The "Two Philps,"	273
"The Two Colemans,"	275
Rev. James Musgrove,	275
Rev. Wellington Jeffers,	277
Rev. Thomas Jeffers,	279
Rev. Michael Fawcett,	279
Rev. John Gemley,	280
Rev. Lachlin Taylor,	282
Doctor Anson Green,	285
Rev. James Spencer,	289
Doctor Egerton Ryerson,	292
Doctor Ephraim Evans,	296

CONTENTS.

Rev. Sylvester Hurlburt,	300
Rev. Thomas Hurlburt,	301
Rev. Erastus Hurlburt,	304
Rev. James H. Bishop,	305
Rev. Jonathan Scott,	307
Rev. W. H. Poole,	309
Rev. President Nelles,	310
Rev. G. R. Sanderson,	314
Rev. Robert Cooney, D. D.,	316
Rev. I. B. Howard,	318
Rev. William McFadden,	320
Rev. C. Vandusen,	322
Rev. J. W. McCollum,	325
Rev. N. F. English,	227
Rev. R. A. Flanders,	328
Rev. Richard Whiting,	331

PAST AND PRESENT.

PART I.

PRELIMINARY ANNALS.

We had intended beginning our sketches with the article which will now succeed to this; but the wish of some subscribers to the book, communicated through an aged and estimable minister, whose judgment we greatly value, that I "would try and extend my 'RECOLLECTIONS' back to the time when the first Wesleyan Missionaries visited the banks of the St. Lawrence," has induced me to republish some sketches relating to Methodism and written on the very spot where it was first planted in the Province, published in the CHRISTIAN GUARDIAN in 1834—to which we append so much of Dr. Bang's History of the M. E. Church relating to Canada, as to make this compendious chain of Provincial Methodist History general and complete, down to the period from which our own *individual* "recollections" date. We extract now from the GUARDIAN :—

SKETCHES OF THE EARLY SETTLEMENT AND IMPROVEMENT
OF UPPER CANADA.

A few weeks since, we addressed a series of questions to the Methodist Ministers throughout the Province, to which we solicited answers, illustrating the early settlement, improvements, and local advantages of those parts of the Province which were within the bounds of their several circuits; embracing likewise a History of the establishment and progress of the Methodist Church. The Superintendent of the Matilda Circuit has commenced a sketch of the Townships in his field of labor, and we hope he will persevere until he has answered *all* our questions; and that his example will be followed by the preachers on every circuit in the Province:

MATILDA, August 24th, 1834.

Having no more to say on business, I employ the remainder of my sheet in answering the first four questions which you recently proposed.

This circuit is bounded on the north by the townships of South Gower, Mountain, Winchester, and other back settlements; on the east by the eastern part of the township of Cornwall; south by the river St. Lawrence; and west by the western part of the township of Edwardsburg—including within it part of the last mentioned township, Matilda, Williamsburg, Osnabruck, and part of Cornwall.

The part of this section of country immediately on the river, was settled as early as June, 1784. Its original settlers were principally disbanded revolutionary soldiers, belonging to Sir John Johnson's regiment, and of Scotch and German extraction, but most of the latter. The inhabitants of the back parts of the above mentioned townships, which have been settled at different periods from that time to this, are a mixture of almost all nations.

Some of the circumstances connected with the early settlement of this place, which I have learned from some of the *few remaining* first settlers, are rather amusing, and perhaps worthy of record. The first three years the settlers were kindly supplied with provisions by the Government: but as they had no roads, they were provided with two batteaux to each township, in which they used to convey their provisions from Montreal. Their method of serving out their rations was rather peculiar. Their plan was, to prevent the appearance of partiality, for the one who acted as commissary, either to turn his back, take one of the articles, and say, " Who will have this ?" or else the provisions were weighed, or assorted, and put into heaps, when the commissary went around with a hat, and received into it something which he would again recognise, as a button, a knife, &c.; after which, he took the articles out of the hat, as they came uppermost, and placed one upon each of the piles in rotation. Every person then claimed the parcel on which he found the article which he had thrown into the hat. As they had no mills for a long time, Government provided each township with a steel handmill which they moved from house to house: their first milling was done in Kingston. There was a great deal of simplicity and unanimity among the people at that period; but they were very little acquainted with true religion. They were much given to carousing and dancing.

" The agricultural and commercial advantages " of this part of the country are great. The fertility of the soil, and its contiguity to the river St. Lawrence, render it at once one of the most pleasing and prosperous parts of North America. Formerly, it is said, the inhabitants lumbered extensively; but of late years, since the timber in the immediate vicinity of the river has begun to be scarce, they have turned their attention more to agriculture; and the country seems to profit greatly by the change. Many of the persons in business, however, still lumber largely, and, it is said, successfully, back on the Nation and Ottawa rivers. The roads have been universally bad in the interior of this section, till the legislature began to take the subject into consideration, and to make appropriations. They are now in a state of rapid improvement.

It appears, from the best information I can obtain, that this part of the country was one of the first places in Upper Canada visited by a Methodist Preacher, which, from the Minutes, we find to be sometime in the year 1792. At that time, but two regular travelling preachers were sent, viz., Darius Dunham and William Losee. The first was sent from what was then called the Cataraque Circuit; the other was sent to this, which was then called the Oswegochie Circuit. This name it derived from an old Indian village, which formerly stood a little east of where the town of Ogdensburg, on the American side, now stands. What the extent of the circuit then was, I shall not pretend to decide; but it is probable that it included all the settlements in Upper Canada, east of Kingston, excepting those on the Ottawa, if, indeed, they were then in existence. It appears, however, that notwithstanding the Circuit was denominated from a place on the other side, that there were no appointments on that side: for, in fact, it seems, there were no settlements of white people on the south side of the St. Lawrence at that period. The circuit bore the name above mentioned, with the exception of one year, when I find it called the "Upper Canada Lower Circuit," till the year 1808, when it was called "Cornwall," from the town or township of that name within its borders. The propriety of the change in the name was suggested by the Rev. Joseph Sawyer, Presiding Elder, in Canada, for that year, who now, I am proud to say, resides on my circuit, and of whose counsel and communications I am happy to avail myself. The first ministers of the Gospel in these parts were of the Lutheran order; who came in shortly after the first settlement of the country, and who, it appears, knew and preached but little concerning the *power* of religion: for, according to the testimony of those who were converted to God, under the ministry of the early Methodist preachers, the people were greatly sunken in ignorance and vice. It is but just, however, to state, and I feel a pleasure in doing it, that it is said of a Mr. Swartsfager, who was then settled in Matilda and Williamsburg, that he was a person of exemplary morals, and that he used to defend the Methodists after their coming into the country, when he heard them unjustly aspersed; and also, that he was wont to say of their doctrine, that it was the doctrine of the Bible and of the Reformation, which had been too much lost sight of; but which had been revived by John Wesley. If I might be again permitted to digress, I could tell an amusing anecdote concerning this old gentleman and one of his parishioners. The person in question was an old German lady, whose children had been converted, and joined the Methodists. She thought because she had been baptized, and had partaken of the sacrament, that, therefore, she was a Christian; but her children told her that unless she was "born again," and knew her sins forgiven, she would be lost. At this she took great offence, and so excessive was her grief, that she undertook one day to make her complaint to her beloved pastor. Said she, "Mr. Swartsfager, my chiltren says that I must pe pourn akain, and know my sins forgiven!" To which the good man rejoined, "What now, mamma! have I been preaching to you so long, and you have not found that out yet?" He went to his rest a short time after the arrival of the Methodists.

You inquire in your seventh question, "By whom or what *agency* were Methodist Societies first formed?" The *agency*, I believe to have been that which has been employed since the commencement of the gospel dispensation: "the foolishness of preaching." The *person* honoured of God as the "Apostle" in the formation of the first churches, was the individual mentioned in my last—the Rev. William Losee. This appears from the Minutes for the year succeeding his first appointment, 1793, in which we find ninety members returned for this circuit. Hence, his labours must have been much prospered, considering the then scattered state of the settlements, and the comparatively limited period he had to stay with them, occasioned by the distance and difficulty of the way he had to travel, in coming from and returning to Conference, which was on horseback, by the way of Montreal.

Perhaps it would not be altogether irrelevant to give here a list of the names of the early preachers who laboured on this circuit, which my copy of the Minutes only allows me to carry down to the year 1812. It will be seen that Mr. Losee was the first Preacher appointed for this circuit, viz., in 1792; I find no appointment for 1793, but the people inform me that he continued the second year; in 1794-5, James Coleman; in 1796, Hezekiah C. Wooster; who, though I find no appointment in the Minutes for the circuit that year, was, I believe, re-appointed for 1797; in 1798, Samuel Coate; in 1799, Darius Dunham; in 1800, Joseph Jewel, James Heron; in 1801, William Anson, James Aikens; in 1802, for this and the Ottawa, Sylvanus Keeler, Seth Crowell, Nehemiah U. Tomkins; in 1803, Peter Van Est, Luther Bishop; in 1804, Thomas Madden; in 1805, Sylvanus Keeler, Nathan Bangs; in 1806, Gershom Pearce, William Case; in 1807, Daniel Pickett, I. B. Smith, C. Hurbert; in 1808, in which the circuit was abridged, and called Cornwall, William Snow; in 1809, Elias Pattie; in 1810, Bela Smith; in 1811, it appears to be included in the Augusta Circuit, and to which were appointed John Rhodes and John Reynolds; and in 1812, J. Rhodes, E. Cooper, S. Hopkins.

How affecting is the contemplation of the changes which the lapse of a few years have made in reference to those labourers! Some of them literally wore themselves out in their Master's cause, and died triumphant; some were driven by the embarrassments under which they laboured to retire from the itinerant field, and have either died or are now living in retirement; some few, I am sorry to say, have seceded from the Church, of whom, perhaps, some have made "shipwreck of faith;" but a few of them, thank God! are still upon the walls of our Zion, both in this country and the United States, in the faithful discharge of their important functions.

The "opposition" with which the first Methodist Preachers

had to contend in the discharge of their holy and benevolent work, was similar to that which has ever assailed the preachers and preaching of the Gospel, viz.: that arising from the natural hardness, enmity, and unbelief of the carnal mind. This was manifested by pointing the finger of scorn, calling opprobrious names, and, it is said, in some instances, by throwing stones at the Preacher, setting the dogs on his horse, and " hurraing for the Methodists."

Through the deficiency of particular information, I am unable to adduce and give the particulars of *many* " instances of remarkable conversion." But of these it appears there were not a few; for, to use some of the old people's own words, in reference to the conversions of that period: " They were ' cast out' powerful!" I have gleaned a few facts, however, upon this part of my subject. Perhaps I could not illustrate the character of the work in that day better than by giving a narrative of the conversion of a man and his wife, (whose house was the *first* home for the weary, way-worn servants of God, in the lower part of Matilda,) which was given to me yesterday by the old lady herself, who survives her husband, at present, under another name. Her first acquaintance with the Methodists originated from Mr. Losee's calling at the house, and asking her if she would not like to have the word of God preached in her house; to which she replied that she would, not being able to understand the Germans. Upon which she asked him what he was called; and having ascertained that he was a Methodist Preacher, she ran to the barn, to call her husband. Having told him that a Methodist was in the house, he expressed his surprise; and wished to know " how *he looked*." To which she replied, that " he looked like another man, but that he wanted an arm." To shorten my story, suffice it to say that the Preacher stopt to dinner; got acquainted, and left an appointment to preach, on his return from the lower part of his circuit, to which he was then going. And under his preaching, Mr. Wright, (for so he was called,) who had been a professor among the Baptists, before the Revolution, but had backslidden—and his wife, got awakened, and greatly concerned about the salvation of their souls. One Sabbath evening, having returned from a little quarterly meeting, he summoned courage to take up the cross of family prayer. The exercise of both their minds was great. *She* formed the resolution of spending the " live-long night " in prayer and watching; for, as she expressed it, " she was afraid of being in hell before morning." She strenuously adhered to her purpose; but spent the night in the most indescribable *agony*. She truly " drank the wormwood and the gall." The husband rose early from a restless bed, and asked her if she had found any relief. To which she replied, " No;" but expressed a determination, that if she went to hell, she would perish, " crying out for God." *He* went to the barn, not, as she supposed, to fodder his cattle, but to pour out his soul to God in prayer; and *she* repaired to the bed-room, and literally fell upon her face on the floor, and " poured out strong cries and tears to Him that was able to save her." Nor did she cry in vain: suddenly a flood of light and joy broke in upon her soul—she sprang upon her feet—leaped to the bed-room door—crying out to her eldest daughter to run immediately for her father.

The child instantly obeyed the command; and going to the stable, found him just getting out of the manger, where he had been at prayer, and coming to tell his wife the joyful news of the liberation of his own soul. His daughter, meeting him, exclaimed,—" Oh, daddy, come quick, I never saw mamma look so before in my life!" The husband and wife met at the door; and embracing each other, glorified God with a loud voice for what he had done for them. After walking across the floor several times, hand in hand, in inexpressible rapture, said Mr. Wright to his wife, " We do wrong to eat our morsel alone; let us go up and inform Mr. and Mrs. Doran, (a neighbouring man and his wife, both of whom were under conviction,) of what the Lord has done for us." Away they flew, like lightning; and got there just as the woman was preparing for breakfast. But no sooner had she seen them, and before they had spoken a word, discovering their unusual and heavenly appearance, than she threw herself into a chair, and began to weep bitterly on account of her sinful state; the husband, who was smoking in the chimney corner, threw down his pipe, and began to cry to God. They bound themselves under a promise, which was often made in those days, which was, not to eat, drink, or sleep, till God should liberate their souls. The man obtained liberty that night; and, I believe, the woman soon after. There being "four believers," a class was shortly organized, and Mr. Wright was appointed leader. And the work of the Lord began to revive powerfully. For, said the old lady, "There was not a prayer meeting at which there were not one or more conversions; and I used to count the days," continued she, "till the return of prayer meeting night, with the expectation of seeing souls brought to God." And pointing to the roof of the house, "Say, brother, there have been many and many souls converted to God under this same poor old shell!" She then mentioned the names of some of the old, influential members on the circuit who had obtained religion in her house. Your's truly,

J. CARROLL.

Dr. Bang's account, in his History of the Methodist Episcopal Church, supplements the information given above, inasmuch as it shows that Losee was in the country one year before his labouring in Matilda and its neighbourhood. Still, from the information I received from the old settlers, I believe Losee visited the banks of the St. Lawrence while yet an Exhorter, before he was received on trial by the Conference as a Preacher.* And, from the best evidence I can get, a

---

* Since writing this sentence, I find my opinion confirmed by the

relative of his, Joshua Losee, afterwards known as a distinguished exhorter, by the title of "Father Losee," was the first man converted in Canada, under the labors of the Methodists; and it was his (Mr. L.'s) interest in the country that led to his designation to it as a missionary, by Bishop Asbury. We now quote from Dr. Bangs:

Upper Canada was visited by William Losee, a member of the New York Conference, in the year 1791. He went through the wilderness of the western part of the State of New York, suffering many privations and hardships, and crossed the lower part of Lake Ontario, to Kingston. In attempting to form a circuit along the banks of the Lake and of the Bay of Quinte, he found here and there an individual who had heard the Methodist Preachers in England and the United States. By these he was cordially received; and he succeeded in forming a circuit, and establishing a few classes. The next year, Darius Dunham was sent to Canada. He and brother Losee extended their labours from the Bay of Quinte down the banks of the St. Lawrence, forming what was called the Oswegotchie Circuit; and the next year, there were returned on the Minutes of Conference, as the fruit of their labours, one hundred and sixty-five members of the church. From this time, the work of God went on gradually in Canada, until it eventuated in one of the most glorious revivals in religion we have on record in these modern days. It will be noticed more particularly in the proper place." (Vol. I. p. 322.)

In volume *second*, he resumes, " In Upper Canada, a gracious revival had commenced in 1797, chiefly through the

---

following, from the Rev. Mr. Case's Jubilee Sermon:

"Circumstances induce me to believe, and that belief is strengthened by a statement I heard the Rev. Freeborn Garrettson make, that in 1790, while Losee was a local preacher, Mr. Garrettson, at the solicitation of Losee, authorized and recommended him to visit Canada; and under his authority he preached in Elizabethtown, Augusta, Matilda, and, perhaps, in some townships in Bay of Quinte."

instrumentality of Calvin Wooster, whose fervency of spirit led him forth in the work of reformation, in a remarkable manner and with singular success. In company with Samuel Coate, he volunteered his services as a missionary to this distant field of labor, and after enduring almost incredible hardships on their way, for they lodged no less than twenty-one nights in the wilderness, they arrived in safety just in time to attend a Quarterly Meeting on the Bay of Quinte Circuit. After preaching on Saturday, while the Presiding Elder, (Darius Dunham) retired with the official brethren to hold the Quarterly Meeting Conference, brother Wooster remained in the meeting to pray with some who were under awakenings, and others who were groaning for full redemption in the blood of Christ. While uniting with his brethren in this exercise, the power of the Most High seemed to overshadow the congregation, and many were filled with joy unspeakable, and were praising the Lord aloud for what he had done for their souls; while others 'with speechless awe and silent love,' were prostrated on the floor. When the Presiding Elder came into the house, he beheld these things with a mixture of wonder and indignation, believing that 'wild-fire' was burning among the people. After gazing for a while with silent astonishment, he knelt down and began to pray to God to stop the 'raging of the wild-fire,' as he called it. In the meantime, Calvin Wooster, whose soul was burning with the 'fire of the Holy Spirit,' knelt by the side of brother Dunham, and while the latter was earnestly engaged in prayer for God to put out the 'wild-fire,' Wooster softly whispered out a prayer in the following words: 'Lord, bless brother Dunham! Lord, bless brother Dunham!' Thus they continued for some minutes, when at length the prayer of brother Wooster prevailed, and Dunham fell prostrate on the floor—and ere he arose, received a baptism of that very fire which he had so feelingly deprecated as the effect of wild imagination. There was now harmony in their prayers, feelings and views; and this was the commencement of a revival of religion which soon spread through the entire Province; for, as brother Dunham was the Presiding Elder, he was instrumental in spreading the flame throughout the District, to the joy and salvation of hundreds of immortal souls.

"Calvin Wooster was a man of mighty prayer and faith. Frequently his voice was heard by the families where he lodged, in the night season, when, rising from his bed while others slept, he would pour out the desire of his soul to God, in earnest prayer for the salvation of souls. Such, indeed, was the strength of his faith in God, and the fervency of his spirit, as well as the bold and pointed manner of his appeals to the consciences of his hearers, and particularly to the wicked, that few of these could stand before him: they would either flee from the house, or, smitten with conviction, fall down and cry aloud for mercy—while, in the midst of these exercises, the saints of God were shouting forth His praises.

"Nor was he alone in this work. The other preachers caught the flame of divine love, and were carried forward under its sacred impulses, in their Master's work. Many instances of the manifestations of divine power and grace might be narrated, which go to illustrate the authority by which these men of God spoke in his name; one of which I will relate.

"At a Quarterly Meeting in the Bay of Quinte Circuit, as the preacher commenced his sermon, a thoughtless man in the front gallery commenced, in a playful mood, to swear profanely, and otherwise to disturb the congregation. The preacher paid no attention to him until he was in the midst of his sermon, when, feeling strong in faith and the power of His might, suddenly stopping, he fixed his piercing eye upon the profane man, then stamping with his foot, and pointing his finger at him with great energy, he cried out, '*My God! Smite him!*' He instantly fell, as if shot through the heart with a bullet. At this moment such a divine afflatus came down upon the congregation, that sinners were crying to God for mercy in every direction; while the saints of God burst forth in loud praises to His name. This great work may be said to have been, in some sense, the beginning of that great revival of religion which soon after spread through various parts of the United States.

"The doctrine more especially urged upon believers was that of *sanctification*, or *holiness of heart and life*—a complete surrender of the soul and body, and all the powers and affections to the service of God—and this was pressed on them as their *present* privilege, depending for its accomplishment *now* on the faithfulness of God, who had promised to do it. It was this *baptism of the Holy Ghost* which fired and filled the hearts of God's ministers at that time, and which enabled them so to speak that the people *felt* that their words were with 'demonstration and power,' and they could not well resist the influence of those 'thoughts which breathe,' and those 'words which burn.'

"We are not to suppose that this work went on without opposition. In that country, there was a marked line of distinction 'between the righteous and the wicked,' there being but few formal professors of religion to interpose between the two classes. And such was the general state of society, that those who did not embrace religion felt themselves at liberty to manifest their hatred to its doctrines by open acts of hostility, by scurrilous speeches, and, in some instances, by personal violence. One instance among others I will relate. A stout opposer of the Methodists, hearing that his wife was in a prayer meeting, rushed violently into the room, seized his wife, and dragged her to the door, when attempting to open it, he was himself seized with trembling, his knees failed him, and he fell helpless upon the floor, and was fain to beg an interest in the prayers of those very people whom he had so much despised and persecuted. He rose not until the Lord released him from his sins, and made him a partaker of his pardoning mercy,

This very man afterwards became an itinerant minister, with whom I was personally acquainted, and had the relation of these facts from his own lips."

This is, perhaps, the best place to give the Doctor's obituary notice of the orginal instrument in this work, of whom also we have preserved some *traditions* in another article:—

"HEZEKIAH CALVIN WOOSTER also took his departure to another world this year. We have already seen some thing of his character in the notice we have taken of the work of God in Upper Canada. His name is 'like ointment poured forth' to many in that country, and he was spoken of as an extraordinary messenger of God, sent to declare his counsels to a fallen and rebellious world. After exerting all his powers of body and mind in beseeching sinners to be reconciled to God, he returned home with fatal consumption fastened upon his lungs. But even while in this feeble state, so reduced as not to be able to speak above a whisper, this whisper, being announced to the congregation by another, was frequently attended by such a divine energy and unction, that sinners would tremble and fall under the announcement, while the people of God felt the *holy annointing* running through their souls. It is said, indeed, that his very countenance exhibited such marks of the divine glory that it struck conviction into the hearts of many who beheld it.

"'Behold how great a matter a little fire kindleth.' Though Hezekiah Calvin Wooster could not be regarded as a man of more than ordinary talents as a preacher, yet, such was the holy fervour of his soul, his deep devotion to God, his burning love for the souls of his fellow-men, that he was the happy instrument of kindling up such a fire in the hearts of the people, wherever he went, particularly in Upper Canada, that all the waters of strife and opposition have not been able to quench it. This testimony I consider due to such departed worth. The grace of God wrought mightily in him, and great was his glorying in the cross of Christ—nor did he glory in aught else—for he was as much distinguished for his humility, his deadness to self, and to self-applause, as he was for the fervour of his spirit, and the boldness and pointedness of his appeals to the consciences of the people.

"That he enjoyed perfect love was demonstrated not only from the fact of his having recorded the time when he received the great blessing, but also and more especially from the tenor of his life, his constant self-denial, his watchings and fastings, and from the fruit of the Spirit—love, faith, meekness, patience, gentleness, long-suffering and charity, which shone out conspicuously in all his deportment, in the temper of his mind, and words of his lips.

"It could not be expected otherwise than that such a man should be prepared to meet his 'last enemy with firmness,' and 'rejoice in hope of the glory of God,' when drawing to the termination of his earthly career; accordingly when so exhausted as to be scarcely able to speak, on being asked by his father if his confidence was still strong in the Lord; he answered with holy triumph, 'Yes, strong! strong!' And a short time before his eyes were closed in death, he said, 'The nearer I draw to eternity, the brighter heaven shines upon me!' He thus 'fell asleep in Jesus,' on the 6th of November, 1798, in the 28th year of his age, and the fifth of his ministry. Though his race was short, it was brilliant—its brilliancy arising not so much from the splendor of his talents as from the purity of his motives, the fidelity of his private and public life, and the holy and burning zeal with which he pursued his vocation until sickness and death put a stop to his activity. And when he had sunk under the cloud of death, he left such a trail of light behind him as shall, it is humbly hoped, never be extinguished. Such honour God puts on those who honour him."

Of 1802, our historian says, in reference to Canada:—

"Montreal, in Lower Canada, was visited this year by Joseph Sawyer. He found a few persons there who had belonged to the Methodist Society in the city of New York, before the Revolutionary war, who received him cordially, and assisted him in procuring a school-room for preaching. A Mr. Maginnis and his sister, both unmarried, were among the first who attached themselves to the society in Montreal, and they remained faithful through all the vicissitudes through which Methodism was called to pass in that city until their death."

An incident very little known, and never yet in print, was related to the writer by Mr. Sawyer himself, which occurred in connection with his first entrance into Montreal, will show how Methodist preachers were regarded in certain quarters, and the difficulties through which they had often to make their way. Mr. S., who was very apostolic in his appearance and spirit, and very urbane and polite in his manners, thought it might be well to call on and endeavour to conciliate the minister of what is called the "Church of England," in the city—the Rev. Mr. M—. He did call; and when he came into the minister's presence, making a polite bow, he addressed him to the following effect :—" Sir, I am a Methodist minister, sent to labour in this city and vicinity by Bishop Asbury; and as yourself and I are the only Protestant clergymen in the place, I have made bold to call on you, with the desire to have some conversation with you relating to the interests of religion in the country."

Clergyman (with a mingled look of surprise and displeasure.) "You, indeed! I would much rather encourage the Roman Catholics than such as you, Dissenters. No! Get out of my sight!" While these words were being uttered, he was sideling towards the corner of the room, where stood his trusty staff,—when he reached to grasp it, with a design of driving the lowly Missionary from his house. Mr. Sawyer, finding himself "in the wrong box," expressed his "regret for the intrusion"—said he "meant no offence"—and, keeping a cautious eye on the cane, "bowed himself out" backwards as deputations do out of the presence of royalty; till he got beyond the precincts of the parsonage, when he beat a hasty retreat from the scene of his unsuccessful advance.

"The Long Point Circuit, in Upper Canada," the Doctor proceeds, "was formed the latter part of this year, chiefly through the labours of Nathan Bangs, who went into the work under the direction of the Presiding Elder of the District. In the towns of Burford and Oxford particularly, there was a great work of God commenced under his labours, which eventuated in the conversion of one hundred souls."

Of 1804, the same author says :—"This year also, Nathan Bangs solicited and obtained the appointment of a missionary to a new settlement on the river Thames, in Upper Canada. This place had long been on his mind as a promising field for missionary labour, and he had frequently offered himself to explore it in the name of the Lord, but his presiding elder objected, on account of the feeble state of his health, and the unhealthiness of the climate.

"While at the Conference in New York, this year, he made known his desires and impressions to Bishop Asbury, and he appointed him a missionary to that place. He accordingly left the city of New York in the latter part of the month of June, went into Upper Canada by the way of Kingston, thence up the country, along the north-western shore of Lake Ontario, to the Long Point Circuit, and thence on through Oxford, to the town of Delaware, on the river Thames. Here he lodged for the night in the last log hut in the settlement, and the next morning, as the day began to dawn, he arose and took his departure, and, after travelling through a wilderness of forty-five miles, guided only by marked trees, he arrived at a solitary log-house about sunset, weary, hungry, and thirsty, where he was entertained with the best the house could afford, which was some Indian pudding and milk for his supper, and a bundle of straw for his bed. The next day, about twelve o'clock, he arrived at an Indian village on the north bank of the river Thames, the inhabitants of which were under the instructions of two Moravian missionaries. While there, the Indians were called together for worship, which was performed in a very simple manner, by reading a short discourse, and singing a few verses of a hymn. The Missionaries and Indians treated him with great respect and affection, and seemed to rejoice in the prospect of having the gospel preached to the white settlements on the banks of the river below.

"About three o'clock P. M., he arrived at the first house in the settlement, when the following conversation took place between the missionary and a man whom he saw in the yard before the house. After the introductory salutation, the missionary inquired, 'Do you want the Gospel preached here?' After some deliberation, it was answered, 'Yes, that we do. Do you preach the Gospel?' 'That is my occupation.' 'Alight from your horse, then, and come in, will you?' 'I have come a great distance to preach the Gospel to the people here, and it is now Saturday afternoon, to-morrow is the Sabbath, and I must have a house to preach in before I get off from my horse.' After a few moments of consideration, he replied, 'I have a house for you to preach in, provender for your horse, and food and lodging for yourself: and you shall be welcome to them all if you will dismount and come in.' Thanking him for his offer, the Missionary dismounted, and entered the hospitable mansion in the name of the Lord, saying, '*Peace be to this house.*' A young man mounted his horse and rode ten miles down the river, inviting the people to attend meeting at that house the next morning, at ten o'clock.

"At the time appointed, the house was filled. When the Missionary rose up, he told the people that whenever a stranger makes his appearance in a place, the people are generally anxious to know who he is, whence he came, where he is going, and what his errand is among them. 'In these things,' said he, 'I will satisfy you in a few words.' He then gave them a short account of his birth and education, of his conversion and call to the ministry, and the motives which induced him to come amongst them, and concluded in the following manner:—'I am a Methodist Preacher, and my manner of worship is to stand up and sing, and kneel in prayer; then I stand up and take a text and preach, while the people sit on their seats. As many of you as see fit to join in this method, you can do so; but if not, you can choose your own method.' When he gave out his hymn, they all arose, every man, woman, and child. When he kneeled in prayer, they all, without exception, kneeled down. They then took their seats, and he stood up and gave out his text,—" Repent ye, therefore, and be converted, that your sins may be blotted out when the times of refreshing shall come from the presence of the Lord;' and he preached, as he thinks, with the Holy Ghost sent down from heaven. Having concluded his discourse, he explained to his audience his manner of preaching, by itinerating through the country, his doctrine, and how supported, &c. He then said, 'All you who wish to hear any more such preaching, rise up;'—when every man, woman and child stood up He then told them they might expect preaching there again in two weeks.

"Such a commencement, in a strange place, he considered a token for good. He then sent on appointments through the settlements along down the river, which he filled in a manner similar to the above, and was everywhere received with great cordiality. He proceeded down the shore of Lake St. Clair, visited Sandwich, on the Canada side of the outlet of the lake, crossed over to Detroit, and preached in the Counsel House, thence to Fort Malden, and down the shore of Lake Erie, in a settlement made up of Americans, English, Scotch, Irish, and Dutch emigrants. The people everywhere flocked together to hear the Word.

"A more destitute place he had never found. Young people had arrived at the age of sixteen who had never heard a Gospel sermon, and he found a Methodist family who had lived in that country for seven years without hearing a sermon preached. But although the people were extremely ignorant of spiritual things, and very loose in their morals, they seemed ripe for the Gospel, and have received and treated God's messenger with great attention and kindness. He continued among them about three months, when he left them for Niagara Circuit, intending to return again soon, but was prevented. He was succeeded the next year by William Case, who was instrumental of great good to the souls of the people. Societies and a regular circuit were formed, which have continued to increase and flourish to the present time."

Under the date of 1806, our author recurs to Canada again. "This year a new district was founded, called the Lower Canada District, which included Montreal, Quebec, and Ottawa. I have before spoken of Montreal and Ottawa. Nathan Bangs voluntered his services for Quebec. After spending a few weeks in Montreal; to supply them till their preacher, Samuel Coate, arrived, he sailed down the river St. Lawrence, for Quebec; and arrived there on Saturday morning. Having a few letters of introduction, he delivered them, and by great exertions, succeeded in hiring a room and getting it seated that day, and he preached his first sermon on the Sabbath morning following, to a tolerable congregation.

"The majority of people in Quebec were French Roman Catholics, bigotedly attached to all their peculiarities, and of course, opposed to all Protestant innovations. The next in numbers and influence were the members of the Church of England, and next to them the Church of Scotland—all manifesting a deadly opposition to Methodism. He found, however, a few who received him cordially, though with much timidity. Among others, he called on a Scotch missionary, by the name of Dick, who had succeeded in collecting a small congregation, and was treated by him with much affection and respect.

"It would doubtless be uninteresting to the reader to enter into a detail of the difficulties with which he had to contend, the mental trials he underwent, in striving to plant the Gospel in that hardened place, with small means of support, and few to countenance his undertaking. For a while the congregation was respectable as to numbers, but they soon dwindled down to not more than a dozen steady hearers, and not more than three or four of these seemed to be under religious impressions. He has frequently held a prayer-meeting with only one besides himself, when each would pray, and then dismiss the meeting, though inwardly conscious of the divine approbation, yet with but faint hopes of success. He, however, formed a small society, which, under more faithful and skilful labourers, has since increased to a considerable number, and Methodism has now a firm stand in Quebec."

This was the commencement of a regular Methodist cause in that city, but an experienced and intelligent Wesleyan minister, the Rev. John Tompkins, who has spent the most of his ministerial life in Lower Canada, and who has interested himself in all that concerns the rise and progress of Methodism in that section of the Province, has assured the writer that he had good evidence for believing that the Gospel was preached by lay Methodist Preachers, in the army of General Wolfe, in which there was a society of Methodists. This was as early as 1759.

"An attempt was made this year," Dr. Bangs continues, "to establish a mission for the benefit of the French Catholic population of Lower Canada; and William Snyder, who understood and could preach in the French language, was appointed to this service. He entered upon his work in the French settlements in the vicinity of the Ottawa river, and for a time was cordially received and listened to with much attention, so that great hopes were entertained of a successful issue of his labours. Having occasion, however, to be absent from his field of labour for a few weeks, the parish priest took the opportunity to go and warn them of the danger of hearing the 'Protestant heretic,' threatening them with excommunication—which, in their estimation was a sure prelude to damnation—if they did not desist. This so wrought upon their fears, that, upon the return of brother Snyder, not a soul dared to hear him or receive him into his house. He was, therefore, reluctantly compelled to abandon the enterprise in despair, nor has anything been effected for this people since The chains of Roman Catholicism still hold them in bondage to their priests."

We are thankful that the late success of Protestant Missionaries, and Wesleyans among the rest, renders the Doctor's concluding remarks, in their strongest sense, inapplicable to the present time. Enough is being done, we humbly hope, to give earnest of a brighter future for the French Canadians of the Lower Province.

Our principal authority for these summary annals, furnishes nothing very special relative to Canada, till 1809, excepting that in the preceding year, a temporary shock was given to the infant society in Montreal, by a missionary preacher appointed to that city, John Richards, returning to the bosom of the Roman Catholic Church, from which he had been an avowed convert, and entering the ranks of the priesthood. "Father Richards" was a well-known character in Montreal, subsequently to that. In 1809, there was "an attempt to introduce the Gospel at Three Rivers, in Lower Canada, a place about midway between Montreal and Quebec."

Of 1811, it is said, " This year Bishop Asbury crossed the St. Lawrence into Upper Canada. After attending the New England Conference, which assembled this year in Barnard, in the State of Vermont, he took his departure on his intended tour into Upper Canada—a place he had long desired to visit.

On Wednesday, June the 26th, he crossed the Green Mountains, visited Middlebury, and preached in the courthouse, and afterwards set forward a subscription for building a house of worship in that place, fully believing, as he said, that " the Lord would visit Middlebury." He then passed on through Vergennes, Charlotte, and Flattsburg, in each of which places he stopped and preached, until he arrived, after a fatiguing journey through the woods and swampy roads, at the Indian village of St. Regis, situated at the mouth of the river of that name, which empties into the St. Lawrence river. At this place he was ferried across the St. Lawrence, which is here three miles in width. The first place he stopped at was Evan Roy's, (*Roise's*, where the compiler afterwards often stopped with Mr. Roise's son,) "in the town of Cornwall, where there was a flourishing Methodist society, one of the oldest in the province." This is still represented in the Moulinette society.

" On landing in Canada," he (Asbury) says, " my strong affection for the people of the United States came with strange power upon me, when I was crossing the line," and inquires, with much apparent feeling, " Why should I have such new feelings in Canada?" No doubt associations were called up by this visit which he little expected to realize in this world. He had left his native land in his youth —had struggled through the difficulties of the revolutionary war—a war which eventuated in the severance of the United States from the land of his birth—had lived to see these states rising and flourishing, and the Church whose affairs he had been called to superintend, numbering within its bosom six hundred and thirty-six travelling preachers, and 174,560 members—and now, in the sixty-sixth year of his age, and fortieth of his ministry in this country, he found himself once more under the shadow of his paternal government, in a distant province of the empire, among a people who had been raised up by his sons in the Gospel, professing the same faith, and adopting the same modes of worship with those with whom he first united himself in the mother country. Amid such reflections, how could it be otherwise than that 'strange feelings' should 'come over him?' And, more especially, as he must then have anticipated the near approach of another war between the United States and that Government from which he had expatriated himself for the sake of building up His kingdom whose government shall have no end.

The Bishop passed along the banks of the St. Lawrence, [calling on the Rev. Joseph Sawyer, who was now located in the township of Matilda, and preaching in the original "Matilda Chapel,"] as well as stopping and preaching in the most considerable places, gathering information from his own observations and communications of others respecting the state of things in Canada, until he arrived at Kingston, where he preached in a new chapel the people had erected in that place. He says:—" Our ride has brought us through one of the finest countries I have ever seen. The timber is of a noble size; the cattle are well shaped and well-looking; the crops are abundant, and a most fruitful soil. Surely this is a land that God the Lord hath blessed."

The war of 1812, the premonitory signs of which Bishop Asbury is supposed to have observed at the time of his visit to Canada, had a disastrous effect on true religion. Most of the Methodist Preachers, being citizens of the United States, from inclination or necessity left the country, and the societies were neglected and scattered. I myself, though but a child at the time, remember seeing the devoted Methodist Class-leader, at the Cross-roads, near Niagara, made a prisoner by the American Indians, and led away towards Greenbush, in the United States; and of my mother entertaining him with dinner, in the town of York, on his way home, at the close of the war. A tender meeting with this worthy man and some others, from Canada, is mentioned by the Rev. William Case, who chanced to be detained in the United States during the war. His words are as follow:—

"ALBANY, Oct. 26, 1813.

" This moment, I have returned from a visit to the barracks, in Greenbush, in company with brother Merwin.

" Having been kindly indulged by Col. Larned, commandant, to speak to the prisoners, we most joyfully embraced the privilege of proclaiming to them the sweet liberty of the Gospel. As soon as we began to sing, there was weeping; and immediately on our kneeling to pray, they knelt down, and here and there we heard the voice of *Amen* to our petition for their salvation. I could not solve this till after the service. To my great surprise and mingled grief and joy, several brethren and acquaintances from Canada came and made themselves known to us; they were militia in arms, and were taken near Fort George; among these were Messrs. George Lawrence,[*] Leader at the Four-Mile Creek; William Clinton, from the head of the Lake; and Russell Hawley, brother of David Hawley, of Bay of Quinte. Their captivity was an affliction which made friends more consoling. By them I was informed, that in consequence of the troubles, there had been no preaching in that part for some time: that Mr. Ryan and others were travelling and doing all the good they could for God and souls: that none of our brethren in that part had been killed.

---

[*] Mr. Lawrence was not "in arms," but seized by the throat, at his own door, by an Indian, to whom he had held out his hand in friendship.

"So soon as the peace took place, attention to the word became more general; the societies began to resume their former strength; till the more general reformation took place, of which the following are some particulars. In 1816, congregations were unusually large, and great seriousness and meltings of heart portended better days. In June, 1816, while the Genesee Annual Conference was in session at Elizabethtown, many were brought under awakening, and ten persons found peace to their souls. On Sabbath, the church was filled from eight A. M. to eight P. M., during which five sermons and several exhortations were delivered. At eleven, that man of God, Bishop George, delivered a discourse which seemed to move the whole congregation. The following thrilling remarks on that discourse are made by the Rev. Charles Giles:—'Of Bishop George's sermon I wish I could give the whole, but it is beyond my reach. Near the close, as he was bringing the strong points together, he ascended from thought to thought in his towering theme, like an eagle on the wing; then higher and higher still, till it seemed that inspiration would become his chariot, and by the grasp he held on the assembly, he would take all away with him to the third heaven. The hearers appeared motionless, absorbed in thought, and charmed with the grandeur of the theme; while emotions were visible and strong in the congregation. At length, as the man of God was about to descend from his lofty elevation, cries for mercy were heard from the awakened crowd in the gallery; and the mourning penitents were conducted to the altar, where a prayer-meeting was opened, and supplications were made in their behalf. The time was well improved; and it was a season of great power and glory.'

"Through the whole sitting of the conference of five days, the word was delivered with much freedom and power; and so great was the revival that followed, it is believed that more than one hundred were awakened during that conference.

"Conversions now became frequent: whole families were made the subjects of saving grace. The numerous family of a pious widow were among the favoured; five sons and four daughters are among the subjects of grace.

"The neighbouring towns now caught the flame. From attending the preaching at the conference, the people returned to their homes with earnest prayer for their families and neighbours; and the revival was renewed with great power in Augusta, and many were converted to God. The Minutes for July, 1818, shew an increase of 317. The professors drink deeply into the spirit of the Gospel—the youth are making promising improvements. They delight in reading the Bible. At a late quarterly meeting in Augusta, the divine power was gloriously manifest. Among the hundreds of joyful souls were eight above the age of sixty, who had found mercy during the late revivals: among them was one of seventy-five: another of seventy-two, blessed God that all his family, seven in number, were converted. About the same time, a revival began in the fifth town, Hallowell Circuit. It was at a prayer-meeting, when the divine power rested on the minds of those praying, filling their hearts with peace. Their supplications were heard for sinners, and a number were awakened. And so powerfully did the Lord carry on his work, that in a few weeks, about sixty were brought to rejoice in the love of God. In this good work whole families were rejoicing! In all the east part of the township, there was scarce a family where the voice of prayer and praise was not daily heard! A great and glorious work of God was also going on in the Bay of Quinte Circuit. It commenced in the township of Fredericksburg, on the 17th of August, 1817. It began at Mr. Cain's, where a company of young persons were assembled for the purpose of improving in singing. At this meeting, a young man, who had lately found peace, addressed the company on the subject of his late conversion—the joy he felt in the service of God; and invited them to come to Christ, and 'taste for themselves that the Lord was gracious.' The divine power rested on all present, and the company were broken into contrition for whom prayer was made, when six young persons were blessed and made happy in the love of God. The news of this meeting brought many together, till no house could contain the multitude: numbers were converted at every meeting. It spread like a devouring fire through the neighbourhood; thence east; thence north, through the German settlement around Hay Bay, sweeping in its course almost every family. From brother Cain's it took a western direction, and spread the width of Adolphustown, leaving a blessing in many a house. Many hundreds assembled at the prayer meetings, when ten or twelve would be converted. From the fourth concession, boat-loads crossed the bay to the meetings in the chapel; by this means the revival obtained in the north part of the township. O, it was most delightful to hear the solemn praises from the happy converts, as they sailed across the bay, to and from the place of worship!

"This work produced a most happy change in families. On some occasions, while the father would be reading the Bible, praying or conversing with his family, some one would realize the divine power, and experience a saving change. On these occasions, it would be truly affecting to witness the Christian endearment, when parents and children would embrace each other, praising God for his mercy, and rejoicing in its mighty comforts. Some who embraced the Gospel when first introduced into the country, have lived to see the piety of their children and children's children. So true are the words of unerring inspiration: *The mercy of the Lord is from everlasting to everlasting upon them that fear him, and his righteousness unto children's children.*—Ps. ciii. 17.

"By these revivals, great changes were brought about in the state of society. Rude companies, who spent the Sabbath in idleness and revelry, were now seen with their families in the place of worship. Others, who, through the influence of strong drink, had been led to differences and fights, now learned meekness and to forgive. The drunkard's song was changed into loud hosannas, and blasphemies into praise! It was delightful to witness the Christian affection and religious fervour of the people: they seemed to hang on the ministers' lips, as if feasting on every sentence; and as the truths of religion were brought to their believing view, they received them with tears of joy—sometimes with shouts of praise, and " Glory to God," for the wonders of his grace! Our quarterly meetings were attended by such multitudes that no house could contain them. We then had to stand at the door, and to preach to those within and those without,—or divide the congregations.

" Other revivals might be named, but those were the principal, at that day; at least in the Bay of Quinte district. The Niagara country was equally favoured, about four hundred having been added in the Niagara Circuit."

The above extracts from Mr. Case's Jubilee Sermon, bring down the annals of Canadian Methodism to the time when my own recollections begin, with

THE OLD FRAMED MEETING-HOUSE.

" Mother," said a white-haired urchin of some nine years old, who had just returned from an errand, " Mother, when I was in at Mr. Cafrey's store, a man came in and said, they were going to raise the new meeting-house to-day, and that they wanted hands to help in putting up the frame. He said they did not mean to have any rum or whisky at the 'raisin', but only some beer and cakes!" The announcement that there was to be *no rum or whiskey* at the raising, and *only* some *beer*, was the declaration of a purpose so singular for the place and period, that the little boy's mother, who piqued herself on the possession of some little wit, and who, at that time, had anything but a good opinion of the Methodists, remarked, somewhat derisively, "Oh, I suppose they intend to have it like Solomon's Temple, 'without the sound of an axe or a hammer'!" The building referred to was the first Methodist chapel in the then town of York, the present city of Toronto. It was the second place of worship erected in the capital, and must have been erected in the summer and fall of 1818. At that time there was not a Methodist in town. The preachers had preached occasionally in private houses, taverns, &c., but the seed sown had been lost. Elder Ryan, for so many years so distinguished for his zeal, labours, and heroism in the cause, with his characteristic boldness, determined to have "ground whereon to stand" in the capital of the Province; and, it was said, *mortgaged his farm* for a sum to erect the church, and afterwards appealed for indemnification to the Methodist people scattered throughout the length and breadth of the land. One of these, from the country, came and built the church. He was the person the little boy had seen in the store on the morning of the day on which it was raised. Early in the autumn of that season, the chapel was used for preaching. Under the second sermon, a man of intelligence and influence was converted, who became the first Leader; and was for many years an efficient and hearty friend of the cause. And, some few Sundays after it was opened, the woman who had made herself merry at the abstemiousness practiced at the raising, attended the preaching—was so much impressed that she stopped to the class, and joined the society; and in a few weeks afterwards, in that same delightful means of grace, while a hymn was being sung, entered into the liberty of the children of God, receiving the Spirit of adoption by which she could cry Abba Father. The first time the little boy alluded to, in company with many others, entered the house (it was the first time he had been in any place of worship,) was during the following winter, on the occasion of the opening of a Sunday School, organized by that indefatigable friend of the young, the late Rev. Thaddeus Osgood. It was the first ever opened in our Western capital; and it is likely, the first in Upper Canada. It was a day of no small bustle, among big and little in the new meeting-house. The three gentlemen the most active in conducting and sustaining it—the distinction between superintendent, secretary, and librarian, was but little known—were Messrs. Jesse Ketchum, W. P. Patrick, and the late Dr. Morrison.

The writer remembers that the new Meeting-house, which stood on the south side of King-street, about half-way between Bay and Yonge-streets, had no house nearer than Mr. Jordan Post's, on the corner of the square, and that gentleman's watchmaker-shop on the other. It was then without a fence around it—unpainted—and stood up from the ground on some blocks, which supplied the place of foundation, while the wind whistled and howled underneath. The Society for several months augmented very fast; but was again diminished by the formation of a rival one in the Masonic Hall, by Missionaries from England. The controversy occasioned by this measure, we may suppose, had no beneficial effect on either society. Happily, this stumbling-block was taken away, by the arrangement entered into between the General Conference in America, and the English Conference, in 1820, which resulted in the removal of the European preachers from the Upper Province. Few, however, of the society they gathered, took the advice of their pastors on leaving, which was to connect themselves with the other. The original society soon recovered its loss, and in about eight years afterwards, numbered *two hundred*. And the congregation was so much increased as to require an addition of thirty feet to the building. In this interval, the white-headed boy had been converted—joined society—and risen through the successive grades of leader and exhorter, and at this period was sent out to supply a vacancy upon a circuit, as the old Presiding Elder said, "as an experiment to see whether he would make a preacher." About two years after this, the spacious and elegantly symmetrical brick church in Adelaide-street was erected. A decade, recounted backwards from the last-mentioned event, was the most prosperous period connected with the Society in the Old Framed Meeting-house: a period during which they enjoyed the able ministrations of a Richardson, a Metcalf, a Wm. Smith, an Irvine, and the three Ryersons—William, John, and Egerton—then in the zenith of their popularity. The Society, during this period, was the most conspicuous for non-conformity to the world, love to each other, and zeal for God, that the writer had ever the happiness of knowing. Although Methodism has passed through several trying scenes from that time to this, it has weathered all the storms; and the Old Framed Meeting-house is succeeded by five elegant churches, supplied by six Ministers, while the Wesleyan Church in the two city circuits comprises the large number of *one thousand five hundred and thirty-nine members*.* To God be all the glory!

MY SPIRITUAL FATHER.

To whom should we apply such an appellation as the one above? To the instrument of our *awakening* or *conversion*, or *early establishment in the ways of piety?* or all

---

* The number at the time the above was written.

these together? Doubtless, he who stands in *all* the above relations best deserves such a designation. He who has been the instrument of both *conviction* and *conversion*, deserves next; while he who only cherished us after our spiritual birth, may be the least entitled to the name. But of the three separately, he who was the one that effectually pointed us to the Lamb of God, in the hour of uncertainty and distress, best deserves the title. Such was the relation to me of the one of whom I am about to write: a person for whom I have always felt a peculiar sort of attachment, which I never felt for another.

The writer had been awakened by reading a religious tract—had resolved on securing salvation—had left off outward sin and forsaken evil company—had commenced using all the means of grace—had joined the church on probation—and had been seeking God with all his heart, "with strong cries and tears," but amid many discouragements, doubts and perplexities, for about two months—but, up to the time we are about to mention, had sought in vain. Such was his state of mind, when, on one lovely Sabbath morning, he started for the "Old Framed Meeting-house," and took his accustomed seat on one of the forms, *pews* there were none, which ran sideways of the pulpit, on which "the members of Society" usually sat—the men on the right hand, the women on the left. By the way, if a member began to sit off those seats, and further down towards the door, he was immediately suspected of a tendency to backslide. He had not long occupied his seat, when, instead of the usual circuit Preacher for the day, Mr. Slater, a stranger entered the house, and went up into the pulpit. He was very peculiar in his appearance. It is true, he wore the usual summer garb of a Methodist Preacher of that day—a black worsted frock coat, and a broad-leafed grey hat—well worn. He was medium sized, rather stout, but stooped, with a sort of groping manner of walking, occasioned by shortness of sight. His appearance gave him an air of meekness, not without some seeming awkwardness. He was not handsome, having coarse, lightish hair, not very delicate features, and much freckled withal.

He conducted the service modestly, and with great propriety. He read his hymns with emphasis and solemnity—prayed with feeling and power—and preached a sermon which (all glory to God!) led *me* to Christ! It was founded on Gal. iii. 13:— " Christ hath redeemed us from the curse of the law being made a curse for us." It was well arranged, expressed in excellent language, and presented the plan of salvation with a clearness and power such as the writer had never seen or felt before. The whole scheme was unfolded to his vision; and he thought if he had had a thousand sinful souls, he could have cast them all on Jesus. He drank in the balmy sound of mercy, and ere he was aware of it, faith had sprung up in his poor, anxious heart, and he " rejoiced with joy unspeakable and full of glory." Oh, how happy was that hour! In the evening, the stranger preached from the well-known passage, " Except ye be converted, and become as little children, &c.:" in expounding which he *described* A CONVERTED PERSON. The description so exactly tallied with his feelings, that he said, with indescribable satisfaction to himself, " *Now I know I am converted.*" He had often sorrowfully sung before that happy moment,

" 'Tis a point I long to know,
  Oft it causes anxious thought,
Do I love the Lord or no,
  Am I His, or am I not?"

But now he knew he was His; and from that glad hour, " went on his way rejoicing."

The Preacher to whom we have referred was the Rev. ROWLEY HEYLAND, still alive, but laid by from the active work by age and infirmity. He was then about twenty-eight years of age. Aside from our affection for him, because of the good he was the means of doing us, we ever had a high opinion of his abilities and excellencies. Nor do we now think it was any higher than his merits deserved. In the palmy days of his earlier ministry, there were few if any, more effective preachers in the Province than he was. Blessed with a clear, strong, musical voice, a sympathetic spirit and fervent piety—with a ready command of good language—and clear views, with a cogent manner of presenting them, he was, if "eloquence is the power of persuasion," *truly eloquent*. This he was, at times especially, when he seemed to possess the divine afflatus, and spake with an unction and power truly remarkable. On some of those occasions, there were bursts of fiery eloquence, attended with "shocks of power," as they used to be called, that created marked sensation.

We have often been astonished that he did not occupy more prominent places: and could only account for it on the principle of his modesty and diffidence; his short-sightedness from the first, and the total loss of one eye, after some years—and his unfortunate committal, at an early period, to some alleged secular entanglements, joined to a little carelessness of his personal appearance—all of which conspired to hold him back from positions, which otherwise he would have occupied with distinction. Heyland never became the man he might have been, in view of his vigorous mind, fair education, and mighty powers of influencing public assemblies. Had he possessed a little more of what is usually called *ambition*—desire to excel—it would have been better for him and the Church. It would have led him to aspire after higher excellence. As it was, however, that old, farmer-looking man, who now sits in some out-of-the-way place when he comes to Conference, was a host in his day. We remember some of his mighty camp-meeting sermons and exhortations of years long past; and we have in our recollection some later efforts, at missionary meetings, which we could pronounce no other than masterly, in which he "took the shine" off younger and more aspiring men with the utmost ease.

Retired now from public gaze, we pray that he may be an object of special favour from God, and that the divine "consolations" may be neither few nor small. We hope he may finally win the well-fought day, and that he may have occasion to rejoice over our unworthy self, among many others, as a "star in his crown of rejoicing, in the day of the Lord Jesus."

AN EARLY CLASS-MATE.

The phrase at the head of this article would, in the minds of most persons, recall the remembrance of their school-going days. It is only to a Methodist that the sense in which the writer uses it would be perfectly intelligible. In the mind of such a one, it might awaken many pleasing associations. These are certainly awakened in my mind, by the remembrance of the individual of whom I am about to speak. The Wesleyan Church is a sort of *imperium in imperio;* for, while there is a pleasing and profitable acquaintance among the members in general in any given locality, similar to that which subsists among the members of other communities, there is a still more intimate acquaintance between the members of the respective " smaller companies called classes," into which each " society " is divided. But in these smaller divisions of the Wesleyan Church, there are often found coteries still less, of kindred spirits, whom a similarity of sex, age, and disposition, render even more intimate. These disclose their hopes and fears, their joys and sorrows, and declare their faults to each other with a candour, minuteness, and fidelity, that they cannot exercise in the class-room. It was such a relationship and friendship that I now refer to. My class-mate, my best beloved and most profitable early religious friend, was a young Englishman, several years older than myself—for I was yet a lad, when for years *he* was a young man—the child of old, consistently pious Methodists, but only converted about three months before myself. Our acquaintance began with my attendance upon class-meeting. The first meeting of the kind attended by the writer will never be effaced from his memory while that faculty retains its vigor. The young man in question was not at that meeting; he was gone with most of the society in the town, to a camp-meeting, a means of grace in those early days, much prized and owned of God in the conversion and sanctification of souls. But few were at the class-meeting, yet it was a delightful season; and I said involuntarily within my own heart, " This people shall be my people, and their God shall be my God." At the close of this meeting, I heard one commend to another the simple-hearted piety of John R——, and when the brethren returned from the camp-meeting, my attention was caught with the unusually meek and heavenly countenance of a certain young man; and my soul instantly clave to his, like the soul of Jonathan to David. A most endeared friendship sprung up between us, a friendship which never met with the slightest interruption, which was attended with nought but profit to me, and which rather increased than otherwise, up to the time of my " going out to travel,"—nay,

"Till he took his last triumphant flight,
From Calvary to Zion's height."

For, though he married and changed his place of residence and business, and we met not sometimes for years, yet I have reason to know, that an ardent friendship, of the purest and most heavenly character, subsisted between us mutually to the last. I shall never forget the heavenly glow with which he proposed, when we were walking together in a retired place, one starlight night, that whichever should be called away from the toils and dangers of this life first into the world of spirits, should watch over the other, if permitted, as a "ministering spirit;" a proposal to which, in the simplicity of my heart, I assented. And be it enthusiasm, or be it what it may, that promise, so solemnly made on his part, has been often a source of comfortable reminiscence to me, since his death, in my lonely nocturnal rides. Now that he has gone to his account, I may speak of him with freedom; nor have I anything but what is good to say. I never met him and found him dull or indifferent to the interests of his soul. Our second question, after a mutual inquiry about our health—and sometimes it was the *first*—was, "How do you prosper? How are you getting on towards heaven? Are you happy?" or the like: and I never left his company without feeling that I was made better by it. Our meetings, though not formally so, were practically of the nature of a "Band." We told our faults—we admonished each other—we encouraged each other—and we prayed with and for each other. We had not even the convenience of an in-door meeting place; but the fields and woods, under the broad canopy of heaven, were the places of our rapturous communings. Such was my early class-mate, the thought of meeting whom constitutes no small portion of the anticipated bliss of heaven.

"If death my friend and me divide,
Thou dost not, Lord, my sorrows chide,
Nor frown my tears to see;
Restrained from passionate excess,
Thou bid'st me mourn in calm distress,
For them that rest in Thee.

"I feel a strong, immortal hope,
Which bears my mournful spirit up,
Beneath its mountain load;

Redeemed from death, and grief, and pain,
I soon shall see my friend again,
   Within the arms of God.

"Pass the few fleeting moments more,
And death the blessing shall restore,
   Which death hath snatched away:
For me, Thou wilt the summons send,
And give me back my parted friend,
   In that eternal day!"

AN "ELECT LADY."

The person to whom this scriptural epithet is here most deservedly applied, was a member of the first society to which I belonged; by which I mean, not only the society in the town where I was converted, but its characteristic composition at the time I joined it, and for some years after—a society remarkable for its numbers, considering the then population of the town, its usefulness, its peacefulness, and fervent piety,—but a society, which after some years, was fated to pass through a severe ordeal, and to be sadly racked and scattered by Politics, by Irvineism, by Mormonism, by Millerism, and by a number of untoward circumstances that shall be left unmentioned, so as almost to lose its identity. For, though there is now a flourishing Wesleyan interest in the city to which the town has grown up, yet few of the members of the original society remain. A few, however, do remain.* And among the rest, at the date of our writing, the lady in question. *She* has continued steadfast amid all the storms and all the changes, and

---

* This can hardly be said now, in 1860.

contributed more than any *one* person, in some of its seasons of greatest prostration, to keep the cause from totally sinking. So great is the good that may be done by a pious lady.

We are often challenged for *examples* of the entire holiness we teach; and it must be confessed there are too few on whom its defenders might boldly fix as proofs *of the truth* of their doctrine. But she was one who might have been pointed out with the utmost confidence. The writer saw her at the moment she sprang up from the midst of a camp-meeting " praying circle," which they were in those days, and otherwise called " the ring," exulting in the pardoning mercy of God. He was acquainted with her while yet unmarried,—when in the conjugal relation —and during the continuance of her long widowhood. He knew her in very moderate circumstances, and in wealth and plenty; she was the same cheerful, humble, heavenly-minded creature in all circumstances. She had, there is reason to believe, a good natural disposition or temper; and she had been rendered still more amiable by a superior moral and intellectual training; but her excellencies were principally the fruits of grace divine. I shall never forget the joy of countenance with which she bounded up from her knees at the time of her conversion, to which I have referred; and, after giving glory to God, the alacrity with which she commenced praying and labouring with the still unpardoned penitents around her. From that time she went steadily on. She never seemed to falter, or stumble, or even to lose ground. She is supposed to have been, instrumentally, the salvation of her husband. And after he was taken from her, being left in somewhat affluent circumstances, she was " full of alms-deeds." Often was her generosity imposed on. Although she might have excused herself on the ground of very delicate health, yet she literally " went about doing good." In whatever company she was, she was useful. He never knew a person who so completely united gravity with cheerfulness; and who contrived to do so much good with so little of ostentation or eccentricity. She *never* spake ill of an absent person. There was nothing sour or morose about her; her piety was bland and inviting. Though a person of great endowments, yet she never presumed to *preach*. The good she accomplished was in visiting awakened persons from house to house, and gathering them together in classes, which she met with great acceptability and profit; in praying in the prayer meeting, for she had a most lovely and powerful gift in prayer; and by collecting the poor and neglected of her own sex, in some by-part of the city, and labouring for their edification, by reading a sermon, and superadding exhortation and prayer. Nor was her labour in vain in the Lord. He has no doubt many hundreds of souls will bless God in heaven for the good done them through the instrumentality of this angel of mercy.

The writer remembers with gratitude how often his heart was cheered by intercourse with her, to go on in his arduous toil, during a very trying time, which happened at a somewhat advanced period of his ministry, when appointed to the place of his spiritual birth. He was about to say that "take her all for all, he ne'er will look upon her like again." But why should he say that? The grace of God is sufficient for all; and what she was enabled to be by the grace of God, all may be. May the earth be filled with such Christians. Amen, and amen!*

---

* Since this was written, she has sweetly fallen asleep in Jesus, and rests from her labours.

"SAMMY" RICHARDSON; OR, THE ZEALOUS IRISHMAN.

Zeal without talent will effect more good than talent without zeal. An instance of the good which may be effected by humble abilities, is to be seen in the career of the simple-hearted, fervent little man, whose name stands at the head of this paper: we venture to give this familiar sobriquet, because it is one which he would not have scorned himself, and because it was the one by which he was distinguished by his friends and neighbours, who loved him dearly. He was a native of Ireland, where he was converted in his youth. He came to this country single, I think, in the fall of '24 or '25. It was about that time we first saw him at a Quarterly Meeting in the "Old Framed Meeting-house." We shall never forget his prayer in the Saturday night prayer-meeting, and his experience in the love-feast next morning. A young man, who was in an unhappy state of mind, was so cheered with his prayer, that he remarked, "If that little Irishman had kept on praying a little longer, I believe I should have got deliverance." There was nothing remarkable in what he said, but he spoke with such a heartfelt sense of earnestness and enjoyment, that, while speaking in the love-feast, the flame spread among the people in all directions.

There were several useful young exhorters in and about the town of York, at that time, but none of them equalled Sammy for being "instant in season and out of season."

The first camp-meeting he attended after his arrival in the country, a little staggered him at the first, as he had never seen it on that fashion in his own country; but he soon rightly concluded that it would never do to stand and look on. He was quickly, therefore, in the thickest of the battle, with his coat off, pointing penitent sinners to Christ, or pouring out strong cries and tears on their behalf. One instance of his usefulness at that meeting might be recorded. He and his friends had settled in a neighbourhood in which there was no class, and the inhabitants of which, at that time, were any thing but religious. There chanced to be one of these at the meeting, a young man of respectable, but irreligious family. His heart was stricken with conviction, and he stood looking wishfully but hesitatingly into the prayer-meeting. Sammy perceived this, and pressed him hard to show his submission to God by going forward to seek mercy and be prayed for. But as he still lingered, Sammy did the part of the angels to Lot and his family, he "laid hold of him." Seizing him around the waist, he literally pitched him within "the ring," as it was then called. The ice being broken, the young man began to seek God for salvation. With what success at the meeting I cannot exactly say; but this I know, that the same young man died in peace only ten days after the meeting was over, thus justifying the unusual method taken to "pluck him as a brand from the burning."

That was the commencement of a work of God which issued in raising up a society which has existed with more or less prosperity to the present time. A chapel was erected after some years, which still stands. "Sammy" was the leader, I believe, till the day of his death, and is embalmed in the memory of his friends. And several of that society are useful Local Preachers in other parts of the country.

The writer has not the materials for a consecutive history of his friend, nor can he give the particulars of his death, beyond this, that he knows he lived faithfully and died happily. But a few instances of his fidelity and zeal may be given as a willing tribute to his memory on the part of the writer; and may be incentives to others to activity in the cause of Christ. Sammy was passing along one day, on his way from a neighbourhood in which he taught a school to the one in which his relatives resided, when, being thirsty, he called into a little house by the road side, in a neighbourhood settled mostly by people from the old country, and in which there was no preaching. After asking for and receiving a drink of water, he inquired if they "loved Jesus." This soon brought the old man of the house, who was a backslider, from Ireland, first to tears, and then upon his knees. After a season of melting prayer, the old gentleman was reminded of his sick son, in a house at the top of the hill, whom he invited what appeared to him the almost angelic stranger, to visit. The stranger readily complied, and was soon praying by the side of the sick man, who had been a leader and exhorter himself in other days, but who was then bitterly mourning his "leanness," and crying out, "Oh that it were with me as in the days that are past." Sammy made an appointment for prayer and exhortation on his return to his school on the following Sabbath. He left an appointment for the following Sabbath after that, to be held by a friend of his, a young Irishman, lately out, then very zealous for God, who used to fly over the country like a hart, to publish a Saviour's love. The *second* appointment was duly kept. At the *third* meeting, the writer was present by invitation, and made his *first* attempt to exhort. This meeting was kept up by the spontaneous zeal of a few pious lads for two years before a preacher went near them. There were no Local Preachers' Plans in those days. But the sick man was *restored* in body and soul. An awakening commenced which resulted in a number of conversions, and when the stationed preacher went out from York one Sunday afternoon, and preached among them, he had the satisfaction of joining no less than twenty-nine believers in class. That sick man is now in the evening of his days a gentleman of a highly respectable social position, and a Local Preacher. And one of the converts in that little revival, has been for many years a truly efficient Wesleyan Minister—the Rev. John Lever.

Sammy was truly instant in season and out of season. The writer remembers his being kindly conducted by a young man through a piece of woods, after nightfall, to the house of a friend which he was anxious to reach. The young man was not converted. When we arrived at our place of destination, who should be there but Sammy. It was Saturday night, and he had come thus far, a distance of some miles from his own house, on his way to his Sabbath appointments. I was glad to meet him. Soon an animated conversation sprung up, on experimental religion, sudden conversions, revivals, and the Lord's wonderful doings that he had seen in various parts of the land. My guide became interested and somewhat impressed; and when the hour for family devotion arrived, Sammy did not forget to remember him in prayer; and while the writer followed in prayer at his bidding, Sammy walked across the room on his knees, and began to point him to Christ and urge him to seek the Lord with all his heart. I am not prepared to say it issued in the young man's conversion at that time; but if it did not, it was not from any want of fidelity on the part of the hero of my story.

An instance of a more successful effort was related to the writer by Sammy, on the afternoon of the day on which it happened. I had spent four months on a bush circuit to the west of the capital, and was ordered by connexional authority a hundred and twenty miles to the east. This journey we had to perform on horseback. It was a squally, half-rainy half-snowy afternoon in the fall of 1828, that we were splashing our way through seas of muddy water, in a dreary sort of mood, without an umbrella, for our apology for one had turned completely inside-out by the first gust that swept the street after we left our mother's door, in the town of York, on which we just rode back, pitched the wreck into the house, and rode on without it. It was a maxim with us in those days, that as we were neither sugar nor salt, a little water would not melt us. Well, as I was saying, as I rode along, splash, splash, splash, moody enough, I met Sammy's ever joyous face, like a gleam of sunshine through the surrounding gloom. Sammy withdrew from the raising of the log-house at which he was assisting, and came to " bring us on our journey," for a short distance at least, after a truly " godly sort." He told me that that morning he had gone to a neighbour's to borrow the use of a yoke of oxen; but forgetting his errand, he had begun to talk to him about his soul, and finding him in distress, they both went upon their knees, and continued to pray till, to use Sammy's words, "the Lord set his soul at liberty." He gave us his blessing, and we went on our way rejoicing. To his kind directions I owed my comfortable quarters that night, in the shanty of a pious new settler, in the front of Pickering, where I slept with a pile of corn husks at my head.

Soon after this, Sammy married; and the writer had the pleasure of twice enjoying his hospitality in his journeys up and down the country. These were our only interviews with our heavenly minded friend, till he exchanged mortality for life. Our last was in the winter of '37, when the country was in a disturbed state after the rebellion. We arrived at a late hour, but met a cordial welcome. We had a season of delightful intercourse throughout the evening. Before the morning light, we rose, poured out our souls together in prayer, and the writer went on his way, never more to see his friend on earth. Peace to thy memory, simple, loving, praying Sammy!

ONE OF MY FIRST PASTORS.

The mention of the "Old Framed Meeting-house" has suggested the idea of sketching the Preachers who laboured in Canada West thirty years ago, especially those who preached in the chapel referred to, who have passed off the stage of action, and are now where they cannot be affected by the praise or blame of mortals.

The first we shall call up in memorial, is WILLIAM SLATER. He was on the York and Yonge Circuit, at the time the writer set out for heaven, and was present in the very Love-feast in which he joined the church. Mr. S. was then comparatively young, and yet single; nor would he be among the very oldest if he were still alive. But death, "the insatiate archer," who "loves a shining mark," laid him low in the midst of his days. He was from old England; and a noble person of a man he was—tall and well proportioned, with florid complexion, and full, open, strong voice. As a preacher, he was considerably above mediocrity for his day, though not very moving. His preaching was plain, lucid and able, but truly practical. Some of the texts he used to preach from are as fresh in the recollection of the writer, as if he had heard them preached on but yesterday. Pardon him for reciting a few of them. They may do us good. "Whom having not seen we love; and in whom believing, though now ye see him not, we rejoice with joy unspeakable and full of glory." "Almost thou persuadest me to be a Christian." "Follow peace with all men, and holiness, without which no man shall see the Lord." "Open thou mine eyes, that I may behold wondrous things out of thy law! These four furnish a pretty fair sample of the kind of texts on which he loved to dwell; plain and full of gospel truth. Although by no means a canting, long-faced person, but the very reverse; yet there is good evidence to believe he was a man of sterling moral worth and piety. The writer being then a boy, never had the pleasure of being in his company but *once;* on that occasion, he remembers his conversation to have been intelligent, serious, and characterized by manly sense. He died from home, and rather suddenly, but, he believes, *in great peace.* The messenger did not find him unprepared. The friends on the Ancaster Circuit, with a praiseworthy consideration, erected a tombstone to his memory, which may be seen in the rear of the "old chapel," in the *now* city of Hamilton; *then* one of the preaching places in the above-named circuit, in which Mr Slater fell.

At the time the writer first saw him, and also the following year, Mr. S. was the colleague of our present [1854] much respected Co-Delegate; and he has reason to know, he remained his attached personal friend till the day of his release from earth. How joyful will be the meeting of such fellow labourers, in the "rest that remaineth for *the people* of God."

A NATION BORN IN A DAY!

"Shall a nation be born at once?"

Yes, so it was with the conversion of the native Indian tribes of Upper Canada to the Christian faith; particularly so with the Chippeways. Perhaps, on the whole, there has not been a more extraordinary work since the apostolic age. It commenced about thirty-one or thirty-two years ago; and in a very few years comprised all the tribes or bands within the settlements on the borders of the Province. The work took all beholders by surprise, and gave a new impulse to the Methodist body, through whose instrumentality it was effected. It was the theme of conversation and the burden of prayer. The Indian converts visited our camp and quarterly meetings; and their altered appearance diffused a general joy. And well it might produce joy and thanksgiving in the minds of every pious and benevolent person. For a more degraded and miserable people than the Chippeway Indians, at least, could scarcely be imagined. They had no arts but the most rude and savage ones—no literature—no property—and it might be said, no houses, no home. When an Indian was asked where he lived, he responded, " All up the river."

The writer has a lively recollection of the Mississagua tribe of the Chippeway nation, which hovered about the town of York and its vicinity. They were drunkards to a man—their women totally devoid of virtue—and the whole of them sunk in poverty and filth beyond expression. At the time of their receiving their "annuities and presents," which was in the town above named, a bacchanalian revel took place, which usually lasted many days, and issued in squandering every copper of money and selling or pawning every article they had received, for the deadly "firewaters," and in the death of several, from exposure and violence. It was not uncommon to see a dozen of them engaged in one melee, tearing each other's hair and flesh to pieces. In a word, they were so debased and even more than embruted, that for any one, at that period, to have expressed a belief of their being susceptible of religious ideas or emotions at all, would have been to expose himself to derision.

Still, it would appear, a few holy men revolved the desirableness and possibility of this event in their minds; among whom was the Rev. Mr. Case. The Rev. Joseph Sawyer, lately gone to his reward, some sixty years ago or more dedicated a little Indian boy, who then lived with a pious white family, to God in the ordinance of Christian baptism, and gave him his own name "Joseph Sawyer." This he told me with his own lips. And it is somewhat curious and interesting to know, that though that Indian boy soon broke away from the oversight of the Christian gentleman under whose guardianship he then lived, and returned to the habits and haunts of savage life, yet his mind was the subject of strong solicitude on the subject of things divine and eternal; and he was the very first of that tribe, after Peter Jones, to embrace Christianity, on the Gospel being preached to them in their own language. His influence was strenuously and successfully exerted in promoting the work among his countrymen. He still lives, the patriarch of his tribe, and efficiently fills, I believe, the offices of Leader and Local Preacher.

As has already been incidentally hinted, PETER JONES was the first of the Chippeways, and, I believe, the first Indian of any kind, converted to God in Upper Canada. There had been a few Mohawks on the Grand River brought into connection with what was then called "The Established Church;" but their knowledge, experience, and practice of Christianity, all who knew them must confess to have been very deficient. The wisdom of God was shown in the selection of the first vessel of mercy, through whom His truth and grace were to be made known to his countrymen. Peter seemed a connecting link between the white man and both the Chippeways and Mohawks. The son of a Welshman, a surveyor; his mother a Chippeway of the Mississagua tribe, with whom he had lived the whole of his boyhood in the woods; and subsequently domesticated under a Mohawk step-mother, some of whose language he is believed to have understood. No wonder, therefore, at the joy said to have been expressed by the devoted Elder Case, when the news was brought into the "Preachers' Tent," at the Ancaster Camp Meeting, in 1823, (celebrated by that event,) that Peter Jones *was converted!* " Glory be to

God!" exclaimed the servant of God, "a door is now open to the Indian tribes." It is not the writer's intention to present anything like a history of that work. He is by no means competent, and if he were ever so much so, it would be unseemly to forestal one who is preparing to do so, and to whom the work naturally and properly belongs. All the writer intends to indulge in is a few reminiscences interesting to himself, and, the record of which may be so to those who were not privileged to witness the events to which they refer. There are many now living who remember the joy felt and expressed in the "Old Framed Meeting-House," when it was said the work of conversion had commenced at the Credit; and that such men as the Herkimers, the Kishecos, Tobeco John, Governor Muskrat, and the desperate Blue Jay, were taught to bow before the truth and power of God. A more lively, lovely, happy and holy community than that Indian society at the Credit was for many years, I do not believe ever existed. To hear them sing and pray, although you could not understand their language, was thrillingly delightful; and the displays of divine power manifested in their assemblies were truly wonderful. The rapidity with which the work went on at this place—the equally speedy manner in which the Belleville or Kingston Indians were converted—but especially the conversion of nearly all the Rice Lake tribe in one Sabbath day, during the session of the Conference in the "Old Chapel" back of Cobourg, township of Hamilton, in 1827, fully justifies the motto we have chosen. The writer will never forget the impression made on his boyish imagination by the conversion of a whole band or tribe in a few hours, which he had the happiness to witness. It must have been in June preceding the Conference just referred to. The Methodists of York and Yonge Street had prepared for a great camp meeting near Cummer's Mill. The Indians from the Credit turned out to a man, woman and child. A band of pagans also, from the shores of Lake Simcoe somewhere, had heard that their brethren had found something which made them "glad in their hearts," and made them happy in other respects; for they had given up the *firewaters*, and were living like white folks. These had heard of this great meeting and had come into the neighbourhood a week beforehand, to make sure of being at it. The Yonge Street friends very kindly supplied them with food, and considerately prepared for their accommodation at the camp meeting. I shall never forget the solemnity with which they attended on the first service, on the afternoon of the first day. When the horn sounded for preaching, they came pouring out of their camp. The old bald-headed chief led the van, followed first by his warriors, and then by the women and children. They seated themselves on the left of the "preachers' stand," prepared for the Indians, surrounded by converted ones of other tribes. The white people were first addressed by one of the preachers in English. Then the venerable Elder Case arose, and began to address the Indians through the youthful Peter Jacobs as his interpreter. He told them of the Great First Cause—of the creation—of the fall of man—of the flood—of the incarnation of the Son of God—of his sufferings and death—of his resurrection and ascension to heaven—of his power and willingness to save; and told them that if they would lift up their hearts in prayer to the GREAT SPIRIT, he would have mercy, and pour out his Holy Spirit upon them. Solemnity sat upon every face from the first. But soon the head of the old chief, and then of one and another was bowed in penitential sorrow, while tears channeled down the cheeks of those who had never wept before. Soon the power from above seemed greater, and the agitation stronger; quaking, trembling, falling, were seen all through the Indian congregation. The preacher's voice was drowned with strong cries and shouts of joy from the liberated. He ceased, and a prayer meeting began which lasted with very little intermission till morning, and the whole of the pagans were happily converted to God. This is but a specimen of the way in which the work took place at the Credit, at Belleville, at Rice Lake, Lake Simcoe, Munceytown, &c. The extraordinary physical agitations and effects above referred to characterized the work in every place on its first breaking out; and were calculated to remind one strongly of the surprising occurrences which attended the preaching of the early Methodists, as recorded especially in John Wesley's journals; occurrences which have more or less marked all great revivals of the work of God.

The eloquence and power with which the native labourers, raised up in the work itself to promote it, prosecuted their efforts—some for a short time and in a limited sphere only, while others laboured more at large, and have continued their labours to the present time—was not the least remarkable feature of the work. A Jones, a Jacobs, a Sunday, a Herkimer, a Sickles; and for a short time, or to a limited extent to the present, a Beaver, a Toney, a Magee, a Doxtater, and many others, were characterised by an eloquence, judging from its effects, of the first order. Or was it not rather, that they preached with the Holy Ghost sent down from heaven?

The mention of Doxtater, not now, I believe, connected with our church, reminds me of the sudden and gracious work among the Mohawks of the Bay of Quinte, or in the well-known "Indian Woods," commenced by his instrumentality, which the writer, in connexion with his superintendent, had the pleasure of assisting to promote, under circumstances of privation and " without fee or reward." We connected the " Woods " with the Belleville circuit, which we were appointed to travel, and each went down once in four weeks, which gave them fortnightly preaching. The road from Salmon River to the Mission at that time, in spring and fall especially, I pronounce to have been the worst one to be called a road at all, that I ever travelled. The land was very low and level. It had once been causewayed; but it was decayed, and the logs were all afloat; so that it was at the jeopard of a man's life that he undertook to ride through some parts of it. My method was to drive my horse before me, and jump from log to log. It was a country, too, something like Cornwall, in England, in Wesley's and John Nelson's day, "an excellent place for getting an appetite, but the worst for getting anything to eat." The Indians were miserably poor and poverty stricken, from the failure of their corn crop the summer preceding. So that we were in "fasting," as well as "perils" the live-long day. Nor was there any after remuneration, except what we had in the pleasing reflection that we had been doing good; for we had no missionary exchequer in those days, and no brother received anything for missionary labour unless it was *exclusively* such. But we never thought of complaining then; and do not complain now. The love and gratitude of these simple sons of the forest were an ample compensation. An invitation to a feast, the last time I went down, consisting of damaged corn and rusty salt pork, in which the dogs had stuck their noses sundry times while the kettles stood on the hearth during divine service, which preceded the dinner, was much the most formidable difficulty I had to dispose of the whole year. I am sure I would have chosen three days' fasting to one spoonful of that abominable soup. But I contrived to beg off—wrote my name on the blank leaf of a book, at the request of the old chief, that they might not forget it—and left amid their tears and blessings.

A CANADIAN CAMP-MEETING THIRTY-FIVE YEARS AGO.

This was the first one held so near Toronto, and the first the writer ever attended. Every scene and circumstance was novel, and, therefore, made a deep impression on his young and susceptible mind and memory.

It was held in the summer of 1825, near Cummer's Mills, considered at that time, the way the road went round Hogg's Hollow, about twelve miles from town. "York and Yonge Street" were then one circuit; and the town society interested itself very much in the coming meeting. Several young men were sent out a week beforehand, to assist in preparing the ground; and to erect a large board tent, which they did, *fifty feet long*, with every convenience. Prayer was offered to God for His presence and blessing on the meeting, for days, if not weeks beforehand. And at sunrise on the morning of the day on which it was to commence, the society of the "Old Framed Meeting-house" were all on the *qui vive*, and very soon *en route* to the camp-meeting. Between carts and waggons, and equestrians and pedestrians, the procession looked quite formidable. We arrived at the place about noon; and without wishing to institute any invidious comparison between "modern" camp-metings and those of former days, farther than is necessary to convey correct information or to impart needed admonition, I must say it had an imposing appearance compared with many encampments of the present time. This arose from the character and necessity of the times, when there was no law for punishing the disturbers of public worship, or the sale of articles on the Lord's-day. As you entered the ground, it sloped downward from the front gate to the "Preacher's stand," with "tent" attached, which stood at the other side of the area. The seats for the congregation (of new slabs from the mill) consequently rose with a gentle elevation from the stand; and they were prepared with a view to accommodate a vast number. The ground, though thoroughly cleared of small trees and rubbish, was delightfully shaded by the wide-spreading branches and thick foliage of the straight and towering forest trees that were left standing. The whole of the cleared space was encompassed with a strong fence *eight* or *ten* feet high, made of slabs, resting against stakes crossing each other, and driven firm in the ground. The slabs, which were also driven in the ground at an angle of forty-five degrees from the perpendicular, were sharpened at the top, thus constituting a sort of *chevaux de frise*, which no intruder, however bold, might dare to scale. Each of the openings for egress and ingress, whether for wood, water, or retirement, as well as the main entrance, particularly the latter, were furnished with gates strongly framed together, and secured by strong pins and massive bars. These were carefully guarded by a strong "watch," a sort of camp-meeting police, that relieved each other at intervals, and kept watch and ward the live-long night.

The tents were nearly all of boards, and completely encircled the ground. I would not like to attempt estimating the numbers, but the ground was alive with people from early the first day to the last. The Methodists turned out numerously from the Yonge Street and from the Toronto Township, then the nearest circuit, on which a glorious revival was in progress at the time. "The Toronto Methodists" were celebrated for being all alive in those days.

The meeting was superintended by the Rev. Thos. Madden, who combined order with energy. I have often thought that he would have made a good general: and so he was, in a more glorious though bloodless conflict. The other travelling preachers were Gatchel, Culp, William Ryerson, Corson, Heyland; and W. H. Williams and J. Richardson, the preachers on the circuit.

The local preachers who assisted were R. Bofield, J. J. Neelands, C. Flummerfeldt, and D. Youmans, then in the local ranks, and Cline, a Dutchman. This meeting was characterised by the most extraordinary displays of God's power, and the accomplishment of much good. The work of conversion began in the first prayer meeting held after the preaching the first night. The spirit of conviction seemed to rest on all the unconverted within the enclosure. They might be seen in little groups all over the ground, pleading with God till near the morning light. It progressed with increasing interest and power through the several stages of the meeting to its close—that is to say, from Thursday night to Monday—on which day no less than 140 persons came forward as the subjects of converting grace. The sacramental and farewell services at the close were the most exciting and intensely affecting that I ever witnessed. And I should think such times are not often seen. The valedictory charge was delivered, at the request of the Presiding Elder, by the Rev. William Ryerson, whose preaching at that time was characterized by a pathos and persuasiveness that seemed to bear down all before it. There was much powerful preaching at that meeting. Mr. Madden's will be mentioned in a succeeding sketch. Rowley Heyland was at that period a thunderbolt for energy. He truly preached "with the Holy Ghost sent down from heaven." May we never forget the obligations we are under to our aged ministers and departed worthies! It is too much the fashion to discard a man as soon as he begins to fail of his natural force: but it is irreverent and ungrateful.

The effect of such meetings is to promote acquaintance and brotherly love between all the church, both ministers and members: and to check a tendency to secularism, and to promote heavenly-mindedness. The writer remembers the regret he felt at going back into the world after the meeting was over. Some of his most hallowed friendships were formed at that and similar meetings; friendships which have solaced him in this vale of tears from youth up to the present time, and friendships which he believes will be cemented and perpetuated,—

"Where all the ship's company meet,
　Who sailed with their Saviour beneath,
Where, with shouting, each other they greet,
　And triumph o'er sorrow and death."

"FATHER" YOUMANS,

Or, as he was wont to style himself sometimes, among his friends, "*The Old Hammer,*" was one of the preachers whom I used most frequently to hear in the days of my boyhood, in the "Old Framed Meeting-house." He was then, perhaps, fifty years of age—possibly not so much; but as he was plain and old-fashioned in his dress and manners, he really appeared older, and was generally known by the name of "Father Youmans;" or more familiarly still, as a term of endearment, "*Daddy* Youmans." He was of Dutch descent, and originally a blacksmith by trade, which latter fact, with a certain hammering method in the pulpit, may have suggested the use of the *sobriquet* above mentioned—"The Old Hammer."

He was not a "star of the first magnitude," nor, perhaps, of the *second* either; but he was a man of strong sense, which, with the divine teaching of which he was the subject, made him a sound divine. He had also a warm heart, which imparted great fervency to his preaching. His exuberance of good temper prevented all severity in his most earnest addresses, and gave them a genial character. He was beloved of all, and the writer well remembers the smile of affectionate regard that was wont to light up the faces of the congregation when he made his appearance in the meeting-house, and passed down the aisle attired in his "Quaker Snuff," or "Parson's Grey," and well-worn broad-leafed *wool* hat in hand. He loved, and was the favourite of children. It was not uncommon to see a dozen little ones around him, pulling and tugging at his hands and coat-skirts, out of sheer fondness for him, and all emulous to

"Share the good man's smile."

The old gentleman had neither much polish nor learning. He has often put me in mind of Bunyan, to whose portrait, in those days he bore a strong resemblance. His similes were of the most homely character. He has been heard in the pulpit to compare the process of purgatorial purification, taught by some, to that of "burning out an old pipe:" with which operation he was, no doubt, familiar, for he was an inveterate smoker. This was the only habit of a reprehensible kind I ever knew him to be guilty of; and this, I believe, was rendered necessary by some asthmatical affection. Yet he was once heard, in Conference, in a conversation on "needless self-indulgences," to offer to relinquish it, "if it were a stumbling-block to any one."

Our hero was a lovely singer, possessed of a clear, strong, masculine, and yet soft voice, as well as correct ear, capable of carrying the *bass* of a tune with enrapturing effect. How much musical *science* he possessed I am not prepared to say. But this I know, he has often enchained the congregation in the chapel by commencing a *solo* at the close of the service; or by singing a select piece, with two or three other practiced, powerful singers, for the possession of which our society was then distinguished. Oh, with what majesty and what effect I have heard Watts' "Tempest" sung on those occasions!

At the time of writing this, (August 28th, 1855,) my revered friend is still alive,* but little known to the present generation, having been for several years confined to his home, if not to his bed. I hope to hear, when his death is announced, that the

---

* He has since died in the Lord.

expectation I once heard him express in class-meeting, (a means of grace in which he delighted, and of which he was the delight,) has been realized. Said he, on the occasion referred to :—" It will not be long till it is said, ' Old Father Youmans is dead :' and, blessed be God, I expect to go with shouting !" May the reader and writer both of them so leave the world ! Amen.

ONE OF OUR SUPPLIES.

For many years the present City of Toronto methodistically stood in connexion with the Yonge Street Circuit, and appeared on the Minutes, not even as *York and Yonge Street*, but as " Yonge Street and York." It was so, we know, in 1823-4, 1824-5, and in 1825 6 ; in 1826-7 it was reversed, and YORK stood *first*. In 1827-8, it became an independent station. During the whole time, from 1823 to 1827, the Yonge Street preachers, two in number, came each only once a month. There were two Sabbaths in every four which they did not supply. Sometimes this defect was remedied by the two Ancaster preachers, coming each once a month. In 1823, these were the Rev. David Culp, and towards the latter part of the year, *Joseph Messmore*, then a young man supplying under the direction of the Presiding Elder. We heard some of his first sermons, and no ill commencement they were to a long course of laborious efforts in his Master's cause. The arrangement referred to stood also for the following year. But very frequently the alternate Sabbath to that on which the Yonge Street ministers were in there, were supplied by *local* and *located* preachers.

The Rev. David Youmans, as we have already seen, was one of the latter. Mr. Robert Bosfield, a profound and masterly sermonizer, but very slow of speech, was one of the former. But there was yet another, a great favourite with all, whom we shall make the special subject of the present sketch.

He was, we believe, a native of Canada, but of German extraction, as both his family and baptismal name unmistakably indicated. He resided in the woods of Scarborough. He had no advantages of education, beyond what the country parts of Canada afforded fifty years ago: but he was a man of genius for all that. This he showed, we are told, by some very clever poetical effusions. During the war of 1812, he was a very active and enthusiastic militiaman, and composed several patriotic songs. One, of a military character, ascribed to him, we often heard sung in our boyhood, and it struck us as very clever. He was naturally a man of activity and daring. Traditions of his personal exploits, showing his agility and strength, were often recited to the writer. He was then unconverted, and remained in that state until he was twenty-nine years old. Then, an alarming providence, which took away one of his companions at "a raising," aroused him from the sleep of sin. Happily the voice of God's messengers in the wilderness, crying, "Prepare ye the way of the Lord!" was there, as also, " the voice of the turtle was heard in the land." His sin-sick soul drank in the balmy sound and was at once made whole.

He soon began to exhort and preach; nor did the trumpet give any uncertain sound. The preachers knew and appreciated him. They had to be absent from the town a Sabbath at a camp-meeting, and our hero was proposed by them as a supply. To this the richest man in the Society, an old Scotch gentleman, who did not believe in camp-meetings, and did not go to them, made strong objections. He was to stay at home, and wanted a respectable preacher in the pulpit, if possible;

but the proposed supply was a poor man who had to labour for his living, and had been in town only a few days before, with a load of shingles, barefooted. To have such a man, the sturdy Scot thought would not do at all. But there was no other supply; and, fortunately, the poor man "made a raise" of a pair of shoes before Sunday, and his good wife otherwise "fixed him up," making his "auld claise to look a'maist as weel as new." On Sabbath morning, in he came, and succeeded to admiration. And the first news Mr. C. had to tell the ministers, on their return was, what two excellent sermons Brother F. had preached. He was thenceforth in great request in the town, and none of the travelling preachers stood higher.

We well remember our first sight of him. We had been only a few weeks trying to serve God, but long enough to have read the "Life of Wesley, by Coke and Moore," and a volume of the "Lives of the Early Methodist Preachers." We went on the morning referred to, as was our wont, at an early hour, to the meeting house. The congregation had pretty much all assembled before any preacher made his appearance. They had begun to look inquiringly at each other, when a broad, heavy, masculine-looking man, with plain but agreeable features, and a sunburnt, beardless face— perhaps thirty-four years of age—entered, dressed in a well-worn suit of dark-coloured homespun—cut-away coat—and an oaten-straw hat in his hand. I felt to love him at once. He was the beau ideal of one of the early rustic lay preachers, and might have answered to represent the meek but stout-hearted JOHN NELSON himself. And, oh, what a delightful service we had that morning! Our preacher was modest, but composed. His voice was pleasant, and his elocution, or "delivery," as we used to call it, good. An impressive reader was he. Then, such a sermon! So clear, methodical, consecutive, rememberable, and sweetly evangelical. His text was, "Fear not, little flock, for it is your father's good pleasure to give you the kingdom." He treated it in a way that went to our hearts. To this day we can easily remember his texts and the way he treated them. He was an easy, natural, ingenious sermonizer. The secret of his *amplification* was, his always noticing what his text *implied* as well as *expressed*.

We must recite another incident of our friend and the town pulpit. At that time there were two well-educated gentlemen, natives of England, who sometimes came to the "Old Framed Meeting-House." The first was the son of a Wesleyan Minister, and had been classically trained at Kingswood school—had been a popular local preacher himself, but now seldom officiated, and wore his religion pretty loosely around him. His connection with Methodism ended with the removal of the British Missionaries about 1820. The other, was a man of respectable connexions, the brother of an English Church Clergyman, and a sincere enquirer after truth, who ultimately became a Baptist. He was very partial to one of our circuit Ministers in 1825–6, during which year the following scene is laid. We remember the morning well; and of seeing him in the chapel, and the rest that occurred. The Scarborough brother supplied that morning. He was dressed in a heavy suit of home-made; and entered with a coarse wool hat in his hand, the binding around the rim of which was in jinglets. His nether extremities were cased in a large, heavy pair of cowhide boots, which were whole enough, only that one of them was *minus* its heel-leathers. This made his heavy tramp somewhat unequal, and gave his walk a "wabbling" appearance. We observed that Mr. W—m looked fidgetty at the first, but that he staid out the service. Some day that week the following colloquy took place in the streets of "LITTLE YORK." Two gentlemen meet and exchange the usual greetings.

Mr. F—N.—"Where were you last Sunday?"

Mr. W—m.—"I was at the Methodist Chapel. I went expecting to hear Mr. R—n. There was no preacher in when I arrived, but I had not been seated long when a great, rough lump of a man came in dressed in home-spun. I was disappointed and disgusted, and, if it had not been for the looks of it, I should have taken my hat and left. But I staid ; and I was glad I did. He gave us a beautiful sermon. Sir, he opened up the Scriptures rightly."

His text that day was the words of Christ : " If any man serve me, let him follow me ; and where I am there shall my servants be : if any man serve me, him will my Father honor." He truly did open this passage of Scripture "rightly." Many of his texts and his mode of treating them, after the lapse of *thirty-four or five years*, are still fresh in our own recollection.

He was our only preceptor in *Homiletics*. Some reverses had confined him for a time to the city limits, where he was fain to support himself by making the coarser kind of shoes. We had been called out on to a neighbouring circuit, about this time. One day—the only spare one we had in four weeks, we rode into town to see our friends ; but we never failed to go and see this preaching Crispin. We usually told him of all the new texts we had taken during the month, and how we had handled them; as also what other texts we had thought of, but did not know how to extract their sweets. He gave us his judgment on the skeletons we had made, always suggesting some real improvement ; while he taught us how to analyze those passages which we had feared to broach. Talk of Theological Schools, and Professors of Homiletics— no man understood sermonizing better than that wax-begrimed child of adversity. And never did I spend happier or more profitable hours than in that unfinished loft, by that lowly shoe-bench. Our seasons of delightful communion were always concluded with prayer.

Subsequently, this good man—for he was a sanctified soul—

adjusted his affairs, and went into the work as a "hired local preacher," being too old and deficient in learning to enter in the usual way. After some years, however, the rule was dispensed with in his case, in view of his actual preaching abilities and successful labors, and he was made a member of the Conference. After laboring for twenty years upon circuits he is now for several years a Superanuate in retirement, not far from the scenes of his early labors. Scores of more sprightly and better educated men have entered the ministry and thrown those of his School into the shade; yet few can think how useful they were in their day, and how really capable they were as preachers. Our hero's general knowledge was not very extensive; the theme of his delighted conversations, therefore, usually was religion and preaching. He might have found it hard to keep up with all our connexional improvements, and may have lacked a little in that case as a Superintendent: yet a *preacher* he was, both in the pulpit and by the fire side— in the latter he particularly excelled.

Though our subject is not dead, we are anxious to have his *name* upon our pages; and hope he will pardon us for bringing CORNELIUS FLUMERFELT out of his obscurity and making him to figure as *One of Our Supplies*, thirty-five years ago, in the "OLD FRAMED MEETING HOUSE."

"THE VENERABLE THOMAS WHITEHEAD."

These are the terms of respect and reverence by which the person named was usually designated for many years before his death, whenever referred to in public. Privately, he was designated by the ministers' and members of the church who knew him as "Father Whitehead." He was so called when the writer first became a Methodist, some twenty-five years before Mr. W.'s death. His first sight of him also was in the "Old Framed Meeting House" in "little York," at a prayer meeting. Mr. W. was on his way from the lower part of the Province to his residence in Burford. Turning aside as a wayfaring man for a night, he had heard of this social means of grace, and felt it his duty and privilege to attend. We were struck with the peculiar manner of his utterance whenever he elevated his voice, which made him so difficult to be undestood by hearers till they became familiar with its sound. This was the only drawback to his ministry. For his other excellencies were many and great.

He was a man of sterling, unbending integrity. He was not ashamed to be singular, and to stand *alone*, when contending for what he thought to be right. Many of the senior ministers will remenber his standing in a minority of *one* in the great question before the Conference in thirty-three. But he, who always contended so honestly while a measure was under discussion, was equally submissive when it was fairly carried by a majority. In this respect his conduct was in beautiful contrast to that of another member of the Conference at that time, who, to avoid the difficulty of voting against what he did not approve, ran out of the house; and yet, subsequently, left the connexion on account of this very measure, and did all in his power to rend it asunder. Whitehead's genuine, truly evangelical piety was the secret of all this. His habits were very much of the simple, hardy kind, that characterized the early Methodist Preachers on the American continent. He rose early, lived plain, and always rode on horseback. No wonder then, that he usually had excellent health and attained to a great age. It is a curious fact, that Mr. W.'s favourite horse, "Sally-John," so called to commemorate the names of the man and his wife from whom he bought him, although he served his master to the advanced age of *twenty-five years*, had never a harness on his back. Mr. W. was a geat reader and exceedingly well informed on all subjects of general interest. He was partial to our English poets, particularly Young's Night Thoughts, a copy of which he had always about him. He maintained that it was the most replete with thought, and the most suggestive of any book in the language. It was this venerable minister's commendation of it, that led the writer, when a mere stripling, to purchase and give himself to the study of this work; from which he thinks he derived both pleasure and profit.

Mr. Whitehead's healthful flow of spirits, combined with his intelligence, piety, and great conversational powers, made him a most interesting and desirable companion. The writer remembers the pleasure and profit he derived from his company during a visit of his to the circuit he was then travelling in '29. The old gentleman's excursion to the East, as far as Hollowell, had a most salutary influence in counteracting an evil leaven, which had begun to work in the connexion. It was during that visit, he first heard him preach. It was in the town of Cobourg, on his favourite theme, "Behold the Lamb of God, which taketh away the sins of the world."

Mr. W. was eminently social, and although not a "spirit drinker," he was fond of "the cup which cheers, but not inebriates." And we have been told by an intelligent and pious gentleman, who had the strongest affection for him, that dur- the war of 1812, Mr. W. who was almost the only Methodist minister that laboured east of Kingston, and whose circuit extended from that town to Cornwall, and as far back as the Rideau: knowing how destitute the people were of that luxury in the interior, he used to carry some tea in his saddle-bags, (as the celebrated Essayist, Foster, did, in his pocket when he went to see the poorer members of his flock); and to share at least, with the "old folks" of the families where he lodged. But whether old or young, the visits of one whose conversation was so entertaining and improving was hailed by all in those days, when there were few, if any, books and newspapers, and in many parts of the country no mails, not to mention the want of railroads and magnetic telegraphs! Under such circumstances, how inexpressibly beneficial must the itinerant rounds of such a man have been?

The writer, thus late, at the suggestion of an aged preacher, one whom we might denominate his "companion in arms," has endeavoured to pay a tribute of respect to one of a class of men to whom Canada owes much. As he has not dealt in anything like narrative in reference to Mr. W. he encloses the obituary of him published in the Minutes of Conference for 1846, which it is judged best to publish :

"Quest. IV. *What Preachers have died since last Conference?*

"Ans. THOMAS WHITEHEAD.—He died at the house of his son, in Burford, 22nd January, 1846, aged 83 years, and in the 62nd of his ministry. The theme of his long ministry was embodied in his last words—"Glory to God in the highest, and on earth peace, good-will towards men!" He was born in Duchess County, in the Province (now State) of New York, 11th December, 1762 ; was converted and joined the Methodist Church in the 18th year of his age; commenced his itinerant ministry at the age of 21, under the direction of the New York Conference, and laboured about three years in the neighbourhoods of Albany and New York, when he was sent as a Missionary to the Province of Nova Scotia, and continued there and in the Province of New Brunswick about 16 years, when he returned to New York; laboured two years near Albany, and was sent by Bishop Asbury in Sept. 1806 to Upper Canada, where he continued to reside and labour during the last forty years of his useful life. While in Nova Scotia, he married a daughter of Israel and Elizabeth Andrews. At the time of his coming to Canada he had a family of six children; was exposed six weeks in an open boat coming from Albany to Niagara, during the greater part of which time he and his family subsisted on *boiled wheat*. He laboured two years in the Niagara District—two years in the Long Point country—travelled several years on circuits in the Prince Edward, Midland, and Johnstown Districts, when he removed again to the Long Point Circuit—superannuated and settled in Burford in the year 1815.

"Mr. Whitehead's early religious convictions had been deep and strongly marked, and his experience of salvation by faith clear and undoubted. His piety was, in the words of his favourite Dr. Young, as

> "An even spun thread, alike throughout"

fervent, deep, and experimental, during the whole of his protracted Christian life. His gentlemanly deportment was but emblematical of his gentle and affectionate piety, and his fine physical stature but the index of the noble spirit within. He possessed a well cultivated mind, which was richly stored with general knowledge. His pulpit talents were superior; and notwithstanding a slight impediment in his speech, which increased with age, he was a popular as well as highly instructive and animated Preacher. He was industrious and faithful in his public labours, as he was diligent and devout in his private readings and prayers. In all agitations and oppositions, he remained firm in his connexion and attachment with the Church in which he had found the Lord Jesus. Christ crucified was his favourite theme, and preaching his delightful employment. He loved to preach, as the Discipline directs, on the occasions of Christian festivals, and preached no less than fifty-three Christmas sermons on as many successive Christmas days. He preached for the last time in his life on Christmas-day, 1845, from Luke ii. 14. While his body, literally worn out, was gradually sinking beneath the accumulation of years and labours, the vigour of his intellect remained unimpaired—his peace perfect—his hope buoyant. His eye of luminous faith converted the darkness of death into the opening light of Heaven, and transformed its gloomy valley into a highway of triumph; and while he was giving the sign of assured victory, after speech had failed, he fell asleep in Jesus—having furnished a practical commentary during a longer period than any other Clergyman in Canada, on the words of his favourite hymn, with which he was accustomed, for many years, almost invariably to commence public service:

> "His only righteousness I show,
> His saving truth proclaim:
> 'Tis all my business here below
> To cry, "Behold the Lamb!"
>
> "Happy if with my latest breath
> I may but gasp his name;
> Preach him to all, and cry in death,
> · Behold, behold the Lamb!'"

"After the example of the Redeemer himself and his holy Apostles, Mr. Whitehead, with his ministerial brethren, was, for many years, maligned and persecuted as an *American Preacher*—as not well affected to the Government of his birth and choice; but he, as well as his fellow-labourers have long since lived down this calumny; and his mortal remains were followed to the grave by the largest concourse of people, of all ranks and denominations, which was ever witnessed in Burford on any similar occasion.

"It may be added in this place, that those self-sacrificing Preachers who, like Mr. Whitehead, came into this country at an early period, came here not because of their aversion to the British Government, but because of their preference for it, and because of their willingness to endure any privations and labours in order to preach to the then destitute inhabitants of Canada the unsearchable riches of Christ. Volunteer Preachers for the then distant and wilderness Canada, were called for in the Conference of the new American Republic, when those who, from hereditary attachment, or from disappointment at the working of the new American Institutions, and from a noble spirit of Christian enterprise to preach the Gospel to the ends of the earth, offered themselves as labourers in Canada. To them the people of Canada are deeply indebted. Their souls were then cared for by no other class of men. Those venerable men have nearly all gone to their reward; and like Mr. Whitehead, have died in the faith of the Gospel, which they had laboured and suffered so much to preach. It remains for the living members of the Church to serve the present generation as faithfully and as efficiently as their predecessors served the last generation."

We want to say in conclusion, to those who never saw him, that the printed portrait of this servant of Christ is a good one; but it is not so life-like as it would have been, if his hair had been disposed in the meek way he usually wore it.

THE TWO SOLDIER PREACHERS.

There is much in the spirit and accompaniments of war in general at variance with the genius of Christianity. No wonder, therefore, that many good persons should doubt the compatability of the soldier's position with the character of a christian. Yet we cannot deny that there have been truly devout and holy men in the army. Perhaps few, if any such, entered it; but there can be no question that some have *become* such while there. We have one remarkable instance at least in the case of Colonel Gardiner. The Gospel has proved itself sufficient, under the divine blessing, to subdue the dauntless heart of the soldier. And the Gospel preached by Methodist preachers has won more than its share of trophies from the military ranks. This has been the case from first to last during the whole career of Methodism. And some of these trophies have become heralds of salvation in turn. Some of the most zealous and successful Methodist preachers have been soldiers in their time. In proof of this we need but transcribe the name of Haime, of Staniforth; of Captain Webb, of Burgess, and of Bamford of Nova Scotia. Whether it was a heroic spirit which led these men into the army; or whether it was there they imbibed it, certain it is they carried it into their religion and ministry. We have some living instances of this christian heroism in our Canadian connexion in the person of a Harmon, now almost *hors de combat*, and a Hardy, and others, who were once in the army.

Two remarkable men, who had been soldiers, identified themselves with the Methodist ministry, in Canada West, at the close of the last American war, figured largely (the one for a *short* period, the other for a *long* one) in connection with Canadian Methodism. These were JAMES PEEL and GEORGE FERGUSON.

As we have scarcely materials for a sketch of the first; so also in the second instance, we have no disposition to forestall a work which ought to have been attended to long ago; viz: the publication of the Journal of the Rev. George Ferguson. Why is it not done? We therefore mention them together. They must have been nearly of the same age, and they served during nearly the same period. They were both preaching soldiers. They were both purchased out of the army: at least I think so. Ferguson certainly was, by our people in

Niagara and its vicinity; and Peel is thought to have been by friends, if I mistake not, about Montreal and the Ottawa. Be that as it may, they were discharged about the same time— were not unlike each other in point of disposition, being cordial and loving—and commenced their labors together on the old Ottawa circuit. It is certain at least that they were there for a time together.

Apropos of this, a curious incident was related of these two simple-hearted, fervent, believing men, by the family concerned, as having occurred while they were in that part of the country. There is a beautiful tract of land in the neighborhood of La Chute, on the North River, which falls into the Ottawa. This was originally settled by an interesting class of people from the United States; from among whom a large and prosperous society was raised up by the labors of a Sawyer, a Luckey, and others. But a succession of blighting frosts had caused such a failure in the crops for several years prior to the time to which we refer, that one family after another had left, and sought a home in a more genial climate, till the society was not only much reduced in numbers, but very few homes were left to shelter the hapless itinerant in a place which had always been considered "head quarters" on the circuit; and the occupant of the principal one of the few remaining "lodging places for wayfaring men," "Father Waldron," as he was called by his friends, had also resolved to leave. The two preachers were spending a night under his hospitable roof; but the intention of their host to leave, communicated to them, had made them sad; they did their utmost to persuade him to stay, setting before him the evil that would result to the cause if he left, and the consequent good he would be the means of doing if he remained. When the hour of devotion arrived, both of the preachers engaged in prayer, one after the other, and made the subject which lay near their hearts ground of earnest supplication. Ferguson prayed first, and earnestly besought the

Lord to prevent Bro. Waldron from going away. To each petition, Peel subjoined the expressive response, "Hedge him up, Mighty God!" And when his time came to plead in prayer, he told the Lord they could not afford to part with Bro. Waldron—besought him to induce him to stay—and to reward him for so doing with an abundant crop. He enumerated every kind of produce he could think of by name; and prayed that brother W's hay and potatoes, and wheat, and rye, and oats, and peas, and barley, &c., might be abundant. Mr. W. was induced to stay another year; and by a very remarkable co-incidence, with Mr. Peel's request, he had an abundant crop the following season, of everything, both in field and garden, *excepting onions*. When this fact was mentioned to the preacher, "Oh," said Peel, "I *forgot* the ONIONS!"

Though there were so many things in common between these two men, there were also points of dissimilarity. Ferguson was born in Ireland; Peel, in England. The former had but poor advantages for education; the circumstances of the latter had been more favourable in that respect. The former was not distinguished for more than ordinary powers of mind; we should judge the latter had powers above the common. Ferguson had never risen above the ranks at all; Peel was a non-commissioned officer. The former had only served in this, and his native country; the latter had been through the Peninsular campaigns. Ferguson was married, Peel was single. The former had a long career, the latter a short one.

Peel was not personally known to the writer, although he with another was the second appointment to the "framed meeting-house," which was then included in the Yonge-street circuit; but he has heard him rapturously spoken of by earnest Methodists in this and two or three other circuits he chanced to travel in common with him, a few years intervening,—the Belleville, the Ottawa, and the Perth circuits. From these sources I have learned that he was studious, cheerful and affectionate in his intercourse with the people, by whom he was greatly beloved; a very acceptable and interesting preacher, and very laborious and faithful in his work, a thorough visitor from house to house. He sported with privation. Recounting to a pious old lady in the Ottawa country, the adventurous incidents of a pioneering tour up the river, and describing the salt-junk of formidable texture, on which he had dined on one occasion, he was asked by her, "Had you no *sass* (sauce) brother Peel?" "Yes, plenty," was his cheerful response. "Why, what was it?"—Elevating his voice to make her hear,—" The love of God, grandmam." "Brother Peel's good sass," became quite proverbial with her ever after. He was well versed in church history, and very clear on questions of church order. He loved to preach from texts in the prophecies, which he excelled in expounding; so said some of his intelligent hearers. The manner of his death was somewhat tragic, brought about by a persevering determination to go through with his work. It was on the old Bay of Quinte circuit. A cold Saturday night, late in the fall, or early in the winter, found him in the neighbourhood of his Sabbath morning's appointment, at Adolphustown meeting house, on the East side of Hay Bay. During the night the ice "took" so strongly as to prevent crossing in a boat, but not sufficiently strong to support the weight of a horse. Still the preacher determined to reach his afternoon's appointment, at Switzer's chapel on the other side of the Bay. Finding the ice sufficient to support his own weight, he started on foot for the other side, against the dissuasions of his friends. But finding the ice so slippery that he could not possibly walk upon it with his boots on, he took them off and crossed it *in his stockings alone*, reeking as he was with perspiration from his morning's labours. This, with the walk some miles on the other side was enough to occasion his death. He felt indisposed during the afternoon service, and tried to get an old exhorter in the neighbourhood, to do what was then thought indispensable, "*meet the class after preaching.*" The brother, likely from motives of delicacy, declined to do it in the preacher's place. Peel went through with the whole of what he thought his duty— went home to his quarters—and took to his bed, from which he never rose. He died in a few days in holy triumph. The only expression of complaint that escaped him during the sufferings that so abruptly closed the career of this ardent young man, was this, which he uttered in a half upbraiding tone of voice, "Father Switzer *might have met the class!*" He had no *relations* to mourn for him in this country; but there was one who mourned for him till she became bereft of her reason. For it might be said of him as Wesley laconically said of another lovely young man, Joshua Keighley,—

"He was about the marriage state to prove,
But death had swifter wings than love."

The books which composed his small but well assorted library, together with his watch, were sent to his betrothed. And if I mistake not, they are still preserved as precious relics in the family of her brother, Mr. Caswell, in Elizabethtown, where any of the brethren in those parts may see these interesting memorials of JAMES PEEL. Peace to his memory!

By a very remarkable providence the friend of Peel, the weakly and diminutive Ferguson, was spared,

"To linger out below,
A few more years in pain."

It will be our lot to describe a number of large, fine looking men: Ferguson was the opposite, small, very small; and after some years, much emaciated with his exhausting labors. It was strange that he should have ever been taken for a soldier; for he never seemed able to carry a knapsack. How he was enabled to hold out *twenty-six* long years in the active work, such as the work was during the greater part of his time, in all sorts of circuits, from the Ottawa to the Thames, especially considering the way he worked his circuits, it is hard to say. Ferguson preached and laboured in every public service, very much as we might expect a man to do, who meant to kill himself before he stopped. He was always very excitable, but if he got into what he called, " one of his gales," the excitement was tremendous. On such occasions he usually preached himself out of the pulpit, asserting in excuse that he was " a travelling preacher." And he had the power of exciting the people, as well as the susceptibility of becoming excited himself. Nor was it *mere excitement:* there can be no doubt that Ferguson was the instrument of many glorious revivals, of hundreds if not thousands of conversions. But some will say, " How did he effect them ? Was it his eloquence and transcendent ability ? " No, for he possessed neither one nor the other. It was by his zeal and earnestness, and the power from God that rested on him and that accompanied what he said.

He prayed much; and as he thus honoured God, the Great Head of the Church honoured him, and gave him souls, for the salvation of which he constantly travailed in spirit. He had so injured his once clear and powerful voice, (little men have sometimes big voices) that for many years his voice in ordinary conversation was a hoarse sort of whisper. In this tone he began his sermons, but so soon as he became warmed with speaking his voice became clear and loud. Hence he was in the habit of notifying his congregations that they would have some difficulty in hearing at first, but he would warrant them to hear before he was done. Our first sight of this diminutive soldier of Jesus was in the summer of 1824, when Bishop Hedding, Dr. Bangs, and a large number of the Canadian Preachers, held a conference with the York Society on the agitating question of separation from under the jurisdiction of the American General Conference. We next saw him and

8*

heard him preach for the first time, with power, at the Presque-Isle camp-meeting in '29, celebrated for the presence of the eccentric Lorenzo Dow. After this we saw him frequently and enjoyed the pleasure of his faithful friendship till the time of his happy death. A good and holy man was GEORGE FERGUSON; but no adequate justice will be done him till his journal is published.

> "Servant of Christ, well done!
> Thy glorious warfare 's past:
> Thy battle 's fought, thy race is run,
> And thou art crowned at last."

THE REV. THOMAS MADDEN,

Thirty-five years ago, was one of the ablest and ripest ministers of our Canadian Zion. It was on a chilly day in the fall of 1825, that the writer first saw him. It was in the pulpit of the "Old Framed Meeting House," in the town of York, on the Saturday afternoon of a quarterly meeting. The writer had left his work promptly at the hour of meeting, and repaired to the house of God. None of the congregation had yet arrived; but on turning his eyes to the pulpit, he observed it occupied by a portly elderly stranger, whom he naturally and rightly judged to be the newly appointed Presiding Elder. He had crossed the lake in one of the sailing packets that then plied between Niagara and York, and finding it was the hour of meeting, had, with the promptitude that characterized him, gone straight to the chapel, without calling on any of the friends, and planted himself at his post. No sooner had the writer risen up from his knees, after performing his devotions on entering the house, than the stern looking stranger who occupied the pulpit, said with a firm and decided voice, "Boy, make a fire in the stove." This done, the people began to drop in, and as soon as there were enough to "raise a sing," the minister began the service. The whole is as well remembered as if it were yesterday. The prayer was earnest, confident, and short. And the sermon was as short proportionately, not perhaps occupying thirty minutes in delivery. But he said more in those thirty minutes, than many of your wordy, declamatory, showy sort of preachers could say in *two hours*. The sermon was methodical, clear, concise, and truly profitable. We all felt quickened and blessed. The text was, "Grow in grace!" —just three words. But we had no occasion to say, "What are these among so many?" for "we had enough and to spare." In the prayer meeting at night—the good old Saturday night quarterly meeting prayer meeting of other days—he was with us in life and power; but both in that and in the love feast the following morning, (bless the memory of the early love feasts!) in his attempts to innovate on some of our desultory habits, we had an inkling of the love of order, and rigid notions of discipline, which we afterwards found to distinguish the man.

These were much displayed in the management of a camp meeting, which in those days was no sinecure, all may be well assured; and which was not then meagerly attended. The writer had the happiness of attending two where Mr. Madden presided. Every one had to work, and to work by rule. The Presiding Elder always opened them himself, by an appropriate opening sermon. Each of these sermons is well remembered. The text on one occasion was, "Lord help me!" and on the other, "Quench not the Spirit." The compact, energetic, direct character of the man, and his preaching, was seen in the very choice of his texts. These were attributes for which he was disliked by all those who hated restraint, who, unhappily are a numerous class; but for which he was truly respected by all who had sense enough to appreciate his worth. As it is likely some of this generation would wish to know more about him, I shall append to this little sketch the obituary notice of Mr. Madden, published in the Minutes for 1834.

"THOMAS MADDEN was born in Cambridge, N. Y., in 1780. In 1789 his father and family emigrated to Ernesttown, Upper Canada. In the 17th year of his age he visited his friends in Cambridge, where, under the preaching of the Word, he was awakened, and soon after brought to the saving knowledge of the truth, and under its influence he returned to Canada, happy in mind and deeply pious. For several years he exercised his gifts as an Exhorter, and afterwards as a Local Preacher, till the year 1802, when he was admitted on trial at the New York Conference. After two years in the travelling connexion, he was ordained at the New-York Conference, by Bishop Asbury, first as Deacon, and at the same Conference a few days after, was admitted to Elder's orders. This was in view of his returning to Canada as a Missionary.

"Brother Madden has travelled very extensively through this country, having been appointed to the following Circuits and Stations: *Long Point., Niagara, Oswegochie, Montreal, Ottawa, Augusta, Bay Quinte, Hallowell, Belleville, Smith's Creek, the Niagara District, Rideau,* and *Elizabethtown.* And, beside these, he travelled the *Charlotte* and *Brandon* Circuits, in the State of New-York. He has spent 31 years as an Itinerant Preacher. Our junior preachers will form an idea of the toils of their elder brethren, when they know that the *Oswegochie* Circuit once embraced what are now the *Elizabethtown, Augusta, Matilda,* and *Rideau,* including all the country between *Gananoque* and *Cornwall,* and extending north as far as the *Rideau* and the township of *Mountain.*

" To perform this, Brother Madden travelled 340 miles, and filled about 30 appointments every four weeks. In these labours he spent a useful life, and died in Christian triumph at his own house in Augusta, the 22nd May, 1834.

"As a Preacher of the Gospel, Brother Madden was considered a sound divine. On various subjects which he discussed, he showed a clear and discriminating judgment; and was admired for the promptitude and firmness of his proceedings, whether in his pastoral charge or the deliberations of the Conference. These important qualities rendered him peculiarly useful to the Church, and secured the respect and esteem of his brethren.

" During a protracted illness of more than a year, Brother Madden was a severe sufferer; but he endured his affliction with much patience; he often spoke of it as providential, and was greatly supported by the consolations of the Holy Spirit. These were given by his Saviour with increasing measure as he drew near the close of life. In some instances he was so enraptured with divine things, that he was constrained to praise and glorify God with a loud voice. His last efforts were to deliver a solemn charge to his family, which he did with great composure, and took an affectionate leave of his wife and children, one by one, soon after which he expired."

He had a daughter, the precious and now *sainted* Hester, married to one of our ministers; and his only son is also a herald of the Cross, in connexion with his father's Church. The remains of this servant of the Lord rest, along with many other worthies of Canadian Methodism, in the interesting old grave yard in the front of Augusta, about four miles above Prescott, which may be easily identified from the deck of a steamboat, as you pass down the St. Lawrence, by the spire of the tiny church, which peeps from among the beautiful pines with which the spot is shaded.

> "O may I triumph so,
>   When all my warfare's past;
> And dying find my latest foe,
>   Under my feet at last!"

THE REV. JAMES WILSON,

At this writing in '54, but recently gone to his reward, was one of the *active* worthies of the period of which we write. Though but lately deceased, yet living, from extreme age, so long in retirement before his death, those who have come upon the stage of active life since he retired, or who have but lately landed upon our shores might wish to learn something about him.

"He was a native of Ireland, and came to this country about middle life. He entered the itinerant ministry soon after he arrived. We have heard him say, he was converted at the "Methodist Preaching House, Gravel Walk, in the City of Dublin." Although he had only been a local preacher in his own country, yet being a person of good natural abilities, a clear christian experience, and fair education, he had been very active and useful for many years. He had been, I believe, "a cavalry man," or trooper, during the Irish rebellion; and brought a good deal of the martial spirit and bearing into his religion and ministry. No man could be more heartily loyal than he was. It was not only a matter of principle, but of sentiment and feeling with him. He had imbibed it in his infancy. I used to delight in hearing him pray for the King and Government—there was a heartiness about it that was truly refreshing. Perhaps in exercising the discipline of the church, and in his treatment of people in general, there was more of martial authority than ecclesiastical law.

The writer remembers well his first sight of Wilson, of whom he had heard favorable mention before. It was a lovely, sunny, Sabbath morning. It chanced to be our last quarterly meeting for the year. A number of preachers had arrived on the Saturday preceding (on horseback, as they used then altogether to travel) on their way to Conference; and when the doors were opened for love-feast, a number of them came pouring into the church. Among the rest, there was a small sized man, some forty-five or fifty years of age, straight and trim in his build, with a great appearance of determination in his black, fiery eyes, and a most remarkable head, having the crown towering up at an angle of forty-five degrees from the perpendicular, not unlike an Egyptian sphinx, covered with a thick coat of black, glossy hair. After the love-feast, which in those days of healthful activity was always held in the morning, and used to commence at half-past eight o'clock, this same dark complexioned, severe looking little man ascended the pulpit and commenced the service. It was Wilson. I thought I had never heard a man read a hymn with such force and propriety. And then his prayer was so copious, confident and powerful. He excelled in the gift of prayer. But no sooner had he taken his text, than jets of fire began to flash from under his dark, shaggy eyebrows. The foundation of his discourse was, Colossians, chap. i, v. 21–4.—" And ye that were sometime alienated and enemies in your mind by wicked works, yet now hath he reconciled in the body of his flesh through death, to present you holy, and unblameable, and unreprovable in his sight: If ye continue in the faith, grounded and settled, and be not moved away from the hope of the Gospel which ye have heard." From these words he gave us the whole remedial scheme—as indeed he was prone to do, whatever was his text—with a lustre and a power that thrilled through the congregation like electric fire. It was a gracious means of edifying and comforting my poor soul. Oh, how much good I *did* use to get under preaching in those days! The "word" *did* "profit," "being mixed with" the most implicit, cordial "faith" in the youthful hearer. It was our privilege, subsequently to that, to hear the preacher of that morning on various occasions, and always with profit.

Mr. Wilson used to preach the doctrine of entire sanctification clearly; and he professed the enjoyment of the blessing. But, although it is not at all likely his experience was a delusion, yet his mental and nervous constitution and temperament were such, that the fruits of that exalted state of christian attainment did not appear to so much advantage as they otherwise would have done.

A number of incidents of a somewhat amusing character might be told, illustrative of the peculiarities of the man. On one occasion he commenced preaching at a camp meeting, on the afternoon of Sunday, from Zech. ix. and 9th.—"Rejoice greatly, O daughter of Zion; shout O daughter of Jerusalem; behold thy King cometh unto thee; he is just and having salvation; lowly, and riding upon an ass, and upon a colt the foal of an ass." The meeting had been very dead and powerless, but Wilson had not progressed far in his sermon before he obtained uncommon liberty, and the people were much moved; and before his discourse was finished by one-third, the power of conviction so descended on the people that their cries of distress, and believers' shouts of praise were so great as to drown the preacher's voice, and forced him to give over. The other brethren on the "Stand" went down and commenced a prayer meeting, in which some of them received the blessing of full salvation; and, among others, one young man was converted, went home and commenced exhorting the next Sunday. He has been a preacher for many years—was once the Secretary of the Conference—and the Chairman of a District. While the prayer meeting was in progress, Wilson walked the "stand" exulting in what was going on; and some friend overheard him to exclaim, clapping his hand upon his thigh, while his black eyes glistened with joy, "We're the boys!"

On another occasion, he had to pass through great difficulties in getting to his appointment, and arrived a little late and much fatigued. Observing he was a little out of humor, and wishing perhaps to say some good natured, soothing word, one of the by-standers remarked, "You have had to come by a very bad road, Father Wilson." "Yes," said he, pettishly, "but not half so bad as sinners have to go to hell."

On one occasion, it is said, while addressing a congregation in the village of Hallowell, now Picton, he was led to branch out so far in the early part of his discourse, that by the time he had got through his introduction, he had forgotten his text. After several ineffectual attempts to recall it, or to find it, said he, looking around upon the congregation, with the peculiar looking smirk his countenance used to wear, "Brethren, if any of you will tell me what or where my text is, by the grace of God I will try and preach a sermon worth hearing." A brother rose and informed him where it was—Wilson thanked him and went on not in the least disconcerted.

He was capable of a sly sarcastic thrust at error and errorists, by way of inuendo. Once when giving an exhortation, after the Presiding Elder, at a quarterly meeting, (something deemed almost indispensable in those days) who had preached on the subject of Gospel Fishing, perhaps, from the text, "I will make you fishers of men." Wilson remarked, "he had known a great many fishermen in his time, both at home in Ireland, and in this country, and that, generally speaking, they were a *poor despised set of men*; and he had known *some* of these to *make themselves very rich by fishing*, but unhappily while they caught *vast multitudes of fish*, they *let them stink for want of salting.*" The reader, perhaps, can make the application as well as his hearers could.

Preaching one Sabbath, in the "old framed meeting housse," about the time that Dr. Strachan's celebrated "Report," in which he stigmatized the Methodist ministers as incompetent, was exciting no small stir in Upper Canada, on one of his favourite texts—" The priests lips shall keep knowledge, and they shall seek the law at his mouth, for he is the messenger of the Lord of hosts"—while describing the "knowledge" which the true spiritual instructor should be possessed of, said that a large share of human learning, however desirable, was not indispensable, but said that of which he should be possessed was a knowledge of God and things divine. "And," continued he, "it is generally thought that we Methodist preachers are an *ignorant set of men*, but," said he with one of his peculiar leers, while he lowered his voice and emphasised every word " *We-know-a-little-and-they-had-better-let-us-alone.*" This fling derived point and pungency from the fact that a Methodist preacher had been giving the Doctor to feel by a "Review" of his "Sermon" and "Report" that he knew quite enough for the assailants of Methodism.

Father Wilson once performed a feat that somewhat nonplused certain parties. He had spent a year on a circuit, where, as usual, he was the pride of the Methodist people, and where he was also a great favourite with the Baptists and Quakers, who were very numerous within the bounds of the circuit. Both of these denominations claimed him as the advocate of their peculiar opinions, on which account he thought he ought to speak out before he left. A numerously attended *field meeting* was the last public service for the year. Wilson mounted the "stand," announced for his text the words of Elihu, Job xxxii, 10. "*I* also will show *mine opinion ;*" and proceeded to *show his opinion*, and reasons for it, on sundry texts of scripture which had been pressed into the service of these sects respectively in a manner which he thought unwarrantable, and on the subjects of adult baptism, close communion, final perseverance "silent waiting," denial of ordinances, &c., &c., that could not have been peculiarly flattering to the parties mentioned. How his sermon was received by those for whom it was intended, deponent did not say.

These instances, which might be multiplied indefinitely, showed a sound heart and right meaning lurking under modes of expression, which one that did not know his worth, might think were characteristic of infirmity.

Wilson was a most prolific rhymer; and wrote some clever acrostics and rebuses—but *poet* he was not—though I am inclined to think the assertion would not have pleased him very well, or some of his admirers. But he has gone—he has dropped the infirmities inseparable from human nature in the terrestial state, to experience the full development of his excellencies and powers in the celestial world.

It speaks well for the subject of the above sketch, that all his surviving children are staunch friends of the cause which their father so ably advocated. One of his sons is a talented and influential local preacher.

"The saints all in this glorious war,
"Shall conquer though they die:
"They see the triumph from afar,
"And faith presents it nigh."

REV. FRANKLIN METCALF,

Was one of the company of preachers, who attended our Quarterly Meeting on the day referred to in the preceeding sketch, when I first saw Wilson and heard him preach. Metcalf, although not more than half his age, was so distinguished among his compeers as to be selected to preach on the evening of the same day. The subject of his sermon also indicated the estimation in which he was held by his brethren. It was *the evidence of a Divine call to the Christian Ministry*, preached,—I was told by *request*,—from Isaiah, xlviii. 16, "The Lord God and his spirit hath sent me." In this sermon he vindicated the doctrine of a divine call—pointed out the true marks of such a call,—and concluded with directions and encouragements. It was a well argued, lucid, satisfactory discourse, expressed in appropriate language, and delivered with a free and agreeable elocution. Such was my first sight of Metcalf. He was then youthful and ruddy—tall, and elegant in his carriage, though very meek and humble in his bearing. He was far in advance of most of his brethren of that day, in point of scholarship and general knowledge. He had been educated for a physician, the study of medicine being given up to preach the Gospel, to which he felt he was divinely designated. Besides this, he was *naturally* a preacher; or as a plain old brother said of another "It came handy to him."

The biographer, however, would perhaps have the same difficulty in sketching his moral and mental portraiture, that a portrait painter would have had in drawing his personal likeness. I think it is said to be more difficult to paint the likeness of a faultless symmetrical person, than one whose features are prominent and irregular. He was a harmonious, well proportioned character. Bold and faithful, yet mild and bland, intelligent and talented, yet modest and unpretending—refined and genteel, yet plain and condescending. He had the very best taste, and perceived instinctively what propriety required in each emergency.

He was a man exclusively devoted to his work—punctual and laborious; but so easy was speaking to him, and so free was he from all imprudences, excesses, and violent excitements, that his labours did not affect him as did those of many of his more robust brethren. His sermons were very methodical, and easily understood, and very easily retained in memory; and yet they were very *ingenious*. He was decidedly the best *sermonizer* of his day. We speak of course of our own little world. One, at least, of his compeers had more fire and eloquence than he; but less system and general accuracy. Although far from being a fanciful preacher, he often took a quaint, unusual text, which no one knew how to handle better. We give a few specimens:—" A man was famous, according as he had lifted up axes against the thick trees; but now they cut down the carved work thereof at once with axes and hammers." "And an high head, and a proud heart, and the ploughing of the wicked is sin." "I will leave in the midst of thee an afflicted and poor people; and they shall trust in the name of the Lord."

He was a very decided *Methodist*, and held very profound and determinate views on all theological questions. He was one of the ablest expositors of the vexed *baptismal controversy*, the writer ever new—a thorough-going Pædobaptist was he.

No person had fewer enemies. He was an almost universal favourite. Though tenacious of all his opinions, he knew how to maintain them in a manner not to give offence to those who differed from him. Habitually correct in his own language, he loved to tease those with whom he was familiar for their blunders; and had a way of making them appear ludicrously absurd. An Irish preacher one day bragged up his mare, said "she was a good hand to walk." "What!" said Metcalf slyly, "Does she walk on her *hands?*" After hearing Metcalf narrate a certain circumstance one day, a young preacher wishing to ascertain the chronology of the event, said inquiringly, "Was that when you rode the Hallowell circuit?" "No," said Metcalf, "I *travelled* the circuit, and *rode* my horse." Conversing once with a brother about his *height*—Metcalf was tall—the young man using a cant phrase which he had unhappily picked up somewhere, said, "But brother Metcalf, you are not *six feet* 'by a great majority.'" "Why," responded he, "that would make me out only about *two feet and a half.*"

Notwithstanding these sallies of wit and pleasantry, none treated *sacred* things with more reverence. And he has been heard to rebuke his younger brethren sharply for the use of terms in relation to religion, that had a profane allusion. He was a man of much and mighty prayer. His devotions were not hurried and formal. In secret he prayed much, and struggled long and ardently—often going abroad into the woods and fields to pour out his soul to God, where I have heard of his being found on one occasion by an irreligious man bowed with his head to the ground, or prostrated on his face, uttering strong cries with tears, to Him that was able to save him. He cherished ardent aspirations after purity; and enjoyed a rich and remarkable unction from above on his ministry. I never heard him make a distinct profession of his own personal enjoyment of "perfect love;" but I never heard a living preacher state the doctrine so clearly in its *experimental* aspects. He had *too mean an opinion* of his own religious attainments. Once riding with him through a long, lonely, forest road, he got into a pensive, somewhat melancholy mood; and allusion being made to his *office*, he broke out into the subjoined soliloquy, following each exclamation with a sigh and pause:—" I'm not fit to be a Presiding Elder!—I'am not fit to be a Travelling Preacher!—I'am not fit to be a Local Preacher!—and I'm not fit to be a *private member of the Church!*" No one who knew him would join in any one of the above deprecatory declamations. He punctiliously observed the laws of the Church in the execution of discipline; and contended for a scrupulous adherence to the constitution of the body in the doings of the Conference, both legislative and administrative; in which it were well if he had more imitators.

But there was *one* cloud, and *only* one, which in some measure obscured the lustre of this moral luminary—that was his premature retirement (in a moment of some agitation, and bodily infirmity) from the active work of the ministry. This the writer has reason to know, he saw and deplored after it was too late to remedy the evil. But no retired preacher could ever be more esteemed and influential than he was in a local sphere. His ministerial brethren also continued to love him to the end; and his last and only visit to the Conference after his retirement was hailed as a most joyful event.

His sudden death, in his field without a single attendant, deepened the feeling of the tenderness and sadness that would have been felt under any circumstance at the event. It happened during the session of Conference. And being informed of it by telegraph, all its members bowed their heads in sorrow, and went into mourning for him. Marching in the most impressive funeral procession, I ever beheld, (the Chairman and officers of Conference in scarfs, and all the rest with a weed on the left arm) to the Church, the occasion was improved by the then *President*, the accomplished Dr. RICHEY.

The writer had the mournful satisfaction of preaching a funeral sermon for him, two Sundays after, at the head of a circuit the deceased had once travelled, and where he was held in the most fond rememberance, to a large assembly from all parts of the surrounding country. "I am distressed for thee, my brother, very pleasant has thou been unto me!"

EZRA HEALY.

This name always seemed to me to have something substantial in it, and to need no prefix to give it dignity. And certain it is, that the bare mention of it will call up in the recollection of many persons in this Province the idea of a portly, muscular man, of good proportion, and somewhere in the neighbourhood of six feet, (he did not appear to be quite that—it might be because he was so stout), of handsome masculine features, florid complexion, hair with a little tendency to curl, high full forehead, and a head largely developed in the region in which phrenologists locate the moral faculties. Indeed it was a fine well-balanced head in all respects. And if physical stamina is an important accession to intellectual power, he had this advantage to an extent which few can boast. He was the very picture of health itself—possessing a powerful frame, and an excellent constitution. The vital organs were apparently proportioned in strength to the external members; and he used to say, his "*lungs* would wear as long as his *legs*." The reader will not be surprised to hear, that he had a strong, clear, musical, reverberating voice, of such great compass that it could as easily command the ears of an assembly of five or six thousand as of half a dozen. The "camp-ground" was the appropriate theatre for this stentorian orator—a place he was wont and glad to frequent, and where he was always a favourite. And *orator* he was—one of nature's own. But if the writer were requested to classify his preaching, he would find it very difficult to do so. Few would venture to call it great, yet all liked to hear him. His expositions were not very satisfactory to well educated, reflecting persons, yet many thought them wonderful. He was not methodical either; and often his matter was much confused and jumbled up. Yet Healy would be listened to with attention, and often with tears and shouts of joy. The fact is, he had a warm affectionate heart, overflowing with pathos and the "milk of human kindness;" and a lively, if not a lofty imagination, with a great amount of religious fervour. These qualifications, with a deliberate, commanding delivery, without much mental discipline or culture, although he was a pretty extensive reader, made him the truly popular, impressive preacher. His commanding "port and presence," with his affability and kindness, made him a general favourite among the people both in and out of our communion; and furnished such an excellent substitute for a polite education as to cause him to be respected by the most genteel. He was so great a favourite as to lead a person to say, "That the people would rather see Father Healy's old white hat in the pulpit than any other preacher there in person."

Healy was no doubt a man of sincere and fervent piety, yet I believe he passed current for a man of more moral worth than some other men, who, perhaps in " the balances of the sanctuary" would really weigh him down. Men of his naturally obliging disposition desire to please; and fondness of approbation may sometimes be brought to compliances, which men of less reputation for piety, but thoroughly under the influence of *principle* would entirely eschew. I do not say that the tendencies of his nature ever warped him from the straight forward course of duty, and it is certain, that whatever failings he may have had, they "leaned to virtue's side." We wish if possible to be candid and useful.

The writer has not many prominent incidents to relate of a man so bland, and quiet, and kindly as the subject of this sketch. He was laborious and punctual in his work, and no doubt suffered much in the bush circuits he travelled in the early part of his ministry. But he was strong and able to endure, and being loving and beloved, he passed quietly and pleasantly through life. About the only thing I can think of worth recording, in the way of incident, stands connected with the amiable in his nature. Healy was wont to love every thing around him. Among the rest, the faithful beast that carried him (no sinecure office) came in for a share, and the animal in return became attached to him. The first companion of his itinerancy, "Old Buck," was a great favourite,—he kept him till he was blind. Buck, on one occasion showed an affection for his master and a reverence for divine worship, which Healy would sometimes relate in public, as an example worthy of imitation to certain gentry, who avail themselves of the precincts of the house of God, and the hours of Divine worship, to regale themselves with cakes and apples. The incident was this:—Healy's circuit comprised the then newly settled townships between the Rideau and the Ottawa. Arriving at nightfall at his place of destination,—somewhere, I think, in the township of Goulbourn,—the people having no shelter for the animal, put him in the far end of the shanty, and gave him a lock of some kind of provender, which he commenced eating, apparently with a good appetite. But the shanty was not only used as a stable for the horse, and hotel for the visitor, but the place of worship for the neighbourhood. Soon the little congregation was assembled, and the preacher rose to commence the sermon. But no sooner did old Buck hear the sound of his master's voice, as he slowly and deliberately read the hymn, than his teeth ceased their operations, and the sound produced by grinding the corn-stalks was suppressed, till the solemnities of worship were entirely through. Now whether it was from any sense of the occasion, whether it was out of respect only to the sound of his master's voice, or whether it was from the acknowledged power of music on the inferior animals; or from all these combined, I shall leave for those who are more philosophic than I am, to determine; but of the *fact* itself, I believe there can be no question.

Healy's death like that of Dr. Newton, comported with the early associations that cluster around the men ion of the man. There would have been something pitiful, in thinking of the athletic Healy in a state of feebleness and infirmity. He died with his natural force unabated, in the act of running to the assistance of a neighbor whose house was on fire. He fell suddenly, like the giant oak uptorn by a sudden blast. Many a generous heart sighed, when it was said "Father Healy is gone." No doubt he was *ready*, and "sudden death," to him, was "sudden glory." He professed perfect love. His "children are walking in the truth." And it constitutes an additional tie to heaven, to others as well as to them, that EZRA HEALY is there.

THE REV. ALEXANDER IRVINE,

Exercised a somewhat popular ministry in Canada, some twenty-five years ago; and was stationed in York in 1832 and '33—being the *last* to minister in the "Old Framed Meeting House," and the *first* in the new brick church on then "Newgate," now Adelaide-Street.

Mr. Irvine was born in Scotland—this was something in his favour to begin with—and had received with his brothers that good common school education for which Scotland was distinguished long before the countries of much greater pretentions, which have only lately awakened to the importance of this subject. The family emigrated to America while he was yet a very young man, and went first to the United States, where he and his elder brother, William, long so favourably known on the old Belleville circuit, as the enlightened and stedfast christian, were converted to God and joined the Methodists, a people with whom they had no acquaintance in their own country. Not long after their conversion the family came to Canada; where Alexander remained long enough to graduate from the *status* of a private member, through the intermediate office of an exhorter—a course then thought to be indispensable—till he became an accredited Local Preacher of much promise, when he returned again to the United States, where he married. Though "encumbered" with a wife such was the character of his abilities that he was soon called into the itinerant work within the bounds of the old Genesee Conference. He filled a number of very important stations within the limits of that Conference, I believe with great acceptability, so far as ability was concerned. But I fear that a consideration of his entire course, must extort the confession that there was a fickleness of purpose about him unworthy of a Scotchman, and that marred what might have been a very useful and even brilliant career. About 1829 he "located," came to Canada, and settled on a bush farm. He and his friends soon perceived that this was not the sphere for him, and he resumed his itinerant labours again in 1830, and was received into the Canada Conference in 1831.

It was at the Conference in this year, held in "York"—a Conference memorable to him, and *four* others on a certain very interesting account, that the writer first saw Mr. Irvine, and heard him preach. So majestically beautiful was his text, I give it entire:—" Happy art thou, O Israel : who is like unto thee, O people saved of the Lord, the shield of thy help and the sword of thine excellence! and thine enemies shall be found liars unto thee; and thou shalt tread upon their high places." Deut. xxxiii. 29. Does any curious person say, "What was the character of his preaching?" We would answer—a chaste and dignified *declamation*. It was true and correct, and beautiful, and even *useful* to a certain class of minds; but if we write to convey right opinions, we think we are bound to say, that it was not so plain, pointed, and adapted to real practical effect as it might have been. The preacher was kind, amiable, gifted, lively in his way, and sincerely pious; but, like many more of us, he might have been more *deeply* so. And it would have done him no harm if he had been more thoroughly baptised with " the spirit from on high."

Irvine was not *handsome*, but *interesting*—we should pronounce him above the medium height, slight made, thin faced, pock-marked, and very intellectual in his appearance. He was a man of a *fine* and *tasteful* rather than a *strong* mind. He would have excelled in the lighter kinds of literature of which he was very fond. He had a good library of our English classics—Shakspeare, Byron, Burns, and, if I mistake not, even Sir Walter Scott, (I do not mention this approvingly) had a place on his shelves with grave divines. He could rhyme even faster than "Father Wilson," and there was vastly more sprightliness and poetry in it. He never took a very active part in the discussions in Conference; but often amused himself by turning the whole of them into very clever verse. Some of the brethren who were on the celebrated committee that drew up the "Preliminaries of the *first* "Union," in 1832, and who still survive, will remember how musically he made their names to jingle in the clever *jeu d'esprit* he wrote on that occasion. Some others will also remember his adroit conversion of the very remarkable defence "dream" and all, of a certain person, now dignified in other relationships, made at the Conference in 1833 into rhyme. Irvine was a man of some scholarship as well as literature. The writer has a classical work in his possession now, which had been well thumbed by Mr. I——, and which he procured from his library.

This amiable but changing brother "desisted from the work" again in 1835, and removed to some one of the Western States (Iowa,) of the neighbouring union, where he settled, and where he died, somewhere about 1838 or '9. It is, however, a pleasing reflection that he was preparing to return to the full work of the ministry when he was seized with the illness which terminated his life. His end was peace and joy. Happy, that he made good his entrance into the haven of felicity after all the vicissitudes that had passed over him.

With this thought the writer would check his pen, and close with the sentiment of our hero's favourite *Shakspeare*:—

> " Let but your honour know,
> (Whom I believe to be most strait in virtue,)
> That in the working of your own affections,
> Had time cohered with place, or place with wishing,
> Or that the resolute acting of your blood
> Could have attained the effect of your own purpose,
> Whether you had not some time in your life
> Err'd in this point which now you censure him,
> And pull'd the law upon you."

THE OUTSET.

It was a sunny, lovely afternoon in the month of June, in the year 1828, that a dear friend, a young minister, called in to see the writer start for his *first* circuit, and to say " Farewell!" The friend just mentioned engaged in prayer for ourself in the arduous work on which we were now entering and for the family. It was a time of solemnity to the young candidate for a minister's life. He had looked forward to the day when he might be permitted to enter the vineyard of the Lord in the character of an authorized laborer, with ardent expectation. His opportunities for the cultivation of his mind had been small, and those he had possessed had not all been improved as they might have been. This was partly the result of boyish heedlessness, before his conversion; and partly from a mistaken or unfounded dread, for some time *after* that event, that learning would corrupt him and spoil his simplicity. By the time this error was dissipated, he found himself apprenticed to learn a mechanic art, a situation which left him but little leisure for mental improvement. The love of God had been shed abroad in his young and ardent heart about the age of *fifteen*. Impelled by that love he began at once to pray in public—to reprove sin wherever he witnessed it—and, in less than a year and a half after this event, to teach in a humble way, in a Sunday school. His first class consisted of four only, two of whom had a coloured skin and curly heads, and the other two, though white, were troubled with an infection which precluded their associating with other children. The more he did for God and souls the more he felt inwardly prompted to do. These convictions of duty were certainly not diminished by old and experienced disciples telling him, *ever* and *anon*, "*you* have a work to do." No wonder then, if, when an opportunity presented itself of quitting his trade, with the consent of his employer, and of devoting himself to *study*, he had availed himself of it. He had at the period when our narrative begins been eighteen months employed in attending school or teaching. This interval, though short, was rendered a highly favored one through the interest shown and assistance afforded by two or three educated friends, whose kindness (especially the superior kindness of *one* of the three) will never be forgotten while memory holds its seat. During this time nearly every Sabbath, and frequently on the weeknight evenings, found him employed in meeting a class, or publicly exhorting and warning his fellow-sinners to flee from the wrath to come. Sometimes, though not officially authorized, he presumed to "smuggle a text," as it then used to be termed. He always thought he could build the better for having a *foundation*. About a week before the time we are describing, he had received instructions from the "Presiding Elder" to make preparations to supply a vacancy in an adjacent circuit, till the ensuing Conference. He had been now four years converted, and was *nearly nineteen years of age.* A newly presented pocket Bible and Hymn Book, a volume of Sermons, and a copy of Watt's Logic, constituted his whole travelling library.

Having thus cleared the way, we take a fair start once more. The youth received the parting kiss of a fond and pious mother; bad farewell to an aged and unregenerate father, about whom he was very anxious, and with whom he now ventured, though with a faltering tongue, to leave a few words of parting admonition; he received a cordial shake hands from the manly grasp of his brothers, to all of whom he was junior, and having strapped on his valice before, and thrown his saddle-bags (an indispensable part of an itinerant's paraphernalia in those days) across the saddle, he bestrode the back of his rat-tailed, "Arabian Spot," and turned away with emotion from the door.

He rode through the town, at the other end of which was the residence of a talented servant of Christ, under whose pastorship he had been placed for the two years immediately preceding. He went up to the door to receive his parting advice and benediction. The latter was most solemnly and devoutly given; and the former the writer will never forget. It related to his personal piety—ministerial conflicts—his behavior in the families he visited—and his manner in the pulpit, or while preaching. On this latter topic he advised him never to put a chair before him, much less to spread out his pocket handkerchief over its back. Advice which he has religiously adhered to ever since.

Again he turned his horse's head, and is soon on the road. But there is one place more at which he must call, before he can leave the town, and that is the house of his *first* and *best beloved* class-leader. A man of a most affectionate heart, and rare qualifications for helping on young converts. The young man, however, was denied the pleasure of seeing him—he was not at home. But his interesting lady and family came out and gave him " the parting hand." In a few minutes, he is out of town inhaling the balmy air of the country, the cooling influence of which he felt most grateful to his throbbing temples, heated and wearied as he was by the labor and excitement attendant on his morning preparations for departing. His thoughts now became occupied with his purposes of future usefulness.

Just this moment, he was joined by a fellow traveller, an equestrian also. After customary salutations, the young preacher thinking it his duty to be "instant in season and out of season," broached the subject of *personal religion*. Unhappily he found the soil on which he attempted to cast the good seed most unpromising, the subject of his exhortations being already very religious. He was of that class of Unitarians, who call themselves "*Christians*," (as if they alone are such) and at the time of the encounter, *nearly drunk*. The writer was not sorry, therefore, when this worthy professor took advantage of the superior speed of his horse and rode away from him, leaving him to his own meditations. These became increasingly sweet as the shades of evening drew on, and as the sombre forest thickened around him. It was full *four* o'clock p. m., when he cleared the suburbs of the town; and, having about fifteen miles to ride, it was after dark when he got to the nearest settlement in his appointed circuit. He rode to the door of a house occupied by a Methodist family of which he had some knowledge. The kind and cordial reception he met with was very soothing to his agitated feelings, although he blushed when the mother of the family called out to "Billy" to "come and take care of the Preacher's horse."

" A sorry substitute for a *preacher* truly," thought he. After a simple repast of *mush* and *milk*, and the delightful exercise of family prayer, the incipient itinerant *retired*—but not to *sleep*. The heat of the atmosphere—the pain of his flesh and bones from riding, to which he had been unaccustomed—the anxieties of his mind about his future success prevented his taking much rest for that night. Such was the first day of the itinerant life of one who has been *thirty-one years* in the work.

"MY FIRST CIRCUIT."

Where is the itinerant Methodist Minister in whom the pronunciation of these words—"My first circuit"—does not awaken varied recollections and emotions! It is so at least with the writer. The following is an attempt, made some years ago, to transfer some of these thoughts and emotions to paper.

My first circuit lay on the North side of one of our great North American lakes, and extended into the interior some forty or fifty miles. It required between three and four hundred miles travel, in going from one appointment to another, to pass around it. It composed the whole or a part of each of nine townships, all of which were newly settled, excepting the front of *two* which were based upon the Lake. With the exception of this "old survey," the *oldest* part of the remaining ones had not been settled above six or eight years, and some of them not near so long. In these new settlements my colleague and self preached each *thirty-two* times every four weeks, or eight times a week. This was our "regular work"— we had many *et ceteras* beside. And this was all the preaching the people in those settlements enjoyed, excepting the labours of a Presbyterian minister, who preached in two or three places; and an occasional sermon in one place from an Episcopalian minister; or rather, I mean to say, that those townships were wholly supplied by Methodist preachers, with the exceptions I have named. We had several Local and Located preachers, who went far and near on the Lord's day to warn and instruct their fellow settlers, which labors they performed without fee or reward. And the itinerants certainly did not make their fortunes. The writer remembers that his share of the contributions for four months labour was *one dollar and a half* in cash, and the cloth for a pair of *over-alls*—and a scant pattern it was, for he had to make the waist-bands of something else!

Considering the newness of the country, the settlements were pretty dense; still, we had, here and there, some long rides through unbroken forest. These rides to him were the most delightful that could be imagined. The scenery in other respects was not of the grand or imposing kind. There were no high mountains or deep valleys, nor cliffs nor crags. The face of the country was too arable for that. The only diversity was that of a "ridge and swale," with here and there a meandering stream, on which clacking mills and busy hamlets were springing up; and now and then you met with a dreary *swamp*. But the sombre, primeval, interminable *forest*, had always the greatest charms for the writer. Here he could more directly hold converse with nature and nature's God. The soil, as already hinted, was very rich; hence it produced a very thick and heavy growth of forest trees. There was the venerable, rugged oak—the tall and stately pine—the lofty sugar-maple—the "shell-bark hickory," which looked like a beggar in his tatters—the majestic elm—the beautiful birch, with its school-going associations—the storied beech—the prodigious bass-wood—and the solemn hemlock—with a variety of others, generally of a smaller kind, too numerous to mention, mixed up in wild and magnificent confusion.

The forest on that circuit, was to me at once my closet, study, and the place of my hallowed and delightful meditation.

In those days no "home" was assigned the "junior preacher," or indeed the senior either, if (as in the case of my colleague, of precious memory) he chanced to be *single*—they were expected to find a home "wherever night overtook them." A home was a superfluity to preachers when their appointments were daily. The houses in which we lodged often consisted of one room, which served the important purposes of parlor, dining room, kitchen, nursery, and bed-room; and the *best* of them were very small, so as to afford, with a large family their usual appendage, but poor conveniencies for study. The writer remembers that his usual practice was, to select his text for the day in the *morning*—(and be it known he had his whole stock of sermons to manufacture after he began to travel on a circuit)—then to steal out to the grove, where he prayed over it, consulted the parallel passages, and formed his *plan*. His horse was now got up; and he performed the *filling up* of his sermon in the saddle. The silence and solemnity of the forest through which he rode he found to be most delightfully condusive to meditation. And for several years he had no idea of sermons being "got up" any other way. This is the method, it is said by his biographer, that the great RICHARD WATSON, in the early days of his ministry, also got his sermons—"he plucked them," as he termed it, "off the bushes as he rode along."

The simplicity and hospitality of these new settlers, and the sincere joy they manifested at the preacher's arrival, will never be forgotten by me while memory retains her seat. Religion could not be said to have been in a lively state on that circuit at the period referred to. It had enjoyed a general revival two or three years before; but was now suffering under a partial declension. Still, there were some of the most exemplary, pious christians, on that circuit I ever knew. Some of these were "fathers in Israel," who had emigrated from England and Ireland; and some of them had been converted in the wilds of Canada. I shall never forget the cordial and encouraging reception I met with from one of these "old disciples," on coming to his house, a few days after my arrival on the circuit; a man whose sterling piety yet lives on earth in the person of his descendants, both children and grand-children. He had the reputation of being rather knowing, and somewhat hard on incompetent preachers. My appointment fell in his neighborhood on the evening of the day to which I refer; I rode anxiously up to the door and dismounted; there was no person in the house; I passed through it. "Father C." had just returned from the hay-field, and was drinking from "the old oaken bucket that hung in the well;" his eye fell upon me, as he raised his head: "This," said he, "is our new preacher, I suppose." "I have come to endeavor to supply the place of one, sir," I timidly responded, fearing I should not abide the ordeal—"Fear not!" said the venerable man, "any young man in that spirit will succeed." He was a father to me during the four months that intervened between that and Conference. His wife was a mother also. Some of the more recently converted are in my recollection, who regularly kept the Wednesday and Friday fasts, and prayed in their families three times a day.

The number of members on that new circuit, if I recollect aright, was about 350. The Methodists in this country were then *one;* a Methodist was a Methodist, and needed no other term to make his position more definite. They did not have to distinguish them then, as an enemy to Methodism did the various kinds of Methodists the other day in the neighborhood of the little country village in which he lives; viz: as "Mr. White's kind of Methodists, Mr. Brown's Methodist's, and Mr. Black's Methodists"; referring to three of his neighbors. No; there were none of these distinctions then. It was before any of our unhappy divisions; and before any of the different bodies of Methodists in England had sent preachers into the country. And I can bear record, that the Preachers labored as faithfully then as they do now, that they had the spur of emulation to goad them on; and the country was as adequately supplied with preaching, in proportion to the population, as it is now, without any of the present confusion and deformity. In those days the minister in charge was not intimidated from the faithful execution of discipline by the threat, that the discontented would send for a preacher of another sort of Methodists to rend the society. Would that it were in this one particular, as when I travelled MY FIRST CIRCUIT.

MY FIRST COLLEAGUE—A CHARACTER.

Among the various relationships that subsist among men, whether civil, social, domestic, or ecclesiastical, none is more peculiar than that which exists between ministerial colleagues in a Methodist circuit. There is something like it, perhaps, in the "joint pastorship" which sometimes, though rarely, takes place in other communities. It is a relation calculated to afford each other a great deal of pleasure and assistance; or a great deal of pain and annoyance, if not injury. The *former*, if they are congenial spirits and good men, as they generally are; and the *latter*, if they are the reverse, which is sometimes the case with one or the other. No doubt my brethren have had much to bear with in me; I have certainly had something to bear with in *some* of them. But generally they were good and amiable; men from whose society I derived both pleasure and instruction, as well as spiritual profit.

Among them all, however, none are recollected with more pleasure than my *first* colleague. Not only because he was the

FIRST, but because he was perhaps the most *amiable*. Indeed, he was a general favourite, a sort of pet, wherever he was known. This, together with a kind of child-like simplicity in the man, led to his being almost universally designated by the endearing derivative of "Johnny ———."

A strange, though amiable specimen of humanity he was, surely. He was a native of that "green isle of the sea," which has given birth to so many distinguished men. He was from the County of Wexford; and although a man of intelligence and much refinement, he had not wholly thrown off the peculiar brogue of that province—*th* being invariably substituted by "d." This made *with* "wid" in his mouth. This Irish accent, with a certain sharpness or shrillness of voice and quickness of utterance, joined to a style peculiarly terse and laconic, made his colloquial and public discourses very remarkable, and, to a stranger, even laughable. He was known to throw a whole company into a burst of laughter, by asking the Lord, in his usually hurried manner, as a grace at table, to "bless the prodooctions of the land, through Jesus Christ!" A comprehensive request you will say, though short. What added to the laughter-provoking quality of what he said, was the exuberant flow of wit and humour, especially the latter, by which his spirit was characterized. He was innocent and playful as a child, yet no trifler. His was the true christian cheerfulness. He was a man deeply devoted to God, very faithful in his work; and for many years enjoyed the blessing of "perfect love."

I shall never forget the warm fraternal greeting I received from him when I came to his help in the old T—— circuit; or the pathos with which he took his leave of me, at the end of four months, when he took his departure for the Conference. I was to remain alone with the sheep in the wilderness; and he was about to gallop off and meet his brethren. We had met on horseback in the road. I moved slowly and sadly onwards towards my appointment for the evening, I involuntarily turned my head to catch another glance of him and his travelling companion, and observed that he had wheeled his horse around, and waving his hand he pronounced the words "Farewell, Johnny!" with a tenderness that broke up the flood-gates of emotion, and I went on weeping. Oh, he had been kind to me. We had long rides, hard labor, and hard fare, with little pay; but then we met once a fortnight and heard each other preach alternately. And his more than brotherly kindness, sprightly conversation, with his shrill and animating exclamation—"Fine times! fine times!"—comforted me much. No wonder, therefore, that I felt on parting with him.

We were destined to meet and labor together again. It was far, far from our former field of united labour; a land of mountains, and rivers, and forests, comprehending a wide extent of country, peopled by an hospitable class of persons, among whom we labored with much satisfaction; and where we saw some glorious displays of the saving power of God.

When I first saw my friend, he was unmarried, and what would be called young, tall, and graceful. At my second appointment with him, he was married, and his wife was one of the most kind-hearted christian ladies I ever had the happiness to know. Their home was a paradise to me, a lonely wanderer.

I might tell *many* queer things of this amiably eccentric man, but a *few* must suffice. He was distinguished for the use of texts appropriate to the time, or occasion, some of which were odd enough. In the spring time you would have heard him—for he was a great lover of nature and viewed it with a poet's eye, and listened to its voice with a poet's ear—you would have heard him, I say, dilating on the goodness of the Creator, in sending another vernal season, from—"Thou renewest the face of the earth." In this sermon, trees and woods, and lawns, and birds, and beasts, and flowers, were all brought to perform a conspicuous and useful part. He seemed to act on the maxim that there were

> "Books in running brooks
> Sermons in stones,
> And good in every thing."

At a time when there was a great commotion in the country because of a bill brought into the legislature, to place all who were not British-born subjects under great civil and social disabilities, called the "Alien Bill," he lifted up his voice and reminded the people of a still greater danger they were overlooking—their being "strangers from the covenant of promise, and aliens from the common-wealth of Israel." At the exciting periods of election, he was wont to urge with pathetic earnestness the apostolic admonition, "Wherefore, the rather, brethren, give diligence to make your calling and election sure."

He was a great admirer of "Thompson's Seasons," and at the appropriate time, often in that poet's words, he did not forget to remind the husbandman, in his usually rural circuits, of the bounteousness of a gracious Providence in giving them another "golden harvest."

His funeral texts were usually striking and appropriate, though sometimes unusual. I knew him to preach the funeral sermon of a strong-minded, intelligent old Methodist lady of many years standing, from the inspired testimony to Abigal, the wife of Nabal: "She was a woman of good understanding." Our second field of joint labor was not less than fifty miles long; and it was often a puzzle to the friends to know where to find us in an emergency. A highly respectable member of the church had died, the mother of a Captain S———, but neither of us could be obtained to attend to the funeral. However, one of Br. B's appointments falling in that neighborhood the following Sunday, and there being an infant to be interred (for all which it was customary to have a sermon) he disposed of the case of both, from the appropriate words—"The *great* and *small* are *there*"—that is, in the *grave*.

He turned everything to good account. The circuit last referred to was intersected from end to end by a wide and rapid river. This was a never failing source of poetic allusion and pleasing illustration.

His prayers were characterized by simplicity and child-like confidence. Oh, it was a comfort to hear him pray—or rather, to join with him in prayer. They were beautifully appropriate, epescially his domestic ones—his prayers in the several families. He had an uncommon faculty of ingratiating himself with the children (for these he had a great fondness) and servants, of learning their names, every one of which, and all their circumstances, were remembered at a throne of grace. His scripture lessons were short, wisely selected, and well read. He prayed in his own, and the families of those with whom he stopped, *three times a day*; and at noon the obligations to Divine Benevolence were duly acknowledged for the mercies of the *half*-day, and for the *remaining half* at night. Nothing could disturb his equanimity, or ruffle his temper. The striking of the clock while he was praying, has been known to be taken notice of by him, and to furnish food and materials for devotion by reminding him of the flight of time. *Apropos*, of interruptions in prayer I have a story to tell;—when he and I were appointed to the O—— Circuit, we found ourselves planned for two Sundays in the month, at $10\frac{1}{2}$ A. M., in the village of St. A's. We had no church in which to worship at that time; but had to hold our meetings in a schoolhouse, directly across the way from the "English church." Their service began at *eleven*; and they rang their church bell just one quarter of an hour before their service began, to summon the worshippers. It fell to my lot to go to that place before my colleague; and on the first occasion, just as I was in the middle of my opening prayer, the bell, almost over my head, began to *ding, dong,* at a rate that distracted my thoughts and made my head ache. In fact, it in a great measure spoiled my meeting throughout, as it did several times afterwards. After coming out, I learned it had been the same annoyance to our predecessors. But, on coming round again, I learned that Br. B. had expressed no sense of annoyance with it; but that he had made good capital out of it, mixing it up in his prayer with fine effect.

Although on account of his great simplicity of heart and manners, he might have been thought by some, as bad men erroneously are generally by those wanting in penetration themselves, to be deficient in judgement, yet he was most *judicious*, as the successful management of all his circuits indicated. Many of his aphoristic laconisms were fraught with the profoundest wisdom. I can remember his breaking in on a censorious conversation among a lot of preachers of inferior grade, in which they were animadverting on the proceedings of some of the leading members of the Conference in no very guarded terms, by saying, "Brethren, we must uphold our great men. Mind I tell you, if we put them down, we put ourselves down." This remark, every person of reflection will perceive, embodied the soundest practical wisdom. If we disparage those on whose talents and eloquence we depend, under God, for the defence and propagation of the cause, by whom shall it be upheld? Yet this sort of infatuation has more than once appeared among the professed lovers of Methodism. He was no disorganizer, though he was incapable of being an oppressor.

There is a story told of his administration which, though I cannot vouch for its authenticity, is in keeping with the expedients to which his singular genius would resort in difficult emergencies. As the story runs, there was in one of our hero's earlier circuits a member of the church who was no credit to the cause among those who were without; and a constant source of turmoil and irritation to them who were within. Yet he was so guarded and adroit, and so well acquainted with the loop-holes of our ecclesiastical laws, that all attempts to get him out had failed, under these circumstances "Johnny" one day, after this person had been exhibiting some of his improprieties, tried his hand upon him. Said he to him in the presence of the class, "You are a disgrace to the Methodist Society!—you are a disgrace to the Methodist Society!" On which the person started up in a pet, and exclaimed, "Then take my name off the class-book!" This threat no doubt, he thought would subdue the preacher. But he had mistaken his man. Said the preacher, with his sharp, shrill voice, and with one of his polite bows, "Thank you, sir, I will! I will!" And suiting the action to the word, he drew, his pencil across the name. The disturber, though sorry enough, could not complain, for he had requested it; and the society was delivered from an impediment to its prosperity. On one occasion the credit of the cause required that a certain man and his wife should be publicly "read out of society;" to avoid prosecution, he did not specify any crime, but said he laid them aside "*for want of goodness.*"

We might have mentioned that he was a great peace-maker; and his preaching was often made to tell powerfully against censoriousness, contention, and railing. A friend of mine heard him on this subject from the 9th verse of the general epistle of Jude. "Yet Michael, the archangel, when contending with the Devil he disputed about the body of Moses, durst not bring against him a railing accusation, but said, The Lord rebuke thee!" In preaching on which he noticed; "1. The character of the disputants; 2. The subject of controversy; and 3. The manner in which the disputants severally demeaned themselves." The Devil "railed," but Michael only said "The Lord rebuke thee!" Enough has been said to show reason why I love and reverence *my first colleague.*

AN ESTIMATE OF PRINDEL.

At the camp-meeting in Flamborough West, in 1828, I *first* saw Prindel. The meeting began on a Friday evening. The writer had the honor of inaugurating the services by the first sermon he ever preached at a camp-meeting, and from a *text*, as the Brethren said, "big enough for a Bishop:" viz: Hebrews, vi. 18, 20. The next day, a stranger of whom I had never heard before, dressed in a black silk robe, sat in a waggon (for which he was a sufficient load) at the gate of the enclosure, hailing and shaking hands with old acquaintances as they passed. It seems he had just returned from the United States, where he had laboured for several years immediately previous, for the purpose of re-uniting with the Conference in this, his native province. At that meeting he preached twice, one of the sermons I have forgotten, if I heard it; the other was a defence of the extraordinary proceedings sometimes displayed, especially in that day, at camp-meetings, from the words of the prophet, "Cry out and shout, O thou inhabitant of Zion, for great is the Holy One of Israel in the midst of thee!" Isa. xii. 6. He not only defended *shouting* in this sermon, but he afterwards exemplified his doctrine on the grandest scale we had ever happened to witness. It was at the Lord's Supper, towards the close of the meeting, that he "got happy," and uttered some earthquake-like shouts that were perfectly electrifying. His voice was a lion's roar when he gave it scope.

His preaching struck me at that time as very original, clear, and cogent. It was no random rant, for he said he would not preach without timely notice. His conversation also, during the meeting, which turned principally on the best method and manner of preaching, and abounded in reminiscences of ministerial life, was very intelligent and entertaining, to a young man at least. Indeed, the discussions of some of the best minds in our then infant connexion—such as Prindel, Madden, Youmans, Richardson, Wm. and John Ryerson, Soveriegn, Messmore, and Anson Green—were to the writer, then a listening junior, peculiarly instructive. When men have less access to books, do they not naturally avail themselves more of the living oracles? Prindel was more attentive to and agreeable in his personal appearance and habits then than he was in after years; but he was even then most unwieldly in size. I remember on his going to bed one night, which was of course on the floor, he came down with an elephantine crash that made the "Preachers tent and stand" shake on its scantling pillars, on which he gave forth the following utterance in his usually measured style of delivery, "There are *two* things that mortify me—yea, *three*—my sins, and my ignorance, and my *corpulence*.

It was not our lot to hear him often after that period. But the few occasions on which we did were sufficient to deepen the conviction that, though he had his education, according to his own account, "in Canada, when there were no schools and no books," yet that his was a mind of a superior order, most discriminating and philosophical. A mind able to grasp the subjects of metaphysical science, and law, as well as divinity. Two of those admired sermons were preached during the sessions of Conference. One in Belleville, in 1830, on this text, from the concluding part of the Lord's

Prayer, " thine is the kingdom, and the power, and the glory, forever, Amen:" the other in 1831, in York, from, "Save yourselves from this untoward generation."

He had a profound and accurate acquaintance with Conferential usage and our Methodist law in general, and was most expert as a casuist, which earned for him the title of "Attorney General."

We need not be more minute on the case of one who has just passed away from amongst us, and whose life and character have been published in the "Minutes of Conference" for the present year (1855); but we would just remark, he was one of the many instances which show that the prize of popularity is often wrung from the grasp of originality and genius by those who are incapable of going beyond mere common places, by attending to appearances and matters conventional. Yet Prindel had a few friends, who could appreciate his powers and his worth; one only of whom, the *Reverend James Spencer*, now Editor of the *Christian Guardian*, was enough to wegih down a legion of those gossamer-loving people who are taken up with mere prettinesses. Prindel was the unwieldly, but intelligent, and powerful elephant, among gazels and spring-bocks.

"Farewell, old soldier of the cross,
"You struggled long and hard for heaven;
"All things below you counted dross,
"And now the warrior's crown is given."

AN OLD-FASHIONED CANADIAN QUARTERLY MEETING.

There is no institution of the Methodist Church, perhaps, which has felt the influence of the transformation our country has undergone more than the quarterly meeting. There are possibly a few of our larger rural circuits in the interior of the country, where the quarterly meeting remains in something like its primitive integrity; but these I imagine are very few, and in them I think it is scarcely what it was thirty years ago. The writer does not mention this either censoriously or regrettingly, although he might perhaps the latter, but simply as a matter of fact and history. We have scarcely the elements for them at the present. The circuits are less extensive now than then; provision is made for the dispensation of the ordinances in the several neighborhoods more generally in this day than formerly, so that there is not the same motive or necessity for going to a distance; and the absence of the "presiding Elder" or "Travelling Chairman"—an anomalous phrase—has no doubt deprived them of a part of their *eclat*. But, whatever may be urged by the lover of innovation in favor of the changes the quarterly meeting has undergone, perhaps the representatives of a former generation may be allowed to linger in imagination around the hallowed scenes of past enjoyment and blessing, and "declare to the generation following, the days of the right hand of the Most High." Our friends from the Old Country, by the term Quarterly Meeting, must not, when applied to Canada, understand a meeting for buisness alone, or the convention of the official members merely. That was included in the ancient Quarterly Meeting, and was called the "Quarterly Conference," a phrase far more just and deffinite than the one now in use. But the "Quarterly Meeting" comprised the assemblage of the private members from the various parts of the circuit as well, to hear the preaching; to attend the Love-feast, to have their children dedicated to God; and to celebrate the sacrament of the Lord's Supper. In view of this there were chapels erected in certain central positions in the several circuits, much larger than were required to accommodate the ordinary congregations in their several localities, to the erection of which the circuit generally contributed with a liberality which is not common now. There being then but few, if any Leaders' meetings of the description there are now; and as the old Deed really empowered the Chapel and Parsonage Trustees to do nothing, except to hold the property for the connexion, all the business that is now transacted by those several courts, was then disposed of once in three months in the Quarterly Conference. This made its deliberations a matter of considerable importance. No wonder then that it should draw together all the "Preachers, Travelling and Local," as they used to phrase it—the Exhorters, a more numerous class formerly than of late—and the Leaders and Stewards, with "all who had business with the Quarterly Meeting." These often consisted of persons who came to prefer an appeal from some act of discipline by a committee or arbitration. Fortunately, the number of these appellants has diminished of late years, an evidence that the Methodists are less litigious than formerly. As the business of the Quarterly meeting was so large and multifarious, ample time was provided for its transaction. It was preceded by a sermon from the Presiding Elder, and usually employed the whole afternoon of Saturday. At the close of this sermon, the accommodation of the brethren and sisters from a distance was provided for. And when we take into account that it sometimes comprised *hundreds*, it might easily be thought, that it would be found an onerous affair. But it was never so esteemed, and it would surprise one of the moderns to see how quickly and quietly it was disposed of. If there was any exception in the matter of *quietness*, it was in the loving strife among the householders in the vicinity of the meeting who should take most of the guests. And it was surprising to see how many they could accommodate. The venerable Isaac Puffer tells us that the rule used to be that "a man should take as many brethren to lodge as he had boards in his floor." Without the least approach to anything querulous or censorious, we must confess that such wholesale hospitality, in a general way, is of very rare occurence now, and is perhaps impracticable. It may be accounted for in various ways; people were less precise and required less waiting on them than now; householders had no carpets to soil or ruffle; and the whole thing was more required and customary than now. The quarterly meeting business gone through and supper over, the strangers and those in the neighborhood, comprising usually all the Preachers, not often excepting the Chairman himself, met in the chapel for the great "Saturday-night quarterly prayer-meeting," when a good part of the evening was spent in this exercise. These meetings were usually characterized by power and glory; and were seasons of refreshing and sanctification to God's people, and of conversion and salvation to seeking penitents. The prayer meeting was closed at a late hour, only to be succeeded by songs of praise and family prayer in the several houses.

The Love-Feast was held in the morning, after an early breakfast, from half-past eight to the hour for public preaching, which was usually at 11 o'clock, a. m. The Great Master of assemblies used to reward the self-denying worshippers for the consecration of their first thoughts and energies to him. Nothing could exceed the interest of an old-fashioned Canadian Love-Feast. The speaking was so thrilling and varied. Several things contributed to this. There was the exciting presence of so many christian friends, many of whom had not seen each other for a quarter; there was the delightful influence of preparatory devotions, and the stimulous afforded by variety. A Love-Feast in a new country like this, where the persons who compose the meeting are from so many different parts of the world, must necessarily be different from one in an older country. But besides this, the circuits were then so extensive that a greater number and variety of persons were brought together than is possible now. Only think of the Yonge Street Circuit comprising the country between the Highland Creek and the Humber, and from the Ontario to Lake Simcoe—Cobourg including all the country from Hope to the Trent, and as far back as Rice Lake, Percy, &c., &c. Nothing could be more touching or graphic than experiences to which the writer has listened in days past in Canada. He deeply regrets that he has not the verbal memory to recite them, or that he did not take the precaution of setting down at the time the terms in which many of these were expressed, the main facts of which have made an indelible impression on his memory. Some of these perhaps he may try to amplify at some future time.

> "Haste again ye days of grace,
> When assembled in one place,
> Signs and wonders marked the hour,
> All were fill'd and spake with power!"

THE LAST NIGHT OF THE YOUTHFUL HOMICIDE.

Those who resided in "Muddy Little York," from '25 to '28, will recollect the state of antagonism and irritation that was kept up between the conductor and friends of a certain periodical, and certain aristocratic families, usually designated the "Family Compact." This paper, for sundry reasons which seemed good and sufficient to its editor, ever and anon kept reciting certain facts and incidents, either real or pretended, in the former history of these families, which they would much rather have had remain in oblivion. Not being so thoroughly schooled in the christian doctrine, or rather duty, of forbearance as might have been desirable, some of the junior scions of these illustrious houses, proceeded one afternoon, I think in '26 or '27, to the office of the said obnoxious paper and tumbled the press and type into the bay. I need not inform the reading people of Canada the issue of the lawsuit which ensued thereon. But all persons will easily imagine that an tea of this kind was not likely to allay, but greatly to increase the irritation that had previously existed. Sundry squabbles and conflicts took place between the partizans of the two hostile interests, till, at length, one evening in the summer of '28, one Knowlan, a reputed bully for the "Compact," was shot in the street, which resulted in his death in a few hours after. The act was charged upon Chas. French, a very young and a very small man, who had been for some years printer in the office of the newspaper referred to. French with three reputed accomplices, whose names were G——, F——, and G——d. G——d turned king's evidence, and saved his neck, although it appears from the dying testimony of F—— to the writer, he was the prime instigator of the deed. The other three were imprisoned together, and, after the lapse of some weeks, took their trial for the crime of murder. G—— and F—— were cleared, and poor young French was found guilty, and condemned to death. If I mistake not, only about twenty-four hours intervened between the passing of the sentence and its execution.

The writer's personal acquaintance with the homicide was confined to that brief but eventful period of his life. We had been brought up within the narrow precincts of the same little town, and knew each other by sight, but had no intercourse. Being accidentally in town for a few days, the writer gladly availed himself of the invitation to accompany the Rev. Jas. R——, one of our ministers, on a visit to the condemned. He was then far from being in a gracious state of mind. He was alone. His companions had been acquitted and discharged, and he was condemned to death. He was quite disposed to think himself hardly dealt with. Close and searching words were addressed to him, and he was urged to improve his few remaining moments in crying to God for mercy. We then engaged in prayer, and left him very much subdued. And he seems to have taken our advice in flying to the throne of mercy so soon as he was left alone in his cell.

When the writer returned in the evening in company with an excellent Local Preacher, now in the ministerial work, who had constantly visited the prisoners two or three times a week, and preached to them, we found him rejoicing in the favour of a sin-pardoning God. Yes, while the poor young man with the crushing thought of a death out of Christ in a few hours before him, had poured out strong cries and tears to Him that was able to save him; nor had he cried in vain. And every subsequent moment only confirmed the persuasion, that God had freely magnified his mercy in the justification of a repenting sinner.

At his request, my friend and I spent the night with him in his cell. The writer has often watched with those who were expected to expire in a few hours; but the scene never equalled in solemnity that of being locked up with a person in perfect health, in the full exercise of his powers of mind, who knew that at a certain hour on the following day he must be launched out of time into eternity, by the hand of the executioner.

Does the reader wish to know how we felt or how the hours of that last night of the youthful homicide were spent? In answer then, I would say, I never spent a night more full of interest, or one on which I have looked back with more pleasure. That night convinced me that death is by no means so terrible a thing as we imagine; and, that it may be rendered even triumphant by a sense of the favour of God, and the prospect of a blessed immortality.

When the massive doors of the spacious cell were locked upon us, we first fell upon our knees and prayed—we each engaged in prayer vocally, and the prisoner as well as we. When we rose, my friend read and expounded a chapter which set forth God's method of justifying and saving sinners. Next, both my friend and I related our christian experience, enlarging on the mistakes and errors that baffled us for a time in our attempts to come to Christ; this we did for his instruction. We then listened to the recital of the exercises of his own mind, till he came to the point where he found peace to his soul. And we were led to the firm persuasion that he was truly taught of God, and had been made a happy though unworthy partaker of his grace. These statements included an account of his whole career; and he recounted his steps by which he was brought to end his life on the gallows, including a full disclosure of the facts of the murder. This issue was, in short, the result of not making God "the guide of his youth," and by consequence, "his going in the way of evil men." Some ill treatment one evening from Knowlan in the market-place, had awakened both his indignation at, and fear of that person. One night subsequently,—the night of the murder—French and his *confreres* had gone to the theatre, a place of evil resort. Knowlan was there with a pair of tongs in the pocket of his hunting coat; and threatened to "measure them over French's head." The four young men withdrew, and it would have been well, if they had gone quietly home. Pity but they had —two lives would have been saved. But instead of going home, they adjourned to a neighboring tavern, where they prepared themselves for deeds of violence by liberal potations of alcohol, and concerted their plan of operation. One produced a pistol belonging to himself—another loaded it—the third (who was afterwards the King's evidence) gave the pistol to French, and told him, that if he did not shoot Knowlan he would shoot him. Thus stimulated and abetted, this unhappy man sallied out, followed at a convenient distance by his companions, and planted himself by the side of the road along which they expected K—— to pass from the theatre, and awaited his coming out. Soon the people, in parties of two, three, and so on, were seen coming along the way; and among the rest Knowlan was seen in company with another. When he spied French standing by the side of the road, he drew the tongs from his pocket, and made a run at F——, who discharged his pistol under the uplifted arm of the other, who immediately cried out and fell. F—— might easily have made his escape, but a kind of fatality seemed to prevent it. He fled as far as a tavern in the neighborhood of the Blue Bell, where he went to bed, out of which he did not rise till he was aroused from it at a late hour the next morning, by the officers of justice. The rest is known.

The premature death of his body no doubt led to the salvation of his soul. Of this he seemed himself to have the firmest persuasion. A large part of the community sympathized very strongly with the unfortunate young man. They considered his youth and the provocations he had endured; and therefore a petition to the Governor for his reprieve, or a commutation of his punishment, was very numerously signed, considering the short space there was for doing it in. And as there never had been but two executions in the district before, and those for very aggravated cases of murder, it was strongly hoped that the Executive would be induced to interpose and save him from a cruel death. And while we were employed as has been related, the Governor in Council met in the Court House to deliberate whether the sentence of the law should be executed or not. But all this time his fate was in suspense, he seemed to manifest no anxiety on the subject; but on the contrary, seemed rather "desirous to depart and be with Christ." It seemed there were too many and powerful influences in the Council against the prisoner's life; and it was decided that the law should take its course. Accordingly, about twelve o'clock at night the Sheriff came to the door of the cell, and knocking to attract attention, said "Charles, I am sorry to inform you there is no hope." His ready and cheerful response was, "thank God! I dont want to live!" And then informed us he would much rather die; for that he was then happy and knew he was prepared, but that if he was suffered to live longer he might forget his God and relapse into vice and folly. His mind continued in this happy frame to the last; nor did he seem to have any dread of the struggle of death. "Perfect love" seems to have "cast out fear" of every kind. Indeed he was very cheerful, and in the course of the evening he gave us an account of the prison discipline, and took us, (he was not bound,) into the cells which opened into the one we occupied. Finding some fruit in one of them, which he had on hand for some days before, he pressed us to eat, and partook thereof himself, apparently with a good appetite. He and the writer being young, and unusued to watching, nature seemed to require repose. Wrapping himself therefore in a blanket, there was no bed, he stretched himself by the stove and slept for two or three hours, while the writer reclined upon a piece of carpet with his over coat round him. Our elder friend kept watch for the morning, and summoned us at the early dawn. This was the last time our young friend was to greet the day on earth. He rose with as much alacrity and cheerfulness as if it were to be his bridal day. And no doubt that day he met the Heavenly Bridegroom. We hastened to pay our orisons to God, in which we severally engaged again in rotation. After this we both left, and the writer spoke to him no more. He embraced me with tender affection, and expressed a confident hope of meeting me in heaven. My friend returned after breakfast, and found him in the same delightful state of mind, and continued with him until he was led out to execution. He betrayed no trepidation; but proceeded to wash and prepare for execution with the same cheerfulness that he might have been expected to prepare for a morning walk. My friend observed that when he put on the white dress in which he was to be hanged, and reached out his hands to him to have him button the wrist-bands, that there was not the least indication of nervous tremor about him. And the writer accidentally passing the jail saw him executed, (the hour had been kept a secret, perhaps from fear of some demonstration in his favor,) and remarked that as he was lead out by the Local Preacher on one side, and the Sheriff on the other, that there was no unusual paleness on his countenance, and that he mounted the steps of the gallows with a firm tread. He did not undertake to address the assembly, which was not large, being totally unused to public speaking. This was done for him at his request, by the Rev. Wm. Ryerson, who had also devoted much time and attention to him. The substance of this address was this, that his present position was the result of disregarding his employer's advice, to which gentleman he expressed himself under great obligations, and of keeping BAD COMPANY, which had *urged* him on to the crime for which he now suffered. This address being hurried through by the Sheriff, who seemed anxious to expedite the matter, a clergyman read the usual prayers till he came to the Lord's Prayer, in the midst of reciting which the drop fell, and the quivering, palpitating body of this young and beautiful person was left dangling in the air. I regret to add, that the clumsy manner in which it was done, made his death more like a piece of butchery than an execution. The unnecessarily large new rope, which he had scarcely sufficient weight to straighten, was left in such a position that, as he fell, it caught under one of his arms, which were pinioned behind him, and the executioner had to go down the rope and wrench it off. But a few struggles and the pain and dying were o'er; and his rescued ransomed spirit, no doubt, made its escape from sin and suffering forever. The assembly wept and turned away in sorrow. His relatives being quite respectable, his body received a decent sepulture,

REV. WILLIAM SMITH.

A bluff and somewhat comical, but good man, once said to me "Do you not know that some christians are like young wasps, as big when they are first hatched as they ever are afterwards?" This was said in reference to a young man a few months converted, who was spoken of as an exhorter of much promise. It seemed to imply the belief that the young man would never be anything more in point of talent and usefulness than he then was. With regard to him, however, it did not prove true. He afterwards labored for many years in our ministry; and although not one of the most polished, was, nevertheless, one of the most ingenious and forcible preachers among us. Still this odd observation proves true in a great many cases. If applied to their *piety* and *usefulness*, it is too true that many are, when first converted, all they are ever after. Surely this is not right; for if "light is sown for the righteous," it ought, if properly tended and guarded, to bring forth in time a plentiful crop. But on the score of talent and ability for public usefulness, without implying any censure, certainly some attain their intellectual and professional growth much sooner than others. Some very eminent men, instance Dr. James Dixon for one, are reported to have been very slow in rising to their meridian altitude; others, of whom Dr. Jabez Bunting was an instance, seemed to shoot up to meridian splendor at once. Of the last mentioned class, considered as a preacher, must be placed the highly respectable man whose name stands at the head of this paper—WILLIAM SMITH.

The writer can well remember what a talk there was in our little Canadian Methodist world during the Conference years of 1827-8, about a young man, connected with a number of respectable families in our church and ministry, who had returned from the academy in the States, and was astonishing the natives with his powers as a preacher. This young man it was our privilege to see, hear, and form the acquaintance of for the first time during the winter of 1829, under the following circumstances:—During the interval between the two dates above mentioned we had been called out under the direction of the Presiding Elder, and were travelling at the date last mentioned on what was then called the Belleville circuit, which not only comprehended the village but included the townships of Sidney, Thurlow, Rawdon, and as much of Huntingdon, Hungerford, Madoc and Marmora, as was then settled, with also the front of Tyendinaga, and the Mohawk Mission in the Indian Woods. Between extra preaching for several days, and a severe cold, we had induced a pleuritic affection, that placed us quite *hors de combat* for a time, and induced our physician to both bleed and blister us. Being incapacitated for work, myself and another young man planned an excursion across the Bay on the ice to Mississauga Point, on the opposite side, for the purpose of hearing the brother who was attracting so much notice in the Hallowell circuit, which then included the whole peninsula, or the whole of the Prince Edward District, some thirty-five appointments in the four weeks, the supplying of which a brother remarked was "more like horse-racing than anything he could think of." The laborious Ferguson, and the popular Smith, were the circuit preachers.

About an hour before dark, we stepped into our cutter, and were soon gliding across the Bay. We arrived at the schoolhouse at a somewhat early hour, and took a seat not far from the huge fire of burning logs that were piled up against the chimney back—stoves were scarce and wood was plenty in those days—but we carefully concealed all that was clerical in our habiliments in the ample folds of our "fear-nothing coat." A large congregation soon assembled. There was then a numerous class in that neighbourhood, under the care of "Father Vantassel," the old Dutch leader. After some time, a middling-sized, very dark-complexioned young man, some twenty-six years of age, with black, glossy hair, keen eye, and sharp features, nose and chin—made his appearance in riding trim, booted, spurred, and gaitered, with his broad-leafed hat in his hand, and saddle-bags on his arm. Having dropped his wrapper, he revealed his white neck cloth and single-breasted, round-skirted coat, and stood forth the preacher of the evening. His text was Galatians iv. and 6, " And because ye are sons, God hath sent forth the Spirit of his Son in your hearts, crying, Abba, Father." Surely the "Spirit of Adoption" was ably expounded and eloquently commended on that occasion. Mr. Smith's matter was weighty and important, but not recondite and far-fetched. He was clever, but not profound. His great strength lay in his command of language and volubility. It was this that carried away the people. His style was chaste and elegant, approaching the florid, and his utterance, though distinct, was unusually rapid. It was the utterance of acknowledged truth, in a sharp, clear, shrill voice, with very considerable force of diction, and youthful heartiness and energy, that constituted the charm of his ministry at that period.

After the lapse of some eighteen or twenty years, and a long season of separation, when on a visit to this country from the States we heard him again on the same text. Although a good sermon, it was far from interesting us as much as when we first heard him. We may have become more knowing and somewhat hypercritical; and the absence of youthful vivacity in him, and youthful fancy in me, may have made some difference; yet, we are compelled to think, that he preached as well at *twenty-six* as he did at *forty*. But then we must remember he preached well, almost faultlessly well, according to its style, from the first. In this we see the truth of the remark concerning him with which we set out.

We may make our boast of Smith as a native Canadian. His parents, I believe, were Scotch, or of Scotch extraction. He was respectably connected, and his manners, though plain and easy, were insensibly polished by intercourse with good society. He had received in early life a respectable business education. His clever abilities developed themselves early, and when quite young he engaged in trade. But being converted to God soon after, and feeling, it is presumed, that a dispensation of the Gospel was committed to him, he gave up business and sought further qualification for his Master's work by the attainment of a more liberal education. He was one of the first to avail himself of the advantages of that useful institution, Cazanovia Seminary, an institution which has conferred a vast amount of good on Canada, as well as the United States. Smith while there made very considerable progress in science, and very respectable attainments in Greek and Latin, reading and translating the latter especially with great readiness and correctness.

His moral and religious character was as elevated as his intellectual and literary. He was of sterling, though not of a long faced, canting sort of piety. He was serious, without gloom or sadness. Without narrow-mindedness, he was a downright, thorough Methodist of the primitive stamp. A plain hearted, free, unsophisticated man, while the last to make a man "an offender for a word," he was a fearless reprover of what he thought incompatible with christian propriety. The writer well remembers two instances of his fidelity in this particular. The first occurred on the night of our first interview. Being introduced to him, our hearts ran together at once, and he pressed me to come and share his quarters, instead of returning to my circuit. Is there anything more delightful to the youthful itinerant, in his long and lonely rounds, than to meet and spend an evening with a kindred spirit! But to return, when we arrived at the house, our host thinking to do us a kindness, brought his gin-bottle and glasses, and proffered us something to drink. I simply declined, but Smith turned on him with a most withering rebuke, and warned him against what he did not fear to designate "a soul damning evil." In this he showed himself quite in advance of public opinion at that time. No wonder that he proved one of the most decided advocates of the temperance reformation when it afterwards commenced. The next instance relates to the free, though serious and becoming manner in which he expressed himself against certain frivolities in *dress* indulged in by the young ladies (members of society,) of a Methodist family in a very respectable social position. Smith was not one of those who are so much wiser than the fossilated John Wesley, aye, and the Apostles Paul and Peter also, that they regard it as an instance of weakness and narrow-mindedness to give advice on this subject. No. Conscientiously plain himself, he did not fail to exhort Christians to "adorn themselves in modest apparel," and "not with gold and costly array" as persons "professing godliness."

Smith was not only an able preacher, but a good pastor—a thorough, systematic, sympathizing visitor from house to house. Having strong natural good sense, with some experience of practical life, he performed the business parts of his circuits well, and was an enlightened and resolute administrator of the discipline of the church, "without fear or favour." No wonder then he commanded the best stations of the day and was made very useful in them. One of the most able and eloquent of our living ministers claims Smith as his spiritual father. Ancaster, "York," Kingston, Brockville, were among the places he filled with great acceptability and usefulness.

We regret to have to add that he left the country of his birth, and went to a co-ordinate branch of the Methodist family in the United States. A rising storm, which he thought might have been avoided, together with the ties and solicitations of an American wife, most likely led to this step. But it is pleasing to know that he continued our friend—that he remained faithful to his ministerial charge—and that he died happily "*at his post*." His death occurred in the city of Boston, in which he had been stationed some years.

His only sister, his much loved SARAH, shares the joys and sorrows, the toils and consolations of one of our modest and unpretending, but one of our most worthy and truly valuable travelling ministers. Alas, that we cannot use the language of this last sentence any more. Huntington, his brother-in-law, is no more!

SEVERAL DAYS IN THE COMPANY OF THE ECCENTRIC LORENZO DOW.

Who has not read or heard something of this almost world-renowned and perhaps useful itinerant oddity? Some of my readers have undoubtedly seen and heard him as well as myself, but many, especially younger persons, never did, to whom it might not be uninteresting to hear something further about him.

None need be informed that he had been for some years in early life an accredited Methodist Preacher in the United States, and continued a Methodist in his doctrinal opinions to the end of his days; but for many years he was not amenable, at least to the old Methodist body, if indeed to any other, but labored pretty much, as he would say himself, "on his own hook."

I have not learned from any authentic source that he was ever in Canada West more than *once*, during which visit the writer had the privilege, if such it might be called, of being in his company, more or less for five or six days; and might have been longer, but that he got thoroughly satiated with his oddities in that time. It was in the summer of '29, at a Camp Meeting held between what is now the village of Brighton and the beautifully picturesque Presque Isle Harbor, on the land of James Lyons, Esq., and member of the then existing "Saddlebag Parliament," so called, of which some time or other we may venture some Recollections. The spot was then within the bounds of the Cobourg circuit, which at that time extended from Hope to the Carrying-Place. The preachers on the circuit were the Rev. James Norris and the Rev. Ephraim (now *Doctor*) Evans, both of them then in their "probation." In order to give the meeting *eclat*, Lorenzo Dow, then figuring largely in the "Genesee Country," directly across the Lake, was invited to attend. Accordingly on the morning of the day before the one on which the meeting was to begin, with his usual punctuality to his engagements, he made his appearance—he had come across in one of the sailing packets, which then perhaps, more frequently than now, plied between Rochester and Presque Isle —and an odd appearance it was. To begin at the top, the hair upon his *head* and *face* had been left to grow till it was some six or eight inches long, while the former was surmounted with a coarse chip hat. He had on a snuff-colored cloth vest— striped cotton pants—coarse cow-hide shoes—and a long white flannel surplice over all, without pocket or buttons: it was fastened around him with strings; his pocket-handkerchief was tied by one corner to a hole in the breast of it, while it was mainly thrust down one of the sleeves of his outer garment for lack of a pocket.

The news of his coming brought together a great many people from the two adjacent circuits—Hallowell, which then included all the country from the Carrying-Place to the Fifth-Town Point; and Belleville, which extended from the Trent to the Indian Woods, and from the Bay of Quinte to Madoc and Marmora. There were also a goodly number of preachers. There were besides those on the circuit the Reverends William Ryerson, the Presiding Elder, George Ferguson, Robert Corson,

Hamilton Biggar, whom the writer then saw and heard for the first time, the lamented William Smith, and the venerable William Case, then the President of the Conference, with a large posse of Indians from Grape Island, his then residence, as also several of his *staff;* such as Thomas Hurlburt, then on his way to Munceytown, where he learned the Indian language and laid the foundation for his usefulness; and the devoted, heavenly-minded, angelic-looking John Benham, afterwards the Superintendent of Methodist Missions in Liberia. These two last were only *exhorters* then, as was also Conrad Vandusen, who gave his first exhortation from "the stand," after an attempted sermon by the writer, who also was there in the character of a *preacher*.

Lorenzo lodged the first night after his arrival in one of the tents, the only person that did without bed or bed-clothes, and every subsequent one he must have slept in the woods, for no person knew where he lodged. This, we were informed, arose as much from necessity as eccentricity, he being oppressed all his life by an asthmatical affection that made a bed oppressive to him at any time, especially a close *apartment* in summer. He was very much by himself—very taciturn when in company—he only condescended to converse with the oldest and best informed, and that sparingly on the gravest subjects of information. He was very inquisitive in a quiet way. And the facts he gleaned in his extensive travels, I have reason to believe were lodged in a most tenacious memory, as it was astonishing to observe the accuracy with which he would speak with regard to names and dates of the most curious and out-of-the-way occurrences and facts in history.* He was always serious as the grave, but he often made others laugh with his odd expressions, especially in his preaching.

---

* He remarked to Elder Case, at the close of the farewell ceremony, how many Indian women had shaken hands with him, and I dare say, he never forgot it.

But some are naturally saying, "what of his preaching? Was he an *able* and *eloquent* preacher? Or what was it like?" We cannot say whether it was *able* and *eloquent* or not, for the simple reason that it was not "like" anything the writer has ever heard from anybody else. This will be decided by a little detail. He would not tell the Presiding Elder when he would preach, but said he would do so whenever it suited himself. His first address was an exhortation after the Rev. Robert Corson, who had preached on the parable of the Prodigal Son. Dow's remarks were a series of comments on those parts of the parable he chose to take up after the other had gone over them. We may premise that his dialect was the broadest "old Virginia" that could be thought of. He said that his brother had remarked that the citizen of the far country was "the devil," who sent him into fields to feed swine. "Now," said he, "the devil has got a great many swine-feeders now-a-days. There is one character that may be denominated the devil's swine-feeder. He frequents balls, and routs, and assemblies, and screeks on an insignificant piece of wood called a fiddle, while the people jump up and down and turn their backs and faces, and cut up their didos."

When he came to where the "elder brother was angry and would not go in," Dow exclaims with all the *sang froid* imaginable, "Oh, I guess he must have been a close communion Baptist!" He hated all exclusiveness and bigotry in religion. He was very catholic himself, and was very hard on those who were not so.

Late in the afternoon of Saturday, it was quite evident that he had a mind to preach that evening. He sent some young men into the woods to procure a large, long pole, with which they constructed a rude "altar" for penitents in front of the stand. In the meantime he had seated himself on the stand and sang one of his favorite odes, with a sepulchral sort of voice, which made it plaintive enough. Only one verse is remembered.

"One night all pensive as I lay,
　　Alone upon the ground,
　I cried to God, began to pray—
　　A light shone all around."

Having thus attracted a large crowd around him, he rose and sounded the horn employed in convoking the assembly, which he held in his hand. So soon as the people saw that it was Dow that was going to preach, they came scampering from all directions to the preaching place. The introductory part of the service was very solemn. He gave out the hymn commencing with the lines,

"How beauteous are their feet,
　　Who stand on Zion's hill,
　Who bring salvation on their tongues,
　　And words of peace reveal."

When he kneeled down to pray, the first petition he offered was for two young men whom he said "stood there talking." He prayed that God would "convert them, that they might go home and serve him." His text was Revelation, xxii. 2. "And in the street of it, and on either side of the river, was there the tree of life, which bear twelve manner of fruits, and yielded her fruit every month; and the leaves of the tree were for the healing of the nations." It would take up too much space for us to recite what we remember of the sermon. Suffice it to say, it was strictly methodical, although that method was original enough, while every part of it was truly unique. He made some very excellent remarks in the commencement on the Revelation as a whole. Then he came to the New Jerusalem itself, the admeasurement of which he explained, and compared it with several of the largest cities in the world; such as London, Paris, Canton, &c., with the size and population of which he seems to have had accurate acquaintance. Indeed, he appeared to have a remarkable memory for matters of that kind. The tree, from the femenine pronoun "her" being applied to it, he decided to mean the church. The "twelve manner of fruits," he decided to mean just so many particular graces, which he named, counting them on his fingers, and illustrated in a very able, though, it must be confessed in a very *unusual* manner. I need not say that he had fixed attention; but a spirit of conviction also seemed to run through the assembly; and when he gave an invitation for penitents to come forward, which he did at the close of his sermon, there was an instantaneous rush for the "altar,"—a perfect jam. The writer never saw the like before or since. The preachers poured out of the stand into the prayer-meeting. Dow went down himself, passing from one mourner to another. The battle was truly "set in array," and lasted the most of the night. And "signs and wonders were wrought in the name of the holy child Jesus."

His next sermon, I think, was on Sunday night. If I remember right, he began without singing. Certainly he did not sing the second time; but as he rose from prayer he thundered out the following words of Holy Scripture, "Behold ye despisers, and wonder, and perish; for I work a work in your day, a work which ye shall in no wise believe though a man declare it unto you." He then made a full stop, and looked around upon the congregation,—But says one, "Where's your text?" "Go home and brush the dust off your Bible; and between the two lids you'll find it. For there are some people, when they go home from meeting, if they were to be damned for it, couldn't tell where the text was." The sermon was of a piece with this rough exordium. In the course of it, he vindicated camp-meetings, and told a number of remarkable experiences of his own connected with such meetings and revivals in general. Many of the objections he took notice of were ridiculous enough, which he answered in a manner equally absurd and laughable. It would scarcely be becoming to recite some things he came over, but they had a keen edge for those for whom they were intended.

This was more or less characteristic of all his preaching; and those side cuts and home thrusts no doubt were rendered useful. The fame of his eccentricities brought out vast multitudes to hear. Among these were bar-room loafers, gamblers and horse-racers, universalists and other infidels, with all of whom he knew how to deal, and for whom he had ammunition prepared.

Instances of this we had on two or three occasions. In the forenoon of Sunday there was an immense congregation, and the presiding minister found it impossible to get some of them to seat themselves and submit to the order of the meeting, observing which, Dow arose and settled them in the following adroit, though odd manner. Said he, " I have travelled a great deal in my life time, in England, and Ireland, as well as America; and I have remarked that every assembly is made up of three descriptions of characters. The *first* is the gentleman; he behaves well for his honor's sake. The *second* is the Christian; he behaves well for Christ's sake. The *third* class, I might denominate ' Tag-Rag and Bobtail;' these will neither behave well for God nor the devil's sake. Now if you want to advertize yourselves as belonging to this class, begin with your didos." This was enough ; no one seemed disposed to give occasion for his being put down as belonging to that class, and the best of order ensued. During the course of the meeting, Mr. Evans preached on the judgment from Rev. xx. 12, " And I saw the dead, small and great, &c." At the close of the sermon, Dow rose up and gave an address, and remarked, that while his brother was speaking on the judgement, a thought struck his mind on the subject of *witnesses*; and said it appeared to him, that God was to be *witness* as well as *judge*. He then quoted Mal. iii. 5, " And I will come near to you to judgment; and I will be a swift witness against the sorcerers, and against the adulterers, and against false-swearers, and against those that oppress the hireling in his wages, the widow, and the fatherless, and that turn aside the stranger from his right, and fear not me saith the Lord of Hosts." From this text he took occasion to dwell upon each description of character here denounced in a manner as able and searching as it was original. I remember his telling us, when describing the manner in which "the stranger is turned aside from his right," of an instance that happened to himself; said he, " I rode up to a tavern door one day and called for a gallon of oats to feed my horse. The landlord calls out to the boy, ' Take this horse to the stable, and *mind* and give him some oats.' Now I didn't like the way he laid the emphasis on the word '*mind*.' So after a while, I went to the stable and found that my horse had had no oats. I, therefore, went to the landlord and ordered another gallon ; and went and saw him fed. I then went and put myself where I could see him, and he couldn't see me ; and after a little I saw the tavern keeper come and take away the oats again. I then called for my bill, and took my horse and started."

He visited several places intermediate between the camp-ground and Kingston, where I believe he preached in the market-house: at the Carrying-Place, Belleville, Grape Island, and Hallowell. The Carrying-Place was the last place at which we heard him preach. "Quench not the Spirit," was his text. I think there was more laughter than conviction produced by *this* sermon. The school-house was crowded with people, who all remained after the sermon in hopes of having a word with so strange a preacher, or at least the privilege of feasting their eyes with his odd appearance. But after waiting for some time in vain, casting their eyes down the road, they saw him some half a mile distant, bundle in hand, making off as fast as he could walk. While they had stood watching the door, he had slipped out of the back window. He hired a canoe and made his way to Belleville that night.

We might have heard him there, but we were satisfied, and thought we could spend our time as profitable some other way. We don't mean to say his preaching was not useful. We think t was very much so to certain characters. While preaching in

Hallowell on the danger of covetousness, he suddenly stopped and screamed in prayer, "Lord have mercy on the richest man in the place!" There was a gentleman present who was reputedly the richest in the community, on whom this produced a good effect, temporarily at least; for the next Saturday afternoon, being Quarterly Meeting, when the Presiding Elder, according to the custom of the times, was exhorting the people of the village to exercise hospitality to the strangers, this person arose and said, "You can send a hundred to my house if you please." At the same time that we make this admission, we could see that his oddities produced a great deal of merriment; and the young people began using his slang, much of which consisted of the lowest vulgarisms. A *good man* he was, no doubt; and, as we have already said, *useful* in his widely eccentric orbit, yet one such character in half a century is enough.

"FATHER MAGRAW," THE PIOUS SHOEMAKER.

We write the name as it was *pronounced*. It was *spelt* MACGRATH, but the former is more euphonious. Who of the ministers, who have travelled north of the Rideau since the settlement of that country, have not seen or heard favorable mention of Magraw? He was "not a prophet, nor the son of a prophet," gentle reader, of whom we write, but an humble shoemaker who had spent many years of his early life in the army, in which, after several years of daring wickedness, he had, through the instrumentality of Methodism, become converted to God. He maintained his integrity in that trying position, and under the pressure for *many* years of a domestic annoyance of no ordinary character. He was one of the military settlers who first colonized the town of Perth, where he constituted one of the early supporters, as he continued an abiding friend of Methodism till the day of his death. He was known and loved by our venerable Case, by our respected Co-delegate, and especially by the discerning, amiable, and now sainted Metcalf. Ere this, these two friends have hailed each other on the banks of eternal deliverance.

It is strange that a man so well known and beloved, and so very useful as FATHER MAGRAW, should have never had one line published about him in our connexional journal or anywhere else! Yet so it was. A man whose life, if he had had a biographer as pains-taking and able, would have deserved to have been placed by the side of the "Village Blacksmith," the "Wall's-End Miner," "William Carvosso," and "Father Reeves." The writer has neither the time nor materials for such a work. All he can pretend to will be a few *recollections* of one, whose name is yet like ointment poured forth among all classes in that part of the country in which he lived.

It was a drizzling, mizzling, rainy afternoon in the autumn of 1830, that we crossed the Rideau Lake at Oliver's Ferry, passed through the intervening woods, and at length found ourselves at the head of the circuit to which we had been newly appointed—"*the gude town o' Pairth.*" And we are compelled to say, that to the "new preacher," a boy of *twenty-one*, it looked uninviting enough. We put our horse in the stable of an inn; walked round by the chapel—a dilapidated old building, made of round logs, some thirty feet by twenty-five in dimensions—and went to hunt up the leader of the only class in town. He proved to be the hero of my story, FATHER MAGRAW; and the cordial reception I got at his hands, and the simplicity, the faith and love that beamed in his countenance and appeared in his every word and act cheered my desponding heart and made me feel myself at home at once. From that day till the hour of his death, the writer felt it an honor and a privilege to rank MAGRAW among the number of his friends. MAGRAW was an instance of the moral influence that may be wielded, and the good that may be done by simple-minded goodness alone. He was a man of only ordinary education—he was poor—(he was too unworldly and too liberal to be otherwise)—and he was a man of no great powers of mind. He was rather shallow and devoid of penetration naturally than otherwise. But he was amiable, zealous for God and souls, and reliant on divine help and guidance; and he was usually directed aright. He was not afraid to speak for his Master in any place or company; and the confidence that was reposed in his integrity and the respect that was felt for his character, caused him always to be listened to with attention. For several years the Methodists had service only once on the Sabbath, and that in the evening. This allowed MAGRAW to accept the situation of Clerk and Precentor in the Episcopalian Church, whose service was held in the early part of the day. He was very catholic spirited; and having no great scrupulosity about matters of form and ceremony, he felt no hesitancy about accepting this appointment and retaining it for several years. Indeed, he made it a post of considerable usefulness, frequently pressing the parson himself on matters of religion till he had him in tears. He felt himself invested with some authority to restrain what he thought wrong in the house of God; and actually pulled the ears, on one occasion, of a respectable barrister, to recall him from the irreverence of laughing in Church. And the bold act of this privileged, though eccentric servant of God, passed off with impunity! He was so zealous for God that he entered no house on any occasion without recommending religion. And when on business with some of the most aristocratic families, he has been known to introduce religion and to close with prayer,—a privilege which none of them ever denied him. He was a constant visitor of the sick; and there was such a sweetness and unction attending his visits that they were in frequent requisition, from the damp cell of the malefactor in the jail, to the bedside of persons of the highest respectability. An instance is well remembered in Perth of a dying lady, who would see no other spiritual adviser in her last moments, but the humble shoemaker; and though the fashionable sneered, her *learned* and intelligent husband, though not a religious man, promptly complied with her preferences. She died happy. It is not too much to say that there was a time when MAGRAW visited more sick than *any* clergyman in the town. I had almost said, than *all* the clergymen in the town. Many of the wicked who made sport of him while in health sent for him when sick. A very profane young man of a respectable family was heard one day by a gentleman of my acquaintance making himself very merry with the religious peculiarities of "brother Magraw," as he derisively termed him. The gentleman told him he " might see the day when he would be glad to have MAGRAW pray by the side of his dying bed." He passionately swore he "would rather die and be damned than submit to be prayed for by OLD MAGRAW." That young man brought himself to a premature grave by habits of dissipation. But happily he did not verify his presumptuous boast: in his last lingering illness he gratefully accepted the counsel and prayers of this once despised follower of Christ. It is believed there was hope in the sinner's death.

MAGRAW was a model CLASS LEADER; punctual, lively, affectionate, and one who assiduously pursued the declining and absentees in the most alluring manner. He sometimes went a number of miles, and met other classes with profitable effect.

In the early part of his time he went near and far to camp-meetings; and thereby became extensively known to the pious. He was never out of a *revival* spirit, but ever ready to help on so good a work. He was an active agent in the revival in the time of the Rev. Messrs. Metcalf and Waldron,—the revival to which the first Perth camp-meeting gave rise—and the seasons of refreshing and accession in the time of the Rev. James

Currie. Some who are or were able ministers of the word in our own connection enjoyed his fostering friendship when young; such as the lamented George Poole, R. Jones, A. Adams, Harper, Lockhead, and others.

Though not possessed of any powers of argument, yet his simplicity and piety always brought him off "first best," whenever attacked by others. When any person started any point of speculative theology, Magraw would generally answer by asking if they were *converted!* One day a hyper-Calvinist, who was very disputatious, and supposed to be very clever, insisted on discussing some of the points at issue between him and the Methodists, when Magraw, finding that he could not get out of it, proposed that they should engage in prayer before they began; and then dropping on his knees he poured out such a subduing prayer as left his antagonist, when he had done, no heart for disputing. By faith and prayer he often cut the Gordian knot which he could not otherwise untie.

We have already said he was a "privileged character." This appears from the endurance of that in him which, by many persons, would not have been borne in another. Audible indications of religious emotion are usually very unacceptable to irreligious persons, who generally make them a subject of ridicule. But responding, shouting when he was happy, or approving the sentiments of a sermon aloud, were looked for as a matter of course and as perfectly consistent and allowable in MAGRAW.

We have said he was catholic spirited, and perhaps no man was ever more esteemed and loved out of his own communion. He was ready to help wherever he could be useful; and his services were always acceptable. He rendered himself of signal use in the revival in the Presbyterian Church under the pastoral care of the Rev. T. C. Wilson; and was greatly esteemed by that servant of Christ. That gentleman's successor, the Rev. Mr. Bain, stated publicly at the funeral of MAGRAW, that the "community had suffered a loss," and that he felt that "he himself had suffered a great loss in the death of his pious friend." The reader may be informed that at the funeral of Magraw, all the Protestant clergymen of the town, but the High Church, were present; and the mournful event brought more persons together than were ever convened at the burial of any other man, however conspicuous, in the district. His death was gloriously happy, and his memory honored.

> "The pains of life are past,
>   Labor and sorrow cease;
> And life's long warfare closed at last,
>   His soul is found in peace.
> Soldier of Christ, well done!
>   Praise be thy new employ;
> And while eternal ages run,
>   Rest in thy Saviour's joy."

BREAD CAST ON THE WATERS FOUND AFTER MANY DAYS.

"Blessed are ye that sow beside all waters, that send forth *thither* the feet of the ox and ass."—Isaiah xxxii. 20.

The writer is well acquainted with a Canadian Preacher of a good many years standing who sometimes recited the following reminiscences of his own ministerial labors for the encouragement of himself and others; and which I here record to the honor of that God who has said, "As the rain cometh down and the snow from heaven, and returneth not thither, but watereth the earth, and maketh it to bring forth and bud, that it may give seed to the sower, and bread to the eater; so shall my word be that goeth out of my mouth: it shall not return unto me void, but it shall accomplish that I please, and it shall prosper in the thing whereunto I sent it."

(1) "When I was a very young man," said the preacher, "I was appointed to labour on the C. circuit, which extended some *fifty* miles along the shores of one of our great North American lakes. My Superintendent was a cheerful, zealous, working preacher, and successful in his ministry. The circuit was pretty much dilapidated, when we went on, by a recent division. But God gave us favor in the eyes of the people, and soon a blessed revival took place, almost in every part. *One hundred and forty* souls was our net increase for the year. Yet there was one spot, the village of ——, where we had a chapel and a small dead society, where I thought neither of us could boast of any fruit. At the end of the year I left; and for seven long years other fields had my labours and occupied my solicitudes. At the end of that time, I was re-appointed to C. circuit, then much abridged; but still the place above mentioned was included within its boundaries, and not very much improved. Yet the little society comprehended some gracious souls; and among the rest, a very exemplary pious young woman, Miss W. by name, who came forward at once on my arrival and claimed me as her "*spiritual father*," stating that under such a sermon near the close of my year she had been awakened and brought to God. She had immediately identified herself with the church, and had continued a faithful member to the time to which I refer. I had the pleasure of uniting her in marriage to a pious young man who was worthy of her. Their's was a pious household; and the last I heard of them they were holding on their way. So here was a healthful plant out of a dry soil."

(2) "In 1831 I rode on horse-back from a circuit to the east of Kingston some one hundred miles, to the capital, where the Conference sat that year. I travelled in all about 300 miles, and returned by the same conveyance. On my way back, my

rough-going horse having shaken me very much, I went very slowly and took frequent and long stoppages to rest. In the town of B. my friends detained me several hours, and at their request I gave them a week-night sermon. My subject was, *the soul and its loss*. I did my best, but was not much inclined to congratulate myself on my performance. I was afraid that it was not of a character to do any good; but I left it with God, and in the morning went on my way. *Eighteen* years had passed away, and I had nearly forgotten the week-night sermon in the town of B. I was appointed as the sole deputation to hold the missionary meetings in a large rural circuit. Our previous meetings had been very encouraging, for which I felt very thankful. And my pleasure was still more increased, on arriving at a thriving country hamlet, to renew my acquaintance with religious friends of other days and places. I also made the acquaintance of an intelligent lady, who I found bore an excellent character for active piety, who reminded me of the occasional sermon referred to, and said: " I was then a stranger in B., a backslider; but I was induced to go and hear the traveller —the sermon was instrumental in arousing me from my dangerous slumber, and in bringing me back to that happiness which I have enjoyed ever since." How truly did this relation enforce upon my mind that scriptural exhortation, " Sow thy seed in the morning, and in the evening withhold not thy hand; for thou knowest not which shall prosper, this or that, or whether they both shall be alike good."

(3) " In the winter of 18'—I was stationed in the city of K. Special services were being held in a neighboring village on another circuit. At the request of the preachers on that circuit I went out one evening to help them. It was near the time of Easter, and I gave them a Good Friday sermon—*on the sufferings of Christ*. But I was almost inclined to pronounce it unsuitable and useless. And the house was so small and crowded that it was impossible to find out much about the penitents.

A young Englishman, however, caught my eye as one who seemed in deep earnest; and as it afterwards appeared, by what we are about to relate, found peace with God that night. *Five years after that*, I was the 'travelling Chairman' of an extensive district, and was conducting the love-feast service in the town of G. Several spoke of the dealings of God to their souls. Among the rest a person arose in a remote part of the house, whom I did not remember to have seen before, and spoke with ability and animation. Said he, "Five years ago I went a giddy young man to a protracted meeting in the village of W., a stranger came and preached, from ' Christ once suffered for sins, the just for the unjust, that he might bring us to God;' my heart was broken, I was led to a crucified Saviour, and found joy and peace in believing. Since then I have held on my way. I often wished to see that evening's preacher; but I was denied my wish—I knew not his name. But, blessed be God! he has given me my desire at last. There he is in the pulpit now'! I need not say, this was a season of mutual rejoicing. And I was glad to learn he had been for some time the useful leader of a little class. May we meet in heaven!"

(4) "Not far from that I met with a singular source of encouragement the same year. In one of my quarterly rounds I took an appointment for the stationed minister of the city of K. —at one of his outposts. It was a little village with a few stores. One of these was kept by a gentleman, who, with his amiable wife, were exemplary members of the Wesleyan Church. I called at his house by arrangement, to wait till the hour of service arrived. The time was spent in profitable religious conversation. Among other things he told me his own religious experience. From the relation of which I found that he had been brought up a Romanist—had early misgivings of the truth of that system—had been for several years converted *intellectually*, but not *converted to God*. Several years before he had joined the Methodist Church, **as a** *seeker;* but lived without an evidence of

personal acceptance, till about *two years and a half before,* under the occasional sermon of a passing stranger in the neighboring city, on the ' Throne of Grace,' he had found peace with God through believing; and that 'stranger' was the grateful listener to his words. I then remembered to have preached on that subject, on my way from my station to the Conference, on a Sunday evening; and how I had chid myself after I had done for taking so plain and common a subject in such a place and on such an occasion. I now viewed it in another light; for had I taken any other there, this inquirer might not have been *emboldened* to come to a 'throne of grace.'"

(5) "When stationed in the town of B—lle for the second time—both periods of sojourn are made grateful to my mind by the rememberance of seasons of gracious revival—I say, during the period of my *second* sojourn in that place, a camp-meeting took place within twenty miles of the town. And I had a strong desire to go, but dare not leave my pulpit till after the Sabbath, and the meeting was to close on Tuesday. But when Monday came I was in want of a conveyance. About noon, however, I mounted a farmer's hay waggon and rode some dozen miles to his house, where I refreshed myself with a meal; and borrowing one of his horses I rode on to the meeting in time to preach that evening—the last sermon but one. I took a favorite subject, and was much blessed in my own soul; but could not claim that I had been the instrument of any particular good. The meeting closed with a love-feast and farewell procession, and I returned home. Years passed on, and I went a long distance to assist at the missionary anniversaries in that same town of B—lle. Just before leaving I received a note from a person whose name I did not remember to have heard, accosting me as 'spiritual father,' and requesting me to come and see him—he was indisposed. I had to leave and could not comply; but the stationed minister informed me that he was a worthy pious man, who claimed to have been converted at that

meeting under my sermon—that he had been a useful member of another Methodist body, there being no Wesleyans in his own neighborhood—but that having of late come into the town to reside he had attached himself to those by whose instrumentality he had been first brought to a knowledge of the truth."

(6) One more is mentioned. "Lately, on my way to a circuit to which I had been appointed, I spent a Sabbath in a very large city; and in the evening made my first attempt to preach in its largest chapel. I took the *worth of the soul* again. I felt awfully solemn myself. And I heard of one other person, who felt solemn also: a young man, who frequented another place of worship. He came there that evening as if by accident—expressed himself as much impressed. The next day he was seized with the Asiatic Cholera; and after a few hours struggle, he died, *it is hoped in peace*. Is not this a brand plucked out of the fire?"

The narrator of the above does not mention these cases as peculiar to himself. They have often occurred to his brethren; but they serve to encourage those who mourn the want of *visible* fruit, to hope that that fruit may appear at a time when they least expect. Since the above was written, several other cases have come to his knowledge, but he leaves them untold. May we therefore learn

"To labour on at God's command,
And offer all our works to him!"

SCENE IN A FERRY-BOAT.

It was a raw, cold morning in the latter part of November, 18——, after spending nearly a week on a large island, in the River St. Lawrence, peopled with lumbermen and "squatters," which constituted one of the Wesleyan Missions, at a Quarterly

Meeting, whose services had been protracted for several days, that I had the good fortune to ascertain a ferry-boat would start at an early hour for the city of K. opposite. I had been for some days most painfully afflicted with an illness, the result of cold and hardship; for which in that inhospitable region, I could obtain no remedy, and which was becoming worse and worse every day. I had refused to cross on Sabbath, from conscientious motives; and every day since it had been so stormy and rough that no craft of the size of the ferry-boat could possibly live in the swell that set in from Lake Ontario. But the wind falling on the morning referred to, the horn at the ferry-house was blown, and there was a general rush of the weather-bound, and of those who were anxious to cross over to market once more before the river was shut up with ice. A more motley group than that which was huddled together in the little, dirty apology for a cabin, surely was never assembled. It was such a group of "characters" as the pencil of a HOGARTH would have delighted to portray; and would have furnished ample materials for one of the "Pick-Wick Papers" of a "Boz." There were several of the agriculturists and business men of the island, a squad of market-women, young and old—a Romish priest, who looked thread bare and squalid—and the *dramatis personæ* who figure in the following colloquy. The *first* was a burly, dissipated, audacious-looking Scotchman, a wandering stone-cutter, in a round-skirted drab coat, rather shabby. The *second* was a poor squalid emaciated-looking old Irish Roman Catholic, in an old flapped hat and fear-naught pea-jacket, worn through at the elbows. The *third* was a broad-spoken North-of-Ireland man, a professed Protestant, but very ignorant, whose garments bespoke his half-farmer, half-butcher occupation.

We had no sooner pushed out from the wharf than the pedantic Scotchman began to enlighten the company on his anti-temperance, and anti-christian, or infidel principles. After a few ineffectual efforts to reason with this impracticable man I gave place to the old Roman Catholic in the fear-naught jacket. As the infidel boasted a great deal of his knowledge of "Aljaybra," the old Irishman took him up on certain mathematical questions (I confess, beyond my depth) on which, to use an Americanism, he "used him up" in about "five York minutes." The wily Scot finding himself worsted in this particular, transferred the debate to religion and objected to the truth of the doctrines and institutions of Christianity. Here the Roman Catholic was not equally at home. He urged the authority of the Church. The infidel called for proof of its authority. The old Irishman was non-plussed. At this juncture the greasy butcher came to the rescue, and talked of using *striking* arguments, saying he could "bate a dozen" of the Scotchman, and that he would "knock his two eyes into one." SCOTCHMAN.— "You'r a butcher, are you?" BUTCHER.—"Yes." SCOTCHMAN.—"Then I don't want to have any thing to say to you, or any man that takes the life of living creatures." BUTCHER.— "Don't *you ate mate?*" SCOTCHMAN.—"I eat nothing but *fish.*" BUTCHER.—"But don't the Scripture say, 'That except these days be shortened, there can be no flesh saved?'" SCOTCHMAN.—"What?" BUTCHER.—"That if these days are not shortened, there can be no flesh saved." SCOTCHMAN.— "I confess that that beats me—you are beyond my depth altogether!" At this an uproarious laugh burst from all the listeners, who had sufficient intelligence and discernment to perceive the absurd ludicrous character of the whole affair; and the rest joined in the laugh from sympathy. The boat having neared the quay the most unique scene I ever witnessed was ended. It served to divert my mind from pain and sea-sickness during the three hours across a Strait of as many miles, which was occasioned by our frequent tackings to gain headway against the wind.

The kind and skilful treatment of my city friends soon restored me to my wonted health. And another thirty-six hours found me at home with my little family and a brother preacher, recounting the *ferry-boat scene*, at the breakfast table, after an absence of four weeks.

ADMONITORY END OF AN EARLY COLLEAGUE.

"We shall not there the fall lament,
 Of a departed friend."

On descending from the pulpit one Sabbath morning in the city of ——, one of our superannuated ministers met me at the foot of the stairs with the inquiry—"Did you know that —— was dead?" "*Dead!*" said I, "*where* and *how* did he die?" "Died in a tavern, in——, in a most awful state of mind!" Oh! what a sense of horror this intelligence produced in my mind!"—although it was such an end as I might have expected from what I knew of his history.

The character of my feelings will not surprise the reader when I inform him, that the individual alluded to was once an accredited and acceptable minister of our church in Canada West; and once my own superintendent for a year; a man whom nature had favored with a vigorous, muscular body, commanding personal appearance, and possessed of two excellent pre-requisites in the character of an effective preacher, namely, good powers of annalysis and a pleasing elocution—including a strong musical voice. Yes, and I had known him to be very successful in the work of saving souls.

I remember well the first time I saw him—at a camp meeting on the old Yonge Street circuit, to which he had come over from an adjacent one on which he was then performing his first year's itinerant labour. Three years after that, having myself in the mean time entered the itinerant work, I was appointed as his colleague on the —— circuit, then made a "*four* weeks circuit" for the first time. A great revival of religion had crowned his labors, especially in the town, the preceding year; and a more happy and holy society than it then was I have never known. The extension of the work created the demand for a second preacher, which led to my appointment to labour with him.

Our journeys were often through the trackless forest, in which once in particular I lost my way and narrowly escaped one snowy night lodging in the woods; yet the time passed upon the whole very pleasantly. For though I often thought he was inclined to be indolent and to "shirk" the performance of his work, a good part of which he contrived to put off upon me, still I loved my colleague, parted with him affectionately; and ever after regarded him as a friend and correspondent, up to the fatal day at the Conference of 183' when he withdrew from the body. He went off in a bad spirit; and I never met with him again, though I often desired an interview to the day when I heard of his death. I had often heard of his bitterness against his former friends—I had heard of his offering, on more than one occasion, to *fight!*—I had heard of his becoming, if not a *drunkard*, at least a *hard drinker*—one who could pour down raw spitits in a bar-room, an act which in this day must be confessed to evince a great depth of moral debasement. I say I had heard all this and more, and therefore was in some degree prepared to hear that he had died at a distance from his family—in a tavern, and in horror of mind.

I heard that he carried a feeling of hatred against some of his former ministerial associates into the very jaws of death, saying, "if he thought they would get to heaven he did not want to go there." No wonder his last exclamation should be, " O my God, where am I going?"

It may be asked, what was the cause of his lamentable fall? I answer, *unfaithfulness to the grace bestowed on him*, no doubt. But I think I observed *several* things, more or less remote or proximate, leading to this unhappy issue. These I will set down for the admonition of all whom they may concern, myself among the rest :—1. He had been, even by his own confession, a person of bad moral habits *before his conversion*. He had been a frequenter of low company. And it is no wonder that a love of stimulating liquors should follow the profuse use of tobacco to which he was addicted. His conversion and union with a pious and excellent young lady operated as a check on his downward tendencies, in this particular, for a time. 2. The loss by death of this priceless wife, who proved a sheet anchor to his way-ward soul in many a storm, that otherwise would have driven him from the true course of integrity, was an evil event that he deplored on his dying bed. He said, she while alive, kept him from quitting the ministry. 3. A departure from the work of God, to which no doubt he had been Divinely called—to a desire to leave which he had been impelled by a spirit of dissatisfaction with his circuits, which were generally very good, arising from a notion that he was qualified for better ones and that his talents were not appreciated—was the immediate inlet to apostacy and vice. No wonder he mourned the loss of his H——t.

The case of this man should teach the young the importance of fostering good moral habits, as a means of giving permanency to their religious character ; and should warn those of us in the ministry from a spirit of distrust and discontent ; while it should put all on their guard against giving any occasion for it. God in mercy fore-fend us against these evils !

MY FELLOW CANDIDATES—WHERE ARE THEY ?

Twenty-eight years ago, in the then metropolis of Upper Canada, sat the Methodist Conference. It had been opened on the appointed day in due form, by the appointment of Rev. William

Case, *President*, and Rev. James Richardson, *Secretary*. The *third* question asked was, "Who are admitted into full connexion?" In answer to this, the names of *five* candidates, who had labored during the probationary term, were read, and a committee struck to examine them. That was the way they did it in those days, when the "Annual Conference" did not much transcend our present District Meeting. The committee also consisted of *five*. *Three* out of the five are in their graves—they died well, and in the work: these were Prindel, Poole, and Smith. *One* is in the ministry of another church. *One only* remains with us, a supernumerary—the Rev. Daniel McMullen, a Nova Scotian, whose early piety and very successful labours ought not to be forgotten.

Nearly as great changes have taken place with the candidates, who of course were younger men, as with the ministers of the committee. One of them is no more. One "located," and after sundry vicissitudes moved to the Western States, where, we are happy to learn, he is useful among his neighbors, a Methodist colony from Canada. One, and he the most respectably connected, the youngest, the best educated, and the most promising of us all, after laboring most successfully seven years in the ministry, went into secular life, made property, and now fills an honorable and useful position in the Legislature of his country. One is "superannuated"—and only one is left on the walls of Zion—the unworthy writer of this article.

Of those who departed from the work we may not further speak. But of my *deceased* and my *retired* friends I would fain preserve some memorial. They were both natives of the United States, nearly of an age, great personal friends, and nine or ten years our seniors. The brother gone to his reward was the REV. SIMON HUNTINGTON. As we were the party who drew up his obituary notice for the "Minutes," and as that account of him received the imprimatur of the Conference, we re-produce it. It is as follows:—" SIMON HUNTINGTON was born about the year 1801 in Norwich, Connecticut, where he was converted at the age of *nineteen*. His excellent moral habits before conversion, joined to deep and fervent piety after he was brought savingly to God, continued to make him a most consistent and exemplary character throughout. At an early period after his conversion he felt a strong desire to be useful, and "pressed in spirit" to warn his fellowmen. This led him to seek the advantages of two years' academic training in the Wilbraham Academy, (then under the principalship of the lamented Wilbur Fisk,) in addition to the benefits of an excellent New-England common-school-education, which he had received in boyhood. He began to preach while at the Academy. In 1829 he came to this province, and was received into the Canada Conference on trial, a close relation to which he sustained till the day of his death. He died August 25, 1856, after a few days illness, in the village of St. Williams. His several fields of labor were, to mention them in the order to which he was appointed to them severally, Yonge Street, one year; Westminster, one; Mississippi, one; Bonchere Mission, one; Augusta, (where he married) two years; Murray, two; Newmarket, one; Toronto (township) two; Whitby, two; Kemptville, two; Prescott and Augusta, two; Grimsby, two; and Wilsingham, where he ceased to "work and live," before the first year had half expired.

Brother Huntington was a plain, sensible, and truly practicable and excellent preacher. The good he accomplished—and he was very useful—was more the result of a combination of faithful and untiring endeavors in every department of a Wesleyan minister's duty, than of any one excellence or kind of effort in undue proportion. He was an example to all who may come after him in our ministry, of cheerful submission to his appointments, patience and self-denial, peaceableness, pastoral fidelity, and punctuality in attending all his appointments. He was not favored with any very particular premonition of his approaching end, or any very rapturous visions of the future, in his last illness; yet death did not find him unprepared, but calm and peaceful. Our much loved brother "rests from his labors, and his works do follow him."

To the above we may append a few recollections. He came to us in company with the Rev. William Case, who had been on a visit to New England. He arrived at a time the Connexion was greatly in want of preachers to follow up the openings which presented themselves on every side; and although he came more as a visitor than otherwise, he was eagerly seized on by the Presiding Elder and appointed to a circuit. His appearance was then very prepossessing. Neat and tasteful in his dress, round-faced and healthy-looking, but slight and small of stature.

We can well remember the start he gave us at our first sight of him. We had been scarcely a year in the work of preaching—we were very young and nervously sensible of our incompetency—and especially timid of preaching before ministers, unless we knew them to be indulgent friends,—when one Sunday morning we were officiating in the "old chapel" in the then village of Belleville, just as we had taken our text a stranger entered the house in the garb of a preacher and much sleeker looking than those of indigenous growth, and took his seat in front of us. He was so bright and observant looking, we could have wished him far enough away. We however stammered through; when on remarking according to the custom of the times, that "if there was a preacher in the congregation we would be glad to have him come into the pulpit and close the service"—giving him an inquiring look the while. To this invitation he responded and concluded the meeting with one of the most richly scriptural and appropriate prayers we thought we had ever heard. This was the beginning of a most (to me) profitable acquaintance and an endeared friendship between us. We met a few days after this interview at one of the glorious camp-meetings of those days, near Cummer's Mills.

He spent the balance of the year on the Yonge Street Circuit. The next year in the West on the great rambling, but non-paying Westminster circuit. The next he was whirled away far to the East and stationed on the Mississippi, which covered the ground now included in the Lanark, Carleton-Place, and Packenham circuits. The writer was that year on the Perth circuit, which then extended to the Mississippi river. Our fields of labor, therefore, lay side by side. This brought us acquainted again. And we chose to be as much in each other's company as our duties would allow. What a solace to me in my lonely position in those then rugged wilds was the occasional companionship of that pure-minded, agreeable, and well-informed young minister. He possessed books, and had had educational advantages that I had not. And he freely imparted both of one and the other. We had a *rendezvous* at the house of a pious Irish brother on the banks of the Mississippi, just where one of the only two rustic bridges that then spaned its rapid waters was, there we used to hear each other preach in turn, and spend a rapturous evening; in comparing notes and forming plans of usefulness for the future.

We often met, and sometimes stood officially related to each other in after years; and every successive interview only strengthened our mutual attachment. We shall not now travel the ground passed over in his obituary, only to say, that his worth was not appreciated. Oh, what a shock was the news of his death to me! He had always been remarkably, healthy and I expected him to out-live me; but he was taken first. Dear, precious SIMON! meeting thee again constitutes one of the anticipated delights of that heavenly world "where saints and angels join."

As we intimated in another article he married the sister of the lovely WILLIAM SMITH, an estimable christian lady, who still lives to mourn the loss of him. Blessings on the memory of my friend!

The Rev. Henry Shaler was one of the *five* who were (*one by one*) examined that 31st of August, 1831, in the upper room in the house of Mr. Perry, in the town of York. He, like Huntington, was a native of the United States—the former of Connecticut, the latter, I think, of York State: if we mistake not, from among the Dutch of Scoharie County—himself also of the Teutonic race. He had come into the country some years before he entered the ministry in the capacity of a school teacher, in which profession he was very efficient and popular. He held the relation of an *exhorter* in the church, and made his first appearance in public at the field meeting in 1825, in the township of Sidney on the Belleville circuit, referred to in our sketch of the Rev. James Wilson, at which that gentleman set himself right with the Baptists and Quakers, and exhorted after Wilson had concluded. His exhortation produced a wonderful commotion among the people. Father Wilson spoke of it afterwards among his friends with surprise. He said "that little squeaking Yankee" had moved the people more with his short exhortation, than he had done with his elaborate sermon.

Three years afterwards, when Shaler went into the work, he was so fortunate as to be appointed with Wilson, who performed a father's part towards his youthful helper, and we have reason to know "bragged him up" among the people. It was when on his way to the old Toronto circuit that the writer first saw Shaler. I had spent four months on that circuit, and was going to Belleville, where he had resided. We met in what was just then "Muddy Little York" truly, at the house of the Rev. William Ryerson, who, thenceforth, was to be our Presiding Elder, where I heard him pray—and it seemed to me with much fluency and power. Surely there is a freshness about the ministrations of young preachers, which is a fair equivalent for the absence of the greater weight and depth of matter which are expected to characterize men of greater maturity. No wonder they are generally so popular. Shaler made a good *debut*, and had he chosen to aim at it, he might have taken a higher position than he ever did. The following summer we heard him at one of the far-famed Cummer's Mills camp-meetings. He preached with energy and power, and his old superintendent, Wilson, prayed for him, and wept all the time he was preaching—the effect on the congregation was great; when the service was ended the old gentleman meeting the writer he said with a look of triumph, "Didn't my little fellow do well?"

We hinted that our friend might have become a greater man than he did, had he labored for it harder—and the same might be said of most—but, in justice to him we must say, he *was great* in the art of awakening sinners. His was a very searching, arousing ministry. He was, however, more for gathering in, than building up; and it is well for him who can do either.

We shall not stop to describe his "wanderings to and fro," from Trafalgar on the West, to Bell-River on the East; or from the St. Lawrence on the South to Pembroke in the North. If the reader wishes to see where his fields of labor have been, let him consult that invaluable book of reference, DOUSE's "REGISTER," and he will learn.

Our friend might have been in the active work at the present time, but for a blow received from a horse *five* years ago, by which he was obliged to forego the pleasure of prosecuting at large his beloved itinerant work. But God has given him a comfortable residence in the midst of kind and appreciating friends, with still a measure of strength to aid his ministerial brethren in their special services in all the region around. We have shared his labors in our own station; and I know not that I ever enjoyed his preaching more than within a few months past. We trust he is ripening for heaven. Yet, may the Lord spare him to the church below for many years to come! God be gracious to that one of my "fellow candidates," who still remains with the writer in the Wesleyan ministry!

TRADITIONARY RECOLLECTIONS.

Pious people are naturally fond of conversation about those who were their ministers in former days, those especially who have gone home to heaven. And so far as my observation extends, I think they are more likely to remember their excellencies than their defects. Whatever fault they may have had to find with them while present, or how much soever those faithful men may have been misunderstood and misrepresented, when present, the maturer reflection of all seems inclined to do them justice when dead or gone. And if there had been any *characteristic* excellency about them (and there always is in every good man) *that*, more especially, would be remembered. This may be a stimulus to us all to " patiently continue in well doing," knowing that God will " bring forth our judgement as the light, and our righteousness as the noon day." Besides, the recitation of these " righteous acts" " to the generation following," may be a means of stimulating others to the imitation of their virtuous conduct.

The writer has been stirred up a thousand times, and cheered in the prosecution of his work as well as entertained, especially in the early part of his ministry, by hearing many of the fathers and mothers in our Canadian Israel speak of the labors, the exposures, the adventures, the wrestlings in prayer, and the successes of the first race of Itinerant Methodist Preachers in Canada, few of whom he had ever the happiness of seeing, and none of whom he ever knew during the day that was peculiarly their own.

Some of the names which he heard dwelt on with glowing language were the following:—William Losee, Darius Dunham, Calvin Wooster, Samuel Coate, Peter Van-Est, William Jewell, Silvanus Keeler, Seth Crowell, —— Densmore, and Nathaniel

Reader, with some others now forgotten. Of none of these has he any *written* memorial, save what has been inscribed on the tablet of his memory. In some instances this consists of a single sentence, and that almost obliterated by the defacing hand of time. Still, he has thought it might not be an unpleasing or unprofitable task to decipher and transcribe in a more legible and permanent form the impressions made on his susceptible youthful memory.

If memory were our only guide, from what was told us by the old people in the Matilda country we should say that LOSEE was the first travelling preacher who labored in Upper Canada, at least in the Eastern part of it. We also judge, for a similar reason, that during the first part of his labors he was not a regularly appointed laborer. He seems to have been only a local preacher, who came at his own instance (by God's providence, no doubt) partly to see some relatives of the same name who had settled in the Province, and partly with a design of being useful to them and others; for he was a fearless, zealous man, who would not confer long with flesh and blood, or wait for human authorization and approval in any enterprize to which he had cause to believe God had called him, and which was likely to redound to His glory. And judging by the result we have no reason to think that he was deceived. His brethren, the Bishops and Ministers of the Methodist Episcopal Church in the United States, seem to have thought the same; for the second year he was sent in armed with proper ministerial authority to feed and govern the flock he had been made the instrument of collecting. One of his first converts, and if I mistake not, the *very first* soul converted to God through the instrumentality of Methodism in Canada West, was a very young man, a kinsman of the preacher, Joshua Losee, so long known on the Rideau as a gifted exhorter—a man, who I verily believe could have talked for half a day without any trouble in any respect! He had been some time under conviction and in great distress of

soul, but had revealed his trouble to none but God. One day being all alone in the lumbering shanty he " poured out strong cries to Him who was able to save him ;" and that God heard and answered to the joy and comfort of his soul. The tide of glory was so great that he was fain to find relief in shouts of praise. I heard him say many years afterwards, when an old man, while relating his experience in lovefeast, that he "verily believed they might have heard him across the river St. Lawrence."
" Old Peter Brouse," " Michael Carman," and " Uncle John Van Camp," were some of the converts in that revival. This work was characterized by extraordinary displays of Divine and saving mercy—or, to use the language of the old people themselves, " they cast out powerful." A very hardened young man came on one occasion to make sport, and tried to attract the attention of the congregation by grotesque grimaces. The preacher turned on him with a withering look and said, " You ought to be ashamed of yourself!" On which the power of God struck him to the floor, where he lay several hours struggling in convulsive agony; and did not rise till he rejoiced in the God of his salvation. And although he was a young man of no education he continued stedfast till the end of a long life; was always characterized by unusual zeal in the service of his Master, and became mighty in prayer and exhortation. That young man was familiarly known in after days to hundreds in Matilda and the neighboring townships, as " Uncle Joe Brouse."

DUNHAM, if I mistake not, accompanied Losee to Canada on the occasion of his second visit, and remained to the end of his life, having married and settled in the country. What a pity that some one of ability who knew him personally, and who has access to the requisite materials, would not give us a life of this extraordinary man. Dunham was a *character*, no doubt. The writer never saw him : but he has heard enough about him to say, that there seems to have been some correspondence between body and mind. He was an undersized, compact, strong, healthy man, with coarse hair, bushy eyebrows, and a grum, heavy bass voice. He was possessed of good talents as a preacher, and very considerable attainments, which enabled him when he desisted from travelling, (as most *had* to do in that day, when their families became large,) to take up the practice of physic; but he was plain of speech, honest, and very blunt. This last characteristic, among those who did not like his plain-dealing, got him the *soubriquet* of " scolding Dunham." But his " scolding," as it was called, was always accompanied with a spice of wit that rather made it agreeable than otherwise. Many instances of his home strokes, both in and out of the pulpit, have been recited to the writer. In the Ottawa country he was remembered, among other things, for his love of cleanliness and opposition to domestic filthiness. Sometimes telling the slatternly to " clean up," or the next time he came he would " bring a dish cloth along." Once in the neigborhood of the " Head of the Lake," after " preaching and meeting class," as there were several strangers present he gave an offer to any who wished to " join the society to manifest it by standing up," according to the custom of the times. Two young women were observed sitting together—one appeared desirous of joining, but seemed to wish her companion to do the same, and asked her loud enough to be heard by the company, if she would join also. Her friend replied in a somewhat heartless manner, "I don't care if I do"—" You had better wait till you do '*care*'," chimed in the grum voice of Dunham. He was for having none even " on trial" who had not a *sincere* " desire to flee from the wrath to come, and to be saved from their sins." But it is in the Bay of Quinte country where he lived so long as a located as well as travelling preacher, that the greatest number of characteristic anecdotes are related of Dunham. His reply to the newly appointed magistrate's bantering remarks is well known. A new made " Squire " bantered Dunham before some company about riding so fine a horse, and told him he was very unlike his humble Master, who was content to ride on an ass. Dunham responded with his usual imperturbable gravity and in his usual heavy and measured tones, that he agreed with him perfectly, and that he would most assuredly imitate his Master in the particular mentioned only for the difficulty of finding the animal required—the government having "made up all the asses into magistrates!" A person of my acquaintance informed me that he saw an infidel who was a fallen Lutheran clergyman, endeavoring one night while Dunham was preaching to destroy the effect of the sermon on those around him by turning the whole into ridicule. The preacher affected not to notice him for a length of time, but went on extolling the excellency of Christianity and showing the formidable opposition it had confronted and overcome, when all at once he turned to the spot where the scoffer sat and fixing his eyes upon him, the old man continued, "Shall christianity and her votaries, after having passed through fire and water, after vanquishing the opposition put forth by philosophers, and priests, and kings—after all this, I say, shall the servants of God, at this time of day, allow themselves to be frightened by THE BRAYING OF AN ASS?" The infidel who had begun to show signs of uneasiness from the time the fearless servant of God fixed his terribly searching eye upon him, when he came to the climax of the interrogation, was completely broken down and droppe dhis head in evident confusion. Dunham was distinguished for fidelity, and faith, and prayer, as well as wit and sarcasm. Religion was much injured by the late American war, and continued very low for some time afterwards; but a few held on, and Dunham continued to preach under many discouragements. One day he was preaching with more than usual animation, when a person in the congregation responded "Amen" to some good sentiment that was advanced. On which the preacher paused and looked about the congregation and said in his usual heavy deliberate manner: "*Amen* do I hear? I didn't know that there was religion enough left to raise an *amen*. Well then, A-MEN—SO BE IT!" He then resumed his sermon. But it really appeared, by a glorious and extensive revival which took place very soon after, that this "*amen*" was like the premonitory rumble of distant thunder before a sweeping, fructifying rain. A pious man told me that a relative of his, who first lost her piety and then her reason, was visited by Dunham and pronounced to be "*possessed with the Devil.*" He kneeled down in front of her, and though she blasphemed and spit in his face till the spittle ran down on the floor, he never flinched nor moved a muscle, but went on praying and exorcising by turns—shaming the devil for "getting into the weaker vessel," and telling him to "get out of her," till she became subdued, fell on her knees, began to pray and wrestle with God for mercy, and never rose till she got up from her knees in the possession of reason and rejoicing in the light of God's countenance. I relate it as I got it; and the reader may make what he pleases of the occurrence.

It is natural in an age like the one of which we write for people to ascribe to satanic influence what *we* should ascribe to natural causes. I shall not decide which of the two is right. An instance of the kind with a supposed disposition at the command of Dunham, was related to the writer by an elderly pious man who said the story was authentic. In some country neighborhood where D. preached he had been disturbed several times successively by the crying of a certain infant at a particular stage of the service, which resulted in the disturbance of the congregation and the marring of the effect of his discourse. Its recurrence in the same way for several times with the same injurious effect, convinced the preacher that it was of the Devil, whom he thought had taken possession of the child for the purpose of destroying the beneficial tendency of his ministry, and his soul was aroused to withstand him. Accordingly, the next time it occurred he advanced towards the child in its mother's arms, and "*rebuked the Devil in it, and commanded him to come out."* And as my story runs, the child ceased to cry and never disturbed the congregation more.

Dunham had once a providential escape from death. He had aroused the anger of an ungodly man, whose wife had been savingly converted under his ministry. The husband came to the house where D. lodged before he was up in the morning and inquired for him. The preacher made his appearance partly dressed, when the infuriated man made towards him and would have terminated his existence with an axe with which he had armed himself, had it not been for the prompt intervention of D's host and hostess, who succeeded in disarming the assailant. Dunham's calm and christian fidelity, with the blessing of God, moreover, brought the man to reason, to penitence, and to prayer at once, and issued in his conversion. His wife was no longer persecuted, and his house became "a lodging place for wayfaring men." This was related to me by a relative of our hero.

Of PETER VANEST he remembers as characteristic that his piety developed itself in a zeal for plainness of dress, which he evinced by example and precept to an extent that, with all our conscientiousness on this point, we cannot help thinking Peter carried to an extreme. He wore no buttons on his coat—but fastened it with hooks and eyes. And he bore hard on all who did not come up to his ideal of plainness. "Father Bailey," late of Moulinette, informed me that when a young man he went some distance to a Quarterly Meeting and VanEst was there. In the course of the evening on Saturday the preacher detected that young Bailey had on his spruce new coat a row of brass buttons too many in front, as well as the superfluous ones behind, and denounced it as a most unallowable instance of pride and vanity. The young convert was very anxious to be a christian in all respects, and thinking the preacher must be right, very deliberately took out his pocket knife and cut them off; and made his appearance among the people the next day *minus* the superfluous buttons.

Calvin Wooster's zeal seems to have displayed itself in a hostility to evils more essential and radical than *supernumerary buttons*. It was an enlightened, determined, and successful warfare on the kingdom of satan and the empire of sin, both outward and inward. He was a rare example of the holiness he preached. Of his piety and devotion the old people were never weary of speaking in terms of the most glowing admiration. And, indeed, his devotion to God and the work of saving souls was above all praise. He seems to have got his soul deeply imbued with God's sanctifying spirit, and to have retained it by maintaining a spirit of continual watchfulness and communion with God. His every breath was prayer. An old lady who entertained him, informed me that on his arrival he would ask the privilege of going up to the loft of their one-storied log building, which was the only place of retirement they had, and to which he had to mount up by the means of a ladder. There he would remain in prayer till the settlers assembled for preaching, when he would descend like Moses from the mount with a face radiant with holy comfort. And truly his preaching was "with the Holy Ghost sent down from heaven." It was not boisterous but solemn, spiritual, powerful. God honored the man who honored him. He was the instrument of a revival characterized by depth and comprehensiveness, a revival of the work of sanctification. Under his word the people fell like men slain in battle. This was even the case when he became so exhausted that he could preach no longer, or his voice was drowned in the cries of the people. He would stand with angelic countenance and upturned eye, bringing his hands together and saying in a loud whisper, "Smite them, my Lord!—my Lord, smite them!" And "smite them" he did; for the "slain of the Lord were many." This is said to have been the case when his voice and lungs had become so enfeebled by *consumption*, which brought him to an early grave, that he used to have to employ an interpreter to announce to the congregation his whispered sermons. But if any person wishes to know more of "Calvin Wooster's Revival," and of his lamented but gloriously triumphant death, let him consult Dr. Bang's History of the Methodist Episcopal Church on those subjects.

> "But his Master from above,
>   When the promised hour was come,
> Sent the chariot of his love
>   To convey the wanderer home.
>
> "Saw ye not the wheels of fire,
>   And the steeds that cleft the wind?
> Saw ye not his soul aspire,
>   When his mantle dropped behind.
>
> "Ye that caught it as it fell,
>   Bind that mantle round your breast;
> So in you his meekness dwell,
>   So on you his spirit rest!"

Of SAMUEL COATE, it is perhaps superfluous and presumptuous for us to write. For, who has not heard the fame of his eloquence and polite accomplishments? His penmanship has, perhaps, scarce ever been equalled. And who, with our slender stock of materials, could presume to do justice to either one or the other? He was evidently a very extraordinary person for such a day and country. He swept like a meteor over the land, and spell-bound the astonished gaze of the wondering new settlers. Nor was it astonishment alone he excited. He was the Heaven-anointed and successful instrument of the conversion of hundreds. His success, in the early part of his career, was truly Whitfieldian. What a pity that so bright a sun should ever have been obscured by a cloud so dark! yet it is cause of grateful gratulation, that it sat *serenely clear* AT LAST.

> "No further seek his merits to disclose,
>   Or draw his frailties from their dark abode;
> (There they alike in trembling hope repose,)
>   On the bosom of his Father and his God."

WILLIAM JEWELL, was really what his name imported, in the estimation of those who knew him. He was a gifted, zealous, hymn-singing, laborious, bachelor-presiding elder, who traversed the land from end to end, preaching, praying, visiting, and singing, and delightfully talking of the things of God in the several families whose hospitality he enjoyed, in such a way as to leave a savor after him which made his name "like ointment poured forth."

The name of SYLVANUS KEELER, converted and raised up into the ministry in Canada, in the Elizabethtown country, not far from where Brockville now stands, is worthy of being rescued from oblivion. He had had no advantages of an early education: and who when he first began speaking in public, it is said, could scarcely read a hymn. But, by assiduously industrous efforts, he so far surmounted this defect as to become possessed of tolerable attainments in English. He had, moreover, endowments natural and of divine bestowment which went far to counterbalance the defect referred to. His person was commanding and even handsome. His voice for *speaking* at least (and, if I mistake not, for *singing* also, a means by which our early Methodist preachers made so lively an impression) was excellent. It was clear, melodious, and strong. The distance at which the old people say he could be heard was marvellous. His spirit and manners too were the most bland and engaging. And his zeal and fervor in his Master's cause knew no bounds and suffered no abatement. He travelled for several years while Canada was yet the newest and the poorest, and the preachers were the worst provided for. He was often three months at a time from his wife and family of small children. The story of their destitution and the shifts they were put to, to exist, in those seasons of destitution, might bring tears from eyes "the most unused to weep." No wonder that his return to them was always considered a Jubilee. When the season of his periodical visit drew near, his little ones, as they informed the writer in after years, would mount the fence, and strain their eyes to get the first glimpse of their returning father, often for hours, and even days, before his appearance. In view of such privations, could any one blame him for "locating," and making provision for those for whom he was the natural provider? But he did not cease to be useful when he ceased to itinerate. He was greatly beloved and respected by the people in the surrounding neighborhoods, and made very instrumental of good to them. And after his family grew up, and were able to provide for themselves, "Father Keeler," as he was now called, extended his labors to greater distances from home, carrying the Gospel into the destitute settlements of immigrants beyond the Rideau. His last labor of love was that of holding a Quarterly Meeting in the "Boyd Settlement"," beyond the Mississippi. His name is even still like "ointment poured forth" in all the region from the St. Lawrence to the settlement beyond the last mentioned river. And his piety lives in the persons of his descendants, who have been the faithful adherents of the Wesleyan cause through every vicissitude. Thus it is, that "he being dead, yet speaks" for that Master whose truth he so zealously proclaimed while living.

Mr. DENSMORE is remembered at a period somewhat later, about the Bay of Quinte, as a little man, young, sprightly, active, cheerful, and faithful in his work. When he could not get to his appointment by the conveyance he liked, he would cheerfully submit to one he did not like; but go he would, if it were within the bounds of possibility.

SETH CROWEL, was the *merest boy* in years; but gifted, voluble, and possessed of a flaming zeal, which attracted the admiration and ensured the grateful recollection of hundreds.

WILLIAM SNOW was remembered as a simple, open-minded young man, from the States, who sometimes preached with such uncommon liberty and power at camp meetings as to extort an ascription of praise from an old *shouter*—" for *snow* in *sum-*

mer," and at other times, was so straitened and embarrassed as to lead him to say at the close—" Brethren, I have done, and I am glad of it!"

NATHANIEL READER came in at the close of the last American War and travelled the first year on the Belleville circuit, which then extended from there westward to Smith's Creek, now Port Hope. He told the people that the Lord promised him a hundred souls that year; and the promise was more than verified. A glorious revival took place in every part of the circuit. He subsequently travelled in the Ottawa country, where he was remembered as so remarkably devout and heavenly in his very appearance, as to arrest the attention of even strangers who chanced to see him riding on the road. "Nathaniel, an Israelite indeed, in whom there was no guile!"

> "Blessings be on their memory and increase!
> These are the moral conquerors, and belong
> To them the palm-branch and triumphal song—
> Conquerors,—and yet the harbingers of peace."

REVIVAL COINCIDENCE.

By this caption we mean the sudden breaking out of a revival under similar circumstances in two several places and on two occasions far distant from each other.

In the year *eighteen thirty-one*, the writer labored alone on the P. circuit. He had been very anxious to see the work of God revived. Still, little good was done, although he labored hard. At length in his youthful zeal and simplicity, he projected a camp-meeting (none had ever been held in those parts) to be convened within a mile of a town where Scotch Presbyterianism was in the ascendant. In this project he was seconded by a few old simple-hearted Methodists of strong faith. We must not be prolix, but hasten to say, that though censured by our Presiding Elder for irregularity, the meeting was a decided success. A number were converted, and that work of conversion gave an impulse to all the surrounding societies.

Among those converted were two Scotch lads, "Johnny A." and Johnny B." They lived in a neglected neighborhood in the township of D——, about seven miles beyond my most distant appointment. They went home in a flame and began to recommend religion to their friends and neighbors. They incurred a good deal of persecution, but God rewarded their efforts by giving each of them a sister to go with him to heaven. They came out from home seven miles and united with the class at the place above referred to. This, however, did not satisfy them: they wanted preaching in their own neighborhood that their friends might hear the saving truth of God.

I was about to leave the circuit for Conference, but sent on word that I would preach to them one sermon before I went. It cost me an extra ride of fourteen miles, but I was well recompensed for my pains. It is true, on arriving there I felt unfruitful in thought and depressed in mind, and wished I had not come. But a walk in the woods and earnest prayer to Almighty God somewhat assured me; I returned and found the congregation assembled in a barn; I took for my text, "How shall we escape if we neglect so great salvation," and began. I had scarcely commenced before I began to feel uncommon liberty of speech and power resting on my soul. It seemed as if I were pulling the words through the roof of the building. The Lord laid too his helping hand—all the unconverted were struck with conviction and "cried with a loud and bitter cry." My voice was soon drowned. And as Jehovah was now preaching I thought I might as well give over. We went to prayer and all cried amain to God. Soon one after another entered into liberty and began to sing praises to God, till all were made happy but one. The whole united in class before I left. They were all Scotch but one.

Now for the coincidence. About ten years after that, nearly a hundred miles from that place, I had gone one evening to a neglected neighborhood, where an old Irish class-leader had settled himself, to fulfil a volunteered appointment. I had selected another subject for the evening. But in the course of conversation after tea, I related the above mentioned occurrence. My host wished I might preach on the same text that night. I feared to promise: the text was never any great favorite with me, or rather, my sermon on it was not; and the thoughts had gone from me. Nevertheless I turned it over in my mind on the way to the place of preaching. When we arrived there I found the school house filled with people. The preliminary devotions were attended to, and I took "How shall we escape, if we neglect so great salvation," and began. And, strange to say, nearly the same state of feeling, as in the former case, fell on me and on the people. I had uncommon liberty and power; and the people wept and cried so loud as to drown my voice. I desisted as before, when about two thirds through, and engaged in prayer. They cried mightily to God—many were delivered—and, after continuing the services a few evenings, a lonely class of *twenty-two* was organized. I mention the coincidence without any remark by way of accounting for it, giving God all the praise.

Would that both these classes had been better handled than they were in after years!

EXPERIENCES OF A SELF-TAUGHT MINISTER

Education is nothing less nor more than the development of powers possessed to some extent by every human being, but existing in different proportions in different persons. Powers which, however, must remain forever latent if they are not drawn out. This work is commenced by others and carried on to some extent by the force of circumstances; but no person can be truly and eminently educated, who does not *set himself* about it with a fixed and untiring determination. The advantages of a regular school and collegiate education are incalculable; as such a course furnishes the tools by which a man may build up the superstructure of a cultivated intellect. There is a sense in which a man who is educated at all, in the true sense of the word, must be *self-educated*. Minds of different casts and calibre require a development each one peculiar to itself. And many a scholar has not discovered the true direction in which his mind ought to grow till he has left college. But then that collegian from his acquantance with the meaning of words, of language in general, of scientific terms, of mathematical principles, of logical forms, and of the leading facts of history, besides having a large development of mind already, has the implements for that particular cultivation which his own individual mind ought to receive.

Religion, besides giving always a mighty impulse to that mind which has been brought under its power, is the only safe guide to the healthy, and useful development of our powers. Every true minister must be supposed to be under its impulses and guidance. The minister's mind, if possible, should be truly and thoroughly cultivated. It becomes his duty, whatever his early advantages, to cultivate his mental powers to the utmost. The early Methodist preachers in this Province entered the work with small educational advantages. Their condition resembled that of the mechanic, who has to teach himself his trade, to manufacture his tools, and to perform the contemplated construction at the same time.

True, there was one thing they did know, before they undertook to teach others. They knew themselves to be ruined sinners—they knew the true source of consolation and help—they clearly understood the plan of salvation through our Lord Jesus Christ—they had a clear experience of the Spirit's work on the heart, and were qualified to comfort, as well as direct, others with the consolation wherewith they themselves were comforted of God. Nor was this all: they were usually persons of good natural parts—of quick perception and ready utterance—whose gifts had been drawn out and exercised in exhortation and preaching in their own localities before they went into the ministerial work. This was the reason why they had been urged to enter the field, and recommended by their several Quarterly Meetings. Yea more, if inquiry were made, it would be found that their literary attainments were considerably in advance of the mass of their hearers. Some of them had been School teachers. This gave them a vantage ground which caused them to be respected. Still, with all these admissions in their favor, they felt their great insufficiency for a work which migh employ the most extensive stores of knowledge and the most highly cultivated powers of mind.

This was felt by the person whose experiences we chronicle. He had learned to read when a child of six years of age, by conning over an old copy of the New Testament with its appended metrical version of the Psalms. The first verse he ever learned to read was this: "Behold the mountain of the Lord, in latter days shall rise." The second was—"Now as it began to dawn towards the first day of the week, came Mary Magdelene and the other Mary to see the sepulchre." His schooling consisted of about two years altogether before the age of seventeen, but distributed into periods of *one*, *three*, and *six* months at a time, with nine and twelve months vacation between. The intervals between the times of attending school were filled up with hard work. So that he lost during vacation what he had learned in term time. No wonder that this alternating system left him at the age above indicated (seventeen years and a half) with the bare ability to read; to scrawl his name with hideous chirography; and with much ado, to count the simplest sum in simple addition. But, thank God! he *could* READ. This art he had possessed from childhood; and the exercise of it was always pleasurable to him, and furnished him boundless stores of enjoyment. How often were the intervals of his toil, which his companions spent in idleness and *ennui*, beguiled with books. True, they were not of the most select or proper kind. They were such as fell in his way. The perusal of them gratified his curiosity, and preserved his appetite for reading. Nor does he now regret the reading of *one* of them. He has learned to extract the precious metal from the dross.

Then came conversion at the age of *fifteen*. This event gave a new impulse to his *intellectual* as well as *moral* powers, the latter of which had either remained dormant, or were distorted and diseased. A taste for a new kind of books was now created, and a conscientious principle established as to the character of the books he should read. He now learned to eschew bad and questionable books, along with injurious companions. A belief that the reading of novels was injurious was the immediate result: and although it cost him a conflict to part with this fascinating sort of reading, to which he had been previously addicted, he triumphed in the struggle, and never read another. His mind, throwing itself into this attitude of defence, went to an extreme in this direction. He was afraid of every kind of reading, however instructive and useful, that was not directly *religious*. This shut him up for some years to the Blessed Bible, to religious biographies, and to works on practical religion. Contiguity to a kind-hearted Presbyterian minister, gave him free access to the parson's old cast off books, which he kept in a passage-way outside his study door. These were all Calvinistic. During that period he read " Boston's four fold state"— the Works of Brooks—of Doddridge, in part, &c., &c. Along with these, he read the Life and Sermons of Wesley—the Lives of nearly all the Lay Preachers—and several Doctrinal Tracts, from the pens of WESLEY, FLETCHER, OLIVER, and BANGS, which neutralizd the Calvinism that his mind might have received from Boston and others. He has never regretted reading any of the Puritan writers, he found a wealth of theological matter, and expression that amply repaid perusal. And the study of these controversies were not unimportant as a means of mental discipline, and occupied the time which more favored ones spend at Latin and Mathematics, and, to some extent, supplied their place.

When midway between seventeen and eighteen years of age, providential circumstances released him from his trade. The time he spent at that, as it comprehended a knowledge of some chemical agents, he does not regard as absolutely lost. Besides, during that period he learned much of the principle and habits of a class of men, which contributed to advance his acquaintance with human nature, a branch of knowledge most important to efficiency in preaching, by furnishing the key, very often, to the conscience and the affections of the hearers; and of skill in pastoral government, by knowing the prejudices of the people in common life, who are always the majority. His ministerial success in after years was principally among persons of this kind. The best part of a year was now spent at school, save what was substracted by a severe fit of sickness—bilious fever, by which his *memory* received a shock which it never wholly recovered. This affliction, however, was a season of healthful moral discipline, which tended to prepare him more fully for his coming work.

In two months time at school, for which he paid two dollars, he qualified himself to teach the juniors, by doing which he defrayed the expense of his own subsequent tuition. During that year, he went twice through the English Grammar—twice through the Arithmetic—learned Book-Keeping in its simplest form—learned something of Geography—and acquired the elements of Latin and Greek. The want of resources, at the end of the space indicated, drew him to adopt the alternative of teaching a country school. Yes, gentle reader, he knows what it is to teach a country school, of the original type, and to study human nature in its domestic phases in rural life, in its newest form, by "boarding around"—that is to say, eating and sleeping one week for each pupil in every house or shanty among Irish, Scotch, Dutch and Yankees, whether tidy or slaternly. If this was not a probation and preparation for ministerial life in its itinerant form, we should like to know what would be. There he developed his talent for lecturing by talking to his pupils, among whom he was as famous as "Goldsmith's Village Schoolmaster." In those days a pious teacher was free to pray with his scholars in good earnest. Our hero nerved himself for after pastoral [engagements, by praying in all the families where he sojourned. The weekly class, with its preceding public meeting for exhortation and prayer, answered our self-taught in the place of the weekly declamations to which our present expectants of the ministry resort. Only that he had to be his own criticiser, which task he performed with severity or lenity as his mind chanced to be depressed or elated with his performances. But it was a rule with him in those days to try and improve on the *last effort* at *every succeeding one*. The only mental advantages of those three months was acquired by teaching what he had learned to others [he thinks it very valuable to alternate teaching with school-going] and the perusal of Mosheim's Ecclesiastical History, which he carefully read, and on which he made notes. The principal idea that impressed him from that reading, was, of the gradual rise of ecclesiastical power and superstitious observances.

A prospect of still further improvement now opened before him: the offer of a more paying school in a much more agreeable neighborhood with the privilege of boarding in the house of a well-educated, studious man, who felt a great interest in all young men anxious for improvement, who promised to give him all the assistance in his power. This person was a plain, unpretending farmer, but one who had enjoyed the benefit of a New England education, and whose only recreations were intellectual pursuits—a man who beguiled the long evenings of a Canadian winter, far from polished society, with Mathematics, Optics, and kindred subjects. Happily he was pious also.

The privilege of this man's society and instructions, this youth, perhaps erroneously, surrendered in obedience to the call of the church authorities, which first designated him to the office of Missionary School-Teacher among the Indians of Scoogog Lake, where had he gone, his career for life might have been very much altered. He might have wandered with THOMAS HURLBERT to the far North West; or with the lamented HURD, the Wesleyan student, he might have found his way to the college and his grave. This order, however, was countermanded. HURD went to the Mission School, and our hero to a circuit. Now opened new sources of mental solicitude and new efforts. As he had to preach eight times a week, his first necessity was to provide the required number of sermons. And they had all to be the fruit of *thought;* for he never had the art of talking without having something to say. He felt ashamed when he found himself rhapsodical. According to his day was his strength. He was now shut up to the necessity of *thinking*, and thinking *closely:* something in which he had long wished to discipline himself. His first sermon was studied on a barn floor. The second and third in the woods; and so on, very much the same with what followed There was little or no opportunity for retirement in the houses, and no facilities for writing whatever. He wrote no sermon— or nothing but the merest outline and the scripture proofs —for several years. His text was usually suggested by his private or domestic devotional reading in the morning of each day—by the wants of the people—or by some remark of theirs in prayer or class-meeting. Next he read the "Brief Commentary" in his little "diamond edition" Bible. Then he searched out the parallel passages, consulted a Commentary, if there was one in the house, (and the Methodists of that time, according to their number and means, bought far more standard religious books than do those of this day,) and then made his plan. By this time it was necessary for him to start for his appointment, for he had one, or two, in every day of the month but two. He *meditated* upon his subjects on horse-back; and the views of truth there eliminated, not only beguiled the journey, but were most sweet to his soul. If time would allow before preaching, when he got to his journey's end, he went into the woods and thought his subject all over again while he beat a path by pacing backwards and forwards, holding his inseparable Bible in one hand, and brushing off the mosquitoes with the other, or otherwise, he prayed it all over on his knees. From that communion with God and truth he went before the people. It is astonishing how fertile of subjects his mind became; and truth unfolded before him. He soon found himself able to make two or three sermons a week, such as they were. His stock of sermons was soon so large he began to feel easy in his circumstances in that particular. Especially so, when, after the lapse of four months, the Conference assigned him a new field of labor. He then began to think of widening his foundation, by something like a fair curriculum of study. The standard qualification in order to admission into the Conference at that day embraced Grammar, Geography, Logic, Ecclesiastical History, and Divinity, only. We do not remember that any text boooks were assigned the Candidates, only that it was supposed Mosheim was the best guide in Church History, and that in Divinity they should use the Bible, with the writings of Wesley, Watson, Fletcher, Clarke, and the rest of the Methodist writers. There were no "printed questions," or "topics" to guide the solitary student. His examination was all attended to at once, and was conducted by a

Committee nominated by the President. Of each of these subjects the young preacher in question had some knowledge excepting *Logic*. This he proposed to learn, with the sciences in general, and to get a knowledge of the original language in which the Scriptures were first written. But how was it to be done? He had no home assigned him; and but little time to spend in it if he had possessed one. He had no teachers, and he might have said no books. Still he resolved on getting every branch of knowledge desirable for a minister. He did not, however, postpone any ministerial duty, or obligation, till he should get such an amount of knowledge. He took for his motto that maxim of our Discipline: " Gaining knowledge is a good work, but saving souls is a better." " Gaining knowledge" was his daily endeavor, but when any particular opportunity for soul-saving occurred, he laid by his books till it was attended to. He found that they might generally both occupy some portions of each day. It was a rule with him to commence as soon as he arose, going over from the beginning to the last lesson, all he knew of any subject he had in hand. He did this particularly with the GREEK language. This occupied the time he was performing his toilet. His Bible and secret devotions of course occupied his first attention after he was dressed. He then employed every leisure and undistracted moment he could secure while in the house in reading and study according to plan. In order to prevent the people from consuming it all in conversation, he had several expedients—such as carrying with him a number of small books, one of which he put into the hands of each member of the family. Or if he was reading a work in which they were likely to feel an interest, he either read to them aloud, or, as this was very hard work, he selected an intelligible reader from among themselves to read aloud to him and the rest, occasionally correcting the reader's mistakes, if he were a young person, thus making it improving to him. Or else, the book elicited a general discussion on the subject of which it treated that was improving to all. He generally studied till he was tired, and thus made the ride to the next appointment, or the work of pastoral visiting, a recreation. But as his time for study in the house was too limited to fatigue him, he contrived to study in walking from one house to another, or on horse-back, in going from one appointment to another. He had always a book upon his person, and read during every interval, when he could do so with safety to his limbs and neck. But his usual method of improving such a time was to have an epitome, on a card, of something he wanted to memorize, or master, and to repeat it over as he went along. It was usual for him, after he had performed his evening devotions, while undressing, and afterwards while composing himself, to go over mentally the studies of the past day, and particularly to charge his mind with the ideas which he had acquired during that day. Another plan he took to imprint any new idea or branch of knowledge on his mind, was that recommended by Dr. Watts in his "Improvement of the Mind,"—a work from which he got many valuable hints— that of relating to another, on the first fitting occasion, any new idea he had received. Such occasions often occur to a preacher, both in private conversation and his public discourses. It is on this account that his occupation is an excellent school. Our subject found it so for another reason—the minister is obliged to *know*, and *must* use research. He is, therefore, educated by the force of circumstances, just like many others placed in responsible positions, in which they must sustain themselves, or sink. He spent, it is true, a great deal of time in vain—unless it were to demonstrate their futility—over two different systems of artificial memory, which he found in books. The first, was a system of technical or arbitrary words; the other, a system of fanciful resemblances, designed to perpetuate and call up the new-gotten idea when required, by associating it with the *mental*, or the *sensuous* symbol. He derived the most assistance from availing himself of the natural laws of association—which are, *similarity, contrariety,* and *contiguity* of *time* and *place.* What these are, and how they are applied, we need not further explain to the intelligent reader. A certain philosophic maxim, which he early adopted was of importance to him: that was, "Never be ashamed to acknowledge your ignorance." By this means he always learned, when he met persons competent to teach; and he met with few who could not impart information on some one subject at least. And on that one he plied them plentifully with questions. Most of people are not only willing but proud to impart what they know. Sometimes he learned the greatest truths, as Dr. A. Clarke, says he did, " by his own blunders." They led some one to correct him; or by accident he found out his mistake, when the mortification he felt so impressed the subject on his mind, that he never went wrong in that particular again. His deficiency compared with others stimulated him. If, in conversation with a man, he found himself inferior on any subject, he went and studied it, if it were possible, till he knew as much about it as the other.

On starting in the work his *elementary* defects were the worst of all. He knew the structure of the English language, its Etymology and Syntax; and had some little knowledge of the Latin and Greek, as also of Geography and History; but his pronunciation was bad, and his spelling was still worse—the fruits of not having had early schooling, and of keeping the company of illiterate people. He set himself to correct these defects. He had learned his Grammar from LENNIE, who has but one short chapter on orthography; he now procured " Murray's Exercises," and committed his Rules of Orthography, while he copied those of Mavor from his spelling book, and kept them by him when he wrote, referring to them whenever he was in doubt. When his piece of writing was finished, he went over the whole with a dictionary in hand. This, which was a pocket edition of Walker, he always carried with him, and kept by him when he read, not only to determine the *meaning* of every word which he did not understand, but to correct his wrong *pronunciation* of words he did understand—or to relieve his mind of doubt on any one, or all, of the above subjects.

The above remarks will conduct us to the method by which he tried to learn *composition*. He had never had but one composition given him to write while at school; and we have already hinted that he had no time or facilities for writing out in full even his sermons. He had travelled seven years, before he fully wrote out a sermon. But he began four years earlier to practice writing for his improvement. He received the first hint of the importance of it from an editorial of the then newly started " CHRISTIAN GUARDIAN," a periodical which has done an incalculable amount of good in improving all classes of people in this Province. It was then in the hands of EGERTON RYERSON. Our hero was at the time indicated *twenty one* years of age. He bought a small pocket blank book, and commenced a Journal, after the fashion of Wesley, making remarks on passing occurrences, and observations on the books he read, as well as recording the varying phases of his own christian experience. He did not write away at random in the book at once—there would have been but little improvement in that. He first carefully wrote his remarks or observations on a slate or piece of blank paper, erasing, adding, transposing, and correcting, till he got it correct—at least in his own estimation. At first he aimed at being *simply correct*. He knew little of enlivening his style with a figure, or of using the least ornament, for several years. So that it was merely plain and neat. Then, as his views expanded, his tastes became more elevated, and composition more easy, insensible to himself at the first, his style began to be more flowing and ornate. On observing which he gave attention to elegance and ornament as well as correctness. It has been said that the ornamented and practical style goes before the prosaic and plain, but it was not so with him. When he first began to compose, the great difficulty with him was, to make his sentences stick to each other! Hence he usually had a conjunction copulative, or disjunctive, between every two sentences, till the *ands*, and the *buts*, and the *fors*, were frightful! Yet he was afraid to do without them! The first hint to direct him was from the pen of EDMONDSON, in his work on the "Christian Ministry," in which he denounces what was our hero's practice, and quotes the words of the famous Bradburn, who used to say "I hate all your *ands*, and your *tos*, and your *buts*, and your *fors*, and all your little feeble expletives." That he knew how to eschew these, was doubtless one of the sources of BRADBURN's energy and impressiveness. To this day, however, the person of whom we write has often to go over the first draft of what he has written, and decapitate the superfluous conjunctions.

He deferred the prosecution of *science* till he should enlarge his acquaintance with the learned languages, from a hint he very casually got at a very early date in his career, that the most scientific terms were derived, or compounded, from the Greek and Latin; and that, consequently, when a person has a good knowledge of those, he can prosecute the study of the Sciences with greater facility. To the former of these, with *Hebrew*, he paid more attention than to *Latin*, as he judged it more immediately necessary to his Bible studies. "And why," he thought, "should not *Greek* be studied before *Latin?* It is the older language, and to a great extent, the purest of the other."

Just at this point, we may as well give the conclusions he came to on the subject of education for the ministry, after many years of anxious inquiry for the right way—of blundering, and of going wrong, for the sake of going right:—"A man," thought he, "should begin with the BIBLE, as the oldest and most authentic of all histories, as containing a picture of primeval manners and primordial civilization, and as being written in *one of the earliest*, if not the *very first* of languages spoken by mankind. "Let him learn," he further thought, "that language thoroughly, with all its cognates—Arabic, Chaldee, Syriac and Persic. Along with these, let him study the Geography of the lands of the Bible, many hints to guide him in which he will obtain from the Scriptures themselves. Next to this," he concluded, "a candidate should study the history of all the earlier nations, with the Geography of their respective countries, at the several epochs of their History. Beginning, if no higher, with Armenia, or Ararat, following JAPHET's posterity till they are settled in Asia Minor and Europe; then let him return," said he, "and settle SHEM in Mesopotamia and Eastward; and after that, follow the descendants of HAM in Arabia, Canaan, Egypt, and Africa in general. The invasions of Nimrod, a son of Cush and grandson of Ham, with the founding of the Assyrian empire, and its history, with those of its cotemporaries, and neighbors—Babylon, Media, and Persia, till the last mentioned swallowed up the rest, and that in turn was swallowed up by the Macedonian, or Grecian. The history of Egypt, to the study of which" (he went on in his musings) "a knowledge of Coptic and Greek would be most desirable, down to its fall—first, under Sardanapalus, and then, under Alexander. A minute acquaintance with the four Kingdoms—the Thracian, Syrian, Egyptian, and Babylonian—into which the Macedonian empire was divided, down to the time of the Romans, with the knowledge of the ever varying civil geography of those times," he concluded, "were most important to a thorough knowledge of the Bible. This," he thought, "should comprehend, not barely a following of the stream of events, but, as far as possible, let it be combined with the study of the manners, customs, civilization, trade, commerce, domestic habits, social manners, &c., of the nations and countries enumerated, at different periods of their history. Then," said he, "should come in the history of the Greeks, Romans, Phœnecians and Carthagenians, with a knowledge of Latin. Then, if a person's means and time would allow it," he mused on, "a journey through those countries, beginning with Armenia, proceeding to Mesopotamia, then to Palestine, thence to Egypt, and then back to Canaan again, by the way of the Red Sea, Horeb, and the Wilderness, till he enters the land from the farther side of Jordan. After which, the land should be explored from Kadesh Barnea on the South, to Hameth on the North. Then let the historical geography of the country be studied under the Judges, as united under David and Solomon—in its divided state, after the Captivity down to the time of Christ—its New Testament Geography—and its subsequent changes and present condition. This, with the Bible in his hand, with all the previous attainments indicated, and a watchful eye to all the new discoveries which are ever and anon crowning the searchers in Bible lands, a man," thought he, "would be prepared to commence the study of Theology proper from the best of all textbooks, the Word of God itself. Then all the general knowledge, if it amounted to universal learning, he could acquire the better, if it were gained by a journey through all lands and the study of their respective languages, histories, and laws, in the best of all places for the attainment of the kind of knowledge desired,—in those several countries themselves,—would be all the better," in his estimation. "All science," according to his views, "should be studied, and in the order in which they are related to each other. As also, the gradual development of society, civilization, commerce, and political economy. These attainments, with a thorough acquaintance with the Spirit's work on the heart; and a proper observation on, and knowledge of all grades of present society, and an acquaintance with the various forms and phases of error and infidelity would make," in his opinion, "a thoroughly accomplished minister of the Gospel, 'for the times.'"

But some will say, "The whole scheme is utterly Utopian and impossible!" Perhaps it is, but our friend's dreaming shows, at least, his views of the relation which the various branches of knowledge bear to each other, and the desirableness of every kind of learning to a minister.

After all we have said of the high standard he raised, we had better reveal no more of his own studies, or attainments, least it should be seen how very far short he has fallen of his own ideal of ministerial perfectness. Only perhaps we are bound to disclose, that his system of *self*-tuition embraced his obtaining the aid of a qualified teacher whenever it was practicable: such as returning the second night to a certain neighborhood, in a country circuit, to have the assistance of an Irish schoolmaster, who had barely missed a Sizar's place in Trinity College, Dublin; reading once a week to a graduate of Edinburgh University in Xenophon's Memorabilia, on his first station in a town; reading Greek and Hebrew, with a student of Trinity College, a fellow boarder, at another time; getting the assistance of the students and Professors of our own Methodist College, when he labored in its vicinity; and of actually spending the most of a year of respite from circuit work within its walls, in studying *Philosophy, Greek,* and *Hebrew.* Of his *divinity* studies, also, we are bound to say, that while he studied Methodist standards, when they could be obtained, which were not always to be had, and all other theological works that came in his way, his decided opinion was, that the BIBLE, expounded by such a grammar of its contents as "HORNE'S INTRODUCTION," a work to which he owed more than to any other, was the *best of all text-books in* THEOLOGY.

GENIUS IN POVERTY AND OBSCURITY.

It is the opinion of some, that if we are possessed of the *moral* qualifications for heaven, our happiness and glory in that holy place will be in proportion to the enlargement of our minds by education. And this opinion is rendered probable by the fact, that otherwise the utility of knowledge would in some cases seem to be doubtful. Unquestionably one reason for acquiring knowledge is, that we may make ourselves more useful in the present life; but when circumstances have placed a person in a position in which he can make but very little use of it for the good of others, we must look forward to another state, as the theatre where his cultivated powers shall receive their appropriate employment and gratification.

The above thoughts are suggested by the recollection of a remarkable individual whom I met with in one of my circuits. He was a local-preacher, and lived in a part of the country settled by people mostly of "Dutch" extraction. The greater part of them had been placed in circumstances in which they had received but little cultivation, except what they had received from the ameliorating influence of religion in the form of Methdism, which had been introduced among them at an early day and produced great results. They were very noisy. Ask one of those old shouting Dutch Methodists what sort of a preacher "Father Gill" was, he would be very likely to answer, "a poor teat, tull, old creatur!" And although there were a few, who from the first appreciated him, there was nothing in his phraseology or manner to attract people excitable, and demanding excitement. His appearance, too, was all expressive of dullness. Imagine a tall old man, "deaf as a stump," who, by the affliction which had deprived him of hearing, had lost all the hair from his head, and even his eye-brows and eye-lashes. The loss of the first was made up by a faded old red wig, which corresponded with his sandy complexion. His manner in the pulpit was rather stationary—his almost only gesture was, now and then, when he became impressed with his subject, striking his open hand on his chest, which always made his hollow frame resound so as to be heard by his audience, and his tones of voice were low and measured.

But that wan and wasted man, with his thread-bare clothing was of a respectable family, and had seen better days. But an undue attention to intellectual pursuits to the neglect of his business, together with the failure of the Linen trade in which he had been engaged in the North of Ireland, the place of his birth, had occasioned his emigration to Upper Canada. When I first saw him, he had, properly speaking, no home. After this, however, through the kindness of friends, a lowly one was provided for him.

I well remember my first sight of him. It was at a Camp-Meeting, the presiding officer at which asked Gill to preach. His answer was, "I am in your hands, but spare my life." Then such a sermon as followed. The manner of reading his first hymn impressed us: it showed an appreciation of *poetry*, which none but a *poet* could evince. His prayer was characterized by awful reverence and spirituality. Next came the text, which was most unusual—" When the unclean spirit goeth out of a man, he walketh through dry places, seeking rest and findeth none. Then he saith I will return into my house from whence I came out: and when he is come, he findeth it empty, swept and garnished. Then goeth he, and taketh with himself seven other spirits more wicked than himself, and they enter in and dwell there: and the last state of that man is worse than the first." After a unique introduction, he told us he proposed "no logical analysis of his text," a thing common with him; but he gave first a bird's eye view of it—then he penetrated its depths, and brought up things new and old. Its effect on my mind, was not pleasure, or tenderness, or fear, but *awe*, an overpowering feeling of intellectual and moral, or spiritual sublimity. The manifestation we received under that sermon almost agonized us. Ever after he was a favorite preacher with me.

He possessed originally one of the first rate order of minds— clear, logical, and yet imaginative, adapted either to the exact sciences, to astronomy, or to poetry. He had received the elements of a classical education, knew much of science, and read extensively, especially the writers of the "Augustin age" of English literature. He was familiar with Johnson, Steel, Sterne, Pope, Addison, and Chesterfield. And he was equally well acquainted with what we might call our Methodist classics, such as Benson, Fletcher, and Wesley. John Wesley was his oracle and admiration. He had heard Wesley and Coke—the latter often—and had been familiar with several of their cotemporaries and companions.

By the loss of his hearing in early manhood, and his obscuration by poverty, the external world and passing events were, to a great extent, shut out. But the world within had inexhaustible resources of occupation and pleasure. He read what books he could lay his hands on; he communed with his own heart; and he beguiled his lonely hours with writing poetry,—for which, in our opinion, he had no inconsiderable genius. He wrote all the acrostics, elegies, and epitaphs, for a large circle of friends; and many of them are dispersed through that region of country at the present time. He had a well-matured and well furnished mind, which enabled him to give a ready and profound view of any subject which came up in conversation.

As it was hard work for the lungs to make him hear, our usual custom was to ply him with *questions* on abstruse and curious subjects, and then listen to his remarks. Ask him of any subject, however new or difficult, and, after throwing himself back in his chair for a moment or two, while his eyes seemed turned on the inner man, his thoughts took a sweep around it, and he would commence and give you a consecutive and analytical view of the whole subject, and lead you to a satisfactory conclusion.

A timid but excellent Methodist minister had been defied by a semi-infidel of some abilities and great pretensions, backed by others like himself,—defied, I say, to prove the doctrines of a *personal* Devil, and a *real*, *local* Hell; and the day was fixed for the exposition. The brother, fearing his want of ability, posted off something like a day's journey for GILL. The old man clambered into the wagon and went without gainsaying. He referred to no books or authorities, but his mind excogitated the subject by the way. On arriving at the place, he met the congregation almost immediately, and preached on one of the topics at once; and, after a brief interval, again on the remaining one. What his line of argument was, I do not certainly know, but it was satisfactory to the hearers, and put a quietus on the champion who had "defied the armies of the living God;" for there was none to move his tongue by way of response.

We might remark, in connection with this incident, that he was very fond of dwelling on invisible things—such as Heaven, God, and Angels; and also Devils and the infernal regions. "The chariots of the Lord are twenty thousand, even thousands of angels," was a favorite text with him. He often took those portions of Scripture which speak of "thrones, and dominions, and principalities, and powers," which led him to speak of the probable ranks and orders of spiritual beings. He would, too, dwell on the nature, powers, and employments of those heavenly existences. While dwelling on these and kindred subjects, after exhausting every proof from Scripture and analogy, he would often say, in his broad, North-of-Ireland accent, "We may now, perhaps, be permitted to venture a little into the *raygions* of conjecture." Then would follow some of the most unique speculations that ever mortal propounded. Still we must say in justice to him, that though he certainly was a little inclined to bold speculation, by times, he never advanced any thing heterodox, and never neglected the practical. The generality of his sermons were highly spiritual, and well adapted to subserve the interests of serious godliness. He knew how to search the "inmost of the mind." A sermon we heard from him "on conscious integrity," from the well known text—"Beloved if our heart condemn us, God is greater than our hearts, and knoweth all things. But if our heart condemn us not, then have we confidence towards God, and shall assure our hearts before him"—was of this character. He himself possessed a truly elevated soul, and knew how to satirize the meanness of wrong actions. We remember his putting a damper on a litigious spirit, in a sermon by comparing the people's complaints to the preacher in charge, as resembling the conduct of children running to the "master" with tales against each other.

Prepared to preach he always seemed to be. Convince him at any time of day, or night, or in any place, that his services were needed in this respect, and he was ready to go about it, on two minute's warning. Gill was the most acceptable supply which the writer could send to one of his town stations when he was absent, although the congregation and society were very select and embraced a large proportion of well informed people. Sometimes they would propose some difficult text to him—perhaps it might be only a quarter of an hour before the time of preaching, and say, "We should be glad to hear you on it the next time you come." After thinking of it a minute or two, he would say, in his usually measured way,—"*I-don't-care-if-I-take-it-to-night*,"—on which he would go into the pulpit and preach them a profound and finished discourse. Every thing seemed finished that fell from his lips. He never wrote a line of his sermons, yet few spoke as correctly. His style was classically pure and elegant. I never knew a speaker who used the *period* so much. His sentences rolled out clear, complete, and round as a coach-wheel. There were never any tags at the end of them.

We have already referred to his *poetical* talents. On this subject we set up for no judge, yet we know he wrote a vast number of pieces, on many different subjects, both grave and gay, which struck us as very beautiful. We once drew up a *prospectus* for an intended volume of his poetry, with the hope of preserving his effusions and of helping the author; but we found the expense of the undertaking more than the subscription list would warrant us to incur. We fear the most of it is now lost, excepting some of those printed *elegies*, which were framed in the houses of the surviving friends of the subjects of them. We present one little relic from his Muse—an *acrostic:*—

"DOUBLE ACROSTIC.

"J-ehovah reigns! Let angel hosts adore;
O-n his perfections gaze forevermore.
H-is boundless love extends thro' earth and sky:
N-ought can escape his all discerning eye.

B-lest are the servants of our Sovereign Lord,
E-xpression fails to paint their great reward:
U-pheld by Him, who sits enthroned in light,
L-ost to the utmost stretch of mortal sight;
A-ll dispensations from his hand are good—
H-elp comes from Him who rules the swelling flood.

C-ontentment, here erect thy peaceful seat!
A-nd let these faithful hearts in union beat!
R-efining fires within their bosoms glow!
R-eturning seasons new delights bestow.
O-bedient to the voice of love divine,
L-ight in eternal splendor on them shines—
L-ife everlasting, to *each* I say, BE THINE!"

Distance from him at the time of his death prevents the writer from knowing much of the circumstances under which he left the world, but as he was one of the purest of mortals, we have no doubt that this child of loss and want has taken his flight to that Heaven of which he delighted so much to speak on earth, and to join in those celestial employments which were, while here below, so often the subject of his pious meditation.

THE BIG SNOW STORM.

At the suggestion of a friend on whose judgement and taste

I place great reliance I transcribe from the pages of the *Christian Guardian*, part of a published journal of a series of Missionary Meetings, embracing an account of what we all used to call "THE BIG SNOW STORM."

"DEAR BROTHER,—Having a few moments leisure in passing through this town, I avail myself of it to transcribe and send you the *fifth leaf* of my JOURNAL.

"*Wednesday*, Feb. 5—Should have gone on to Beverly; but I am laid up by the storm, which continues to rage with unabated fury. Brothers Ryerson and Jeffers, who had intended to start on their return to their families, are also unable to stir an inch. All our interior appointments, viz, Beverly, Bastard, and Crosby, will have to be neglected for this time (we will try and hold them in March); and it will be as much as we can do to get on Friday next to Waterloo.

"*Thursday*, Feb. 6.—Continued to snow and blow all the forenoon. The hope of getting to Waterloo was completely abandoned. The storm subsiding about noon, and hearing that the Stage had come in from Brockville, from which place it had been a day and a-half in coming, (a distance of 12 miles,) we started out. There were *three* sleighs in all: a friend's cutter, who had been weather-bound in Prescott since the meeting, and at whose house we aimed to get for dinner, a distance of 4 miles —he went before; next went the double team, which conveyed my three friends; and I brought up the rear. In this order the procession moved out of the town. First, we had the Stage track alone for about two miles; for the next mile and a-half it was a little better broken by a few sleighs which had turned out for that purpose; but for the last half-mile or more to our friend's house, the road was entirely broken by him, to the great endangerment of himself and lady, who was along, being entombed in the snow. Indeed, to describe the incidents of this four-miles' journey would require a pen far more graphic than mine. The quantity of snow fallen is greater than has ever been known to fall at once by the oldest inhabitants: it cannot be less than three or four feet on the level—if indeed any level there is; it having blown all the time it was falling. The snow has assumed all manner of fanciful shapes and forms. Here the wind in a capricious humour has scooped out a hole to the ground; there it has piled it up like "Alps on Alps;" a little further on, the snow by being driven into some hollow place, forms an almost bottomless ocean. Now, for a few rods we are making a little snail-like progress—there! horses are floundering over head and ears in a snow bank, or groundless sea of snow, where, if they move at all, it is more a swim than any thing else—now we are fast—the horses are unable to "stir a peg"— turn out, boys, and break the road before them—he who has the longest legs and the leanest body is now the best off—but a mis-step, and away we go heels over head in the yielding mass. "Give me your hand, and help me up"—"but I am losing my balance too"—there we are, down together, and up the best way we can, and at it again! After this fashion we wallow on till, after much fatigue, and badly caulking one of the team horses which conveyed my brethren, we accomplished the journey to Mr. Heck's in about two hours' time. Here we are at a full stop. The stage has only gone one mile beyond this to-day, and that not in the road, (which in most places is drifted full from fence to fence,) but on the *ice*. After a substantial dinner, to which we were prepared to do ample justice, four of us went out to reconnoitre. Found the *road* impregnable. Made a detour to the ice; and concluded that something might be accomplished by the Stage track thereon. Resolve on this; but on returning to the house, the friend who brought my brethren refused to proceed, his horse's foot continuing to bleed profusely. Br. Taylor and myself resolved to proceed, in hopes of getting to Brockville before bed-time. Find the stage track only leads a mile—make the attempt to push on to Maitland, a distance of two miles, without a road, *still on the ice*—wallow on a-half-mile—but finding our horse beaten off his legs, and the shades of night coming down upon us, we are fain to retrace our steps to the place where the stage came on the ice. Find a hospitable entertainment for the night with a friend, Mr. Snider. Spent the evening agreeably in religious conversation, and some hoarse attempts at singing.

"*Friday*, Feb. 7.—Rise betimes. Concert the mode of attack on the hitherto-unsurmounted snow-banks between Mr. S's and Maitland—$2\frac{1}{2}$ miles. First, our friend takes his oxen, and breaks down some of the most formidable banks. Then, he takes his able span of horses and sleigh, and goes before: my Br. Taylor rides with him; and I follow in his wake. But the process beggars all description; I therefore leave it undescribed."

I am sorry that here my scrap of JOURNAL runs out, as our troubles were not yet ended. Suffice it to say, that by dint of hard labor, and abusing the several "path-masters" along the road, we got to *Maitland*—$2\frac{1}{2}$ miles—for dinner—to *Brockville* about the middle of the afternoon—and to Yonge Mills, before bed time—perhaps 14 miles in all that day. Lodged in a dirty tavern. The next day turned out cold—we travelled all day and all night—floundering about because of the darkness—and got into Kingston about 2 A. M., more dead than alive. My fellow traveller and I had to pummel each other, to keep the breath of life in our bodies. We were in a poor state for preaching Missionary Sermons the next day, but we had to try it; and the people continued to put up with our efforts.

REMARKABLE ANSWERS TO PRAYER.

Jehovah is "a God that heareth prayer." He has bid us "be careful for nothing, but in every thing, by prayer and supplication, with thanksgiving, to let our requests be made known unto God." Oh, what a privilege is this! But how tardy to avail themselves of it, are the most sincerely pious people! So slow of heart are they to believe, and so prone to think the intervention of the Divine Being is to be expected in matters alone spiritual, and not in matters that relate to our temporal interests and comforts. A delusion this no doubt; and one that has an unfriendly influence on the interests of religion. Infidels will naturally resolve all pretended spiritual answers into imagination, but instances such as I am about to record, constitute a sort of external evidence of the truth of Christianity. They can all be authenticated by living witnesses at the present hour; and more of a similar nature might have been recorded. But these are enough to make up an article and to confirm the position, that we may expect answers to prayer in matters that pertain to this life. Before I specify particular cases, I may say, in a general way, that I remember something like a score of cases, less or more, where recovery, in the case of sick infants, which were given up to die, followed on their *baptism*, and the prayers to God for them which accompanied the ordinance. We simply mention the *fact*, let every person form what conclusion he thinks most consistent. I come now to *particular cases* of apparent answers to prayer.

In 183–, the circuit to which I was appointed had a great deal of week-day work; and on some of those days we preached *twice*. It was so the day on which the incident took place which I am about to record. I had a few miles to ride, from the place where I preached the previous evening, to another neighborhood, where I usually preached in a private house at 11 o'clock, A. M. The family consisted of the man and his wife, and two, or three children. One of these was an infant about six months old. It was very ill, and apparently dying. The parents, but especially the mother, seemed in the deepest sorrow and anxiety. The house consisted of two rooms below stairs. The front one communicated with out doors. The child was in a cradle in the inner room, where the women usually sat during service. The preacher generally stood in the door way between the rooms. And when I rose to begin the service, and, indeed, through the whole course of it, I could hear the afflicted mother sobbing behind me. I resolved when I prayed, to remember the child, and to enlist the intercessions of the congregation in its behalf. But, strange to say, I forgot it, both during the opening and closing prayer! When the service ended, dinner was brought in, and we immediately sat down. My back was still towards the door of the inner room, in which I could still hear the mother's sobs. I felt to upbraid myself for my forgetfulness; and having hurried through my meal, I and the father went into the room where the child lay. The poor babe was black in the face, and apparently near its last. An experienced old lady present said it would assuredly die; but I felt there was nothing too hard for the Almighty. The mother seemed to feel the same; her proposal for prayer in the child's behalf, met my own. We spake at the same instant; and we four were all "agreed as touching what we should ask." We kneeled around and facing the cradle, and made no request but the *one*—that for the recovery of the child. I felt uncommon liberty of speech and unusual faith—I was sure it would be done. The responses of the rest indicated a similar state of mind. We felt that we had got an answer. When we rose, I took the child's hand in my own, and said I thought it would get well. Had I followed the impulse of my feelings, I would have pronounced it with the utmost confidence, but thought it better not. The mother brightened up, and "thought it looked better." It mended from that moment. When I came around, in a month's time, it was perfectly well. It continued so till I left the circuit. Some years after, I met the parents at a Camp-Meeting; the child was then living. It is now, if alive, grown to man's estate. This I always *did* and *will* believe a direct and immediate answer to prayer. Since writing the above, I have stumbled on a reference to this circumstance in an old manuscript journal of mine, written when the facts were vividly before my mind. "Sept. 10. To-day preached at T. J's, whose infant child was very sick, nigh unto death, when I was around last. I prayed fervently and *confidently* for its recovery; and on going there this time, I found it perfectly recovered. They told me it began to amend from that very hour. This is the third instance of a signal answer to prayer, in a similar case, to which I have been a witness."

On that same circuit, a little earlier in the season, we witnessed an evident answer to prayer, relating to a different subject—it was for *rain* in *drought*. This was also on a week day, and at the second of two appointments for the day. It was in the centre of the township of M—, a very clayey soil, which felt the effects of the drought very much, which had now continued several weeks, till the crops had begun to turn yellow prematurely. The meeting referred to was at 3 o'clock in the afternoon, and held in a private house. We usually had a very large congregation at that place. When I arrived on that occasion the men, who were farmers, were standing about the door, engaged in conversation. The subject was *the want of rain*, which they deplored in melancholy strains, while their countenances were suffused with gloom. I felt for them and the country intensely.

Soon the service began, and when we came to pray I did not forget, as on the former occasion, but remembered the state of the country; and pleaded with the God of nature and providence for speedy rain. I felt great enlargement and confidence that it would be. The people responded with great earnestness, and apparently in faith. God also refreshed our souls with a sense of his presence. Before the service was concluded, it had clouded over. The people hurried home, as did Ahab and Elijah from Carmel to Jezreel. When night set in, the darkness thickened; and before morning a copious rain fell for several hours to the extent of several miles around. We all believed it was in answer to prayer. Since then, the writer has always prayed for rain in times of drought. He has also seen what he took to be unquestionable answers to prayer in reference to these requests; but did not charge his mind with the particulars so as to be able to relate them with correctness.

About two years after the last mentioned event, I was stationed in the town of B., whence I went on a visit into the interior of the country about forty miles. On our return, we learned where we stopt for dinner, that " Father T.," an elderly and estimable local preacher, who lived about two miles off the road, was exceedingly ill. Subsequently, too, I learned he had sent off to town, some dozen miles, with the persuasion if the preacher stationed there came and prayed with him he would get relief. This was unknown to me, when a friend proposed that we should go and visit this afflicted servant of Christ.

We set out on foot, to allow my horse to rest and feed the while. When we arrived at the house, we found the old gentleman in dreadful agony. The physician was there. We were not in the house many minutes before we were all on our knees around the sick man's bed. We felt that the Church could hardly spare that excellent member at that juncture, a time of agitation, when she needed "good men and true." How many of us prayed I do not now remember. I and the local preacher did, with great earnestness and faith. And the afflicted brother seemed to have more faith in the efficacy of our prayers than we had ourselves. God in mercy gave an answer. *In less than half an hour after we entered the house, he found relief.* He recovered, and though an aged man, is yet alive after the lapse of twenty-four or twenty-five years.

The writer had forgotten some of the facts, when, about *ten years* ago, they were recalled by an exhorter, who was Mr. T's neighbor at the time of his sickness and recovery, relating the facts in a Love-Feast, in confirmation of the *efficacy of prayer*, which had been the subject of the sermon on the previous Saturday. This was several hundreds of miles West of where the occurrence took place. All who knew the facts, believed that useful man was given back to the Church, from "the gates of the grave," in answer to the prayer of faith.

We now come to an occurrence, among many, nearer the present time. Not more than six years ago, the only child of a very estimable and pious couple—a little girl about nine or ten years of age—was ill. I believe her affliction was a fever at first, but had become complicated, and her life was despaired of. The parents naturally felt much at the prospect of losing their little one. The writer, on the occasion referred to had called at the door, and inquired about the health of Mary; but as she was very low and had been fatigued with company, he thought it not best to go in, but sent his love, and word that he *would pray for her.* On the return of her mother to her bed side, the child wished to know who had called. The answer was, "Mr. C——; and he said he would pray for you." "Well, call him in, and let him pray for me *now*," said she. The pastor was accordingly summoned to return, and to come to the bed side of the sick one. The father, mother, and minister were soon gathered around the couch of that sinking yet intelligent and appreciating child. I do not remember that more than *one led* in prayer, but that prayer was deeply felt, and fervently and believingly offered by each and all. We prayed for the salvation of her soul; but also pleaded with great liberty and boldness, the promise of covenant mercy, for her *recovery.* We felt we had got an answer from the Lord. And from that hour, Mary was convalescent. She went on recovering for several days—when a relapse brought on a new complication in the form *diabetes.* Parents and child were alarmed again. The latter begged that the pastor might be sent for to pray with her again. He went. The former scene was re-enacted. God gave us the desire of our hearts; and in a short time restored her to perfect health. She is still alive, and must be nearly grown to woman's estate. It is to be hoped she will not forget her obligations to that Being, who appeared for her deliverance in the hour of distress and danger; and that she will make prayer and praise the business of her life.

Perhaps we could not make a more fitting close of this article, than by saying it was our happiness to receive, from the subject of the cure himself, an incidental confirmation of an extraordinary case recorded in the Life of that remarkably holy and faithful servant of Christ—the late REV. WM. BRAMWELL. We are sorry we have not his biography at hand, to give the particulars of the passage *verbatim ;* but we give its substance.

It will be remembered, that in a certain house in which Mr. B. used to lodge, I think in one of his favorite Yorkshire circuits, there was a boy whose sight was almost extinguished by an affection of the eyes. Mr. B., on the occasion referred to, had staid over night; and coming out of his room, doubtless from his knees, and going to the front door where his horse awaited him, suddenly stopped and asked where the boy was with the diseased eyes. He was told in a certain "dark room." "Bring him to me," were his words. The boy was immediately brought, Mr. B. made no remark, but put his hand on his head, and continued some time in silent prayer. Then, turning, mounted his horse and rode away. The boy feeling that he was restored to sight, tore off the bandage from his eyes, and found himself perfectly well. When the writer of this article read that case, it impressed him much; but little did he think he should have the truth of it confirmed to him by the party most interested. Yet so it was. When stationed in London, C. W., about ten years ago, I received a beautifully written letter from a gentleman who said he was a commercial agent; it was dated Ayr, Scotland, although his home was in Yorkshire, England, requesting me to make enquiry for a daughter of whom he had not heard for some years, and about whom he was anxious, assigning as a reason why I should feel some interest in him that he was a Wesleyan local preacher, and that he was the identical boy for whose restoration to sight William Bramwell had prayed and was answered. It was signed, if I remember correctly, WILLIAM GREENOUGH. It was the name in the book, which is not at hand. The daughter was found, who confirmed her father's relation, by the tradition that had always been in the family. To her I delivered the letter.

N. B.—When I began, I had the intention to give the *particulars* of a *recent* case, the most remarkable that has occurred to ourself, of an interesting little boy, four years of age, the child of highly respectable parents, and their *only* SON, whose skull was broken through by a blow from a horse, so that a piece of skull came away and some of his brains were spilled, and of whose recovery the most competent to judge had no reasonable hope; whose life was given back in answer to the agonizing prayer of faith, and who may be pronounced recovered. The physicians pronounced his recovery, little less than miraculous. And his intelligent father, who by no means carries his religion to the point of fanaticism, is of the firm persuasion, that *prayer* saved him. But all the parties being well known, we are not disposed to further obtrude it on the public. May it appear that this child was spared for some useful end.

THOUGH REPREHENDED, STILL REMEMBERED.

It is melancholy when from among a truly christian people " men arise speaking perverse things to draw away disciples after them"—" thus separating chief friends," and " scattering firebrands, arrows, and death." This scene was enacted unhappily in Upper Canada, when one of the oldest ministers, and one who had been the most influential member of the Conference, after some years of discontent and agitation, arising from disappointed ambition in not being able to gain the episcopate in the body, withdrew; and after assailing the character of the ministers with whom he had stood connected in labor, set up a church of his own, or one that was popularly called after his name—and thus made the first *permanent* division in Canadian Methodism: we refer to the REV. HENRY RYAN. We do not introduce him for the purpose of censuring him; much less of reviving the animosities engendered by the division and its concomitants, but rather to rescue the remembrance of Mr. R's efficient early labors from oblivion. And that the rather, as we have heard that he viewed some matters connected with those unfortunate events in a different light, on the bed of his last sickness, from what he had done while in the heat of the fray in which he had been a prominent actor. Let this suffice for his *reprehension*—we gladly turn to a brighter picture—his early career.

Since writing the above I have turned up in Bishop Hedding's life to the following reference to RYAN, which not only describes his character and early labors in the States, but shows that those labors were extended into Lower Canada. Some years ago the writer, on a visit to Dunham Flatts, met with several aged persons who remembered his labors and usefulness there, and who spoke of him with enthusiasm. We leave the passage unaltered to speak for itself:—" Mr. Hedding had for his co-laborer and senior in office this year (1802) the REV. HENRY RYAN. Of this colleague Mr. Hedding says: " He was, in that day, a very pious man, a man of great love for the cause of Christ, and of great zeal in his work as a minister. He was a brave Irishman—a man who labored as if the judgment thunders were to follow each sermon. He was sometimes overbearing in the administration of discipline; but with that exception, he performed his duties in every part of his work as a minister of Christ as faithfully as any man I ever knew. He was very brotherly and kind to me—often speaking to me in a manner calculated to urge me on to diligence and fidelity in the great work. When we met in the place of intersection in the route of the circuit, he would occasionally salute me with his favorite exhortation, ' Drive on, brother! drive on! Drive the Devil out of the country! Drive him into the lake and drown him!' The author of the 'Memorial of Methodism' says of this remarkable man: ' He was characterized by an inexhaustible zeal and unfaltering energy. No difficulty could obstruct his course; he drove over his vast circuits, and still larger districts, preaching continually, and pressing on from one appointment to another. Neither the comforts nor courtesies of life ever delayed him. In Canada his labors were Herculean : he achieved the work of half a score of men, and was instrumental in scattering the word of life over vast portions of that new country, when few other clergymen dared to venture among its wildernesses and privations. Not only did he labor gigantically, but he also suffered heroically from want, fatigue, bad roads, and the rigorous winters of those high latitudes. Such was the companion with whom Mr. Hedding was to be associated in the labors and privations of the second year of his ministry. He had but little suavity of manner to render him agreeable to his colleague; but there was a heroism in his daring, and an invincible ardor in his movements, that rendered him not altogether unprofitable as an associate."

The circuit they then travelled is thus described by the Rev. Laban Clark, who had travelled the year preceding:—" Our circuit," says he, " was divided into two parts, nearly like a figure 8 containing a two weeks' appointments in each, and bringing us together every two-weeks; the whole distance about four hundred miles, including all that part of Vermont north of Onion River, and in Lower Canada from Sutton to Missisquoi

Bay, and around the bay to Alsbury and Isle la Motte; embracing about forty appointments for four weeks! Being a newly settled country the roads were exceedingly bad, and to reach some portions of the circuit they were compelled to traverse extensive wildernesses, through which there were no roads." Such was Ryan, and such were his labors, before coming to Upper Canada.

No history of Canadian Methodism, however fragmentary and sketchey, would be in anywise complete, which did not contain some reference to such a leading influence in its early doings as HENRY RYAN—a man who at one time seemed almost ubiquitous in the country, and had unbounded ascendancy over the minds of the great mass of the Methodist people.

He was the first person the writer ever heard deliver a sermon. It was preached in that first meeting house in the town of York, so often referred to in these sketches; and addressed, if we remember correctly to the children of the Sabbath School—they at least were all present. This was as early as the year 1819. He had been in the country from 1805. He entered it in company with the REV. WILLIAM CASE, whose senior colleague he was in the Kingston, or Bay of Quinte circuit. He must have been in the ministry some time before that, as he had been the apostle of Methodism to the new settlements of Vermont three years prior to his coming to Canada; but our not having a copy of the American "General Minutes" at hand, prevents us from determining when he began to travel. And his dying outside the pale of standard Methodism prevented any memorial of him being preserved in our body. The most we have to say is preserved from tradition, the report of his cotemporaries, and our own recollections. He began in the last century, as he was Hedding's senior, who commenced the first year of the present century.

His name indicated a Celtic origin, and he was most likely of Roman Catholic parentage. He was usually supposed to be an Irishman—a colleague calls him such—and he may have been born in Ireland, but he certainly had acquired his dialect some other place than there. An Irishman never calls *endeavor*, "indeevor," which was his pronunciation of the word. He was not a highly educated man, as the composition of some printed circulars, published under his auspices, which we have seen in our time, indicated. He was reported, we know not on what authority, to have been a practiced, if not a professional, pugilist before his conversion to God. And we know of no man who would have been more likely to succeed in that infamous calling than himself, had he turned his attention to it and been trained for it. There can be no doubt but RYAN was one of the most powerful men the race ever produces. He was prodigiously strong; and quick as he was strong; and bold and powerful as either. When we first saw him he was in his prime. We do not like to hazard an opinion about his height, because men so stout as he are likely to seem shorter than they are. He might have been five feet eleven. He was muscular, but plump and compact. His complexion was dark—head massive—forehead rather projecting—his nose curved a little downward—and his chin, which was a double one, with a dimple in the centre, curved upwards. His face was large. He was very quick in his movement—he used to start from his seat to his feet, when an old man of sixty and beginning to be corpulent, without ever putting his hand to his chair. He has been known to fling ordinary sized men, who were disturbing the order and solemnity of divine worship at Camp-Meetings, over the high enclosure with which it was customary in the early days of Methodism to surround them. There was no law for the protection of out-door worshipers at that time, and our hero knew how to protect himself and his friends.

His voice was one of the very best. It was flexible, musical, prodigiously strong, and of fabulous compass. His conversational voice would reach the outskirts of any ordinary congregation, and its tones were very agreeable. He could speak without any effort, the ordinary weight of his voice being enough to carry the sound to the most distant auditor. But when he lifted it up—and he did do it at intervals—"it was as when a lion roareth." We have heard of persons being led to jump from their seats by one of his bursts. He had perfect control of his voice, but being naturally very impassioned, he frequently employed it to its utmost extent; and added to the terrifying effect by vehemently "stamping with the foot and smiting with the hand." Take an example:—In the middle of a sermon he is talking of death as a certainty—but the uncertainty of the time. "It matters not what becomes of the body, whether entombed in marble, or buried in the depth of the sea: "But oh—*the soul!*" (Elevating his voice.) "But oh,—THE SOUL!!" (Elevating his voice still more.) "But oh,—THE SOUL!!!" (Raising it to a terrific shout, and bringing down his weighty hand on the pulpit with a slap that makes the house to ring.) He has been heard distinctly when preaching in the Kingston market house by persons on Navy Point. By the way, the market house was their only preaching place and a butcher's block their only rostrum, when Ryan and Case first tried to introduce Methodism into this ancient town. They were both powerful singers, and they were wont, as Mr. Case informed me, in order to collect a congregation, to take each other by the arm, and walk towards the place of preaching singing the hymn beginning—

"Come let us march to Zion's hill."

They sometimes encountered some annoyance from the rabble, which they however treated with a noble contempt. He never removed after this from Upper Canada; but was one of the very few preachers who remained in the country during the late American war. The Rev. Thomas Whitehead was another. They were Britons by birth and also by preference. Besides, they felt they had an important post assigned them, which they might not abandon. Ryan took the oversight of the whole, calling out Canadian local preachers to supply the work, of whom THOS. HARMON, who had performed prodigies at the battle of Queenstown, whose loyalty to his King, and whose zeal for God, ought not to be forgotten, was one. Elder Ryan's district extended from the extreme West to Montreal, a distance which he traversed to attend the Quarterly Meetings. As his income was very small and precarious, he eeked out the sum necessary to support his family by peddling a manufacture of his own in his extensive journeys, and by hawling with his double team, on his return route from Lower Canada, loads of Government stores, or merchandise. Such were the shifts to which Methodist preachers had to resort in order to sustain themselves in a work which they would not desert. Mr. R. by his loyalty gained the confidence and admiration of all friends of British supremacy; and by his abundant and heroic labors the affections of the God-fearing part of community. But these were not his only sources of influence. He had a rough and ready but real oratory, most admirably adapted to his auditors. He felt strongly and could make others feel. We have seen that he could be most terrific when he liked; and he knew how to melt the people into tenderness, while he addressed them with floods of tears. He was communicative and lively in private conversation, interesting the people with the ludicrous aspects of the checkered scenes through which he had passed. He was perhaps a little too fond of that, but still is was a means of endearing him to the many. Ryan was also witty, and had a ready answer for every bantering remark. Some wicked fellows are said to have asked him "if he had heard the news?" "What news?" "Why, that the Devil is dead?" "Then" said he, looking around on the company, "he has left a great many fatherless children." Sometimes his answers assumed more of a belligerent than witty character. On entering a public house one day, a low fellow, who knew him from his costume to be a minister, thought to insult him with impunity, remarked aloud, while he put his hand to his pocket, "There comes a Methodist preacher; I must take care of my money." Ryan promptly resented it, by saying "You are an impudent scoundrel." "Take care!" said the man. "I cannot swallow that." "Chew it till you can then!" was RYAN's defiant reply. There was often wisdom in his courage. Once in a tavern, he observed that the more than usual amount of profane swearing and blasphemy was evidently perpetrated to annoy him and to draw him into an altercation. He let it pass in silence, till observing one more officious in the matter than the rest, evidently with the intention to elicit his reproof, he turned and accosted him in the following ironical way. "That's right: swear away, my man; you have as good a right to be damned as any one I know of! Go on, and you will accomplish your purpose!" This was doubtless more harrowing and effectual than a milder and more direct form of reproof.

But if he could abate the pride of the haughty, he knew how to sympathize with the humble and contrite ones. I shall never forget it of him, that he turned aside into a destitute neighborhood on one of his long western journeys, about the year 1811, to administer comfort by conversation, singing, and prayer, to my poor disconsolate mother, then in a state of deep religious melancholy. The partial misdirection, to use no stronger word, in his later years, of energies which had made him so effective for good, may serve as a beacon-light to all who have to navigate the same dangerous strait. May all interested learn the lessons taught by the history before us! While we cherish the hope that this wonderful man, after preaching to others, was not finally cast away himself.

THE FATHER OF CANADIAN MISSIONS.

This was a title by which the venerable and REVEREND WILLIAM CASE, otherwise known as "Elder Case," was distinguished for many years before his death. It may seem too broad a title to some, in view of what was achieved by some who preceded him in the Province as Methodist Itinerants—such as Losee, Dunham, Coleman, Wooster, Jewel, Sawyer, Bangs, and others—in so far as the evangelization of the *whites* was concerned; also in view of the labors, at some periods and in several places, of ministers of other branches of the Church of Christ. Yet, when we remember that Case entered the Province so early as 1805, and that he continued to labor in it, with the exception of *six* years, unremittingly down to the day of his death; and that he was almost the first Missionary to the extreme western part of the Province; and when we take into account, that he projected, fostered, and clung to the last to the *Indian* Missions; and that the last mentioned Missions have been almost exclusively connected with the Wesleyan Methodist Church, we must see that the cognomen might pass without much explanation or modification.

Were we to write his life, we should probably divide it into—HIS PRE-ABORIGINAL EFFORTS; *and his Indian Missionary Career.* And what a fruitful subject to one familiar with the political and religious history of Canada, would be the Life and Times of the REV. WILLIAM CASE. "Case and his Co-adjutors," might be its title. He would be a fine central figure, standing out from the rest, while grouped around him might stand the whole array of Canadian Methodist worthies, lay as well as clerical, from one end of the Province to the other, and from *eighteen hundred and five, to eighteen hundred and fifty-five.* Strange that his friends have found no person competent and willing to undertake it.

In the absence of such a life, we furnish a slight memorial. Like the novelists, we begin in the middle—namely, at the time we first saw him, in 1824, when he must have been about *forty-four years* of age. I had heard my mother speak of "ELDER CASE" approvingly, as "a very *mild* man." This was to contradistinguish him from the great majority of Methodist preachers of that day, who were in general very boisterous and particularly so "ELDER RYAN," his coadjutor in the *Presiding Eldership* of the Province; the subject of our last picture, who, as we have seen, was a BOANERGES. At length we saw him for ourself. The writer had set out a few months before to seek and serve God; had joined the Methodist Church, and at the time referred to, was attending a prayer meeting in the house of a Mr. C——, when a tall, somewhat slender, round-faced, pleasant countenanced stranger, genteel looking, in very clerical garb, entered the room; and at the request of the more active of the only two class-leaders then in the town, conducted the meeting. All the older members pressed around him to shake hands, and were most pleasantly received. The youngest member, who stood behind the rest, was led forward by his leader "to speak to THE ELDER." He smilingly remarked to our considerate friend, " I see you have some *young* members." That boy afterwards learned that the good Elder had given his leader a special charge concerning him—predicting by the way, that he would yet preach the Gospel. He took a great interest in young men; and devised measures to bring them forward, often unknown to them, so as not to elate them too much at first. He was the director of the rising ministry of the Methodist Church in Canada before she had a College in which to train them; and he was the friend of that Institution from the moment it was projected to the day of his death, watching its progress and doings with the most lively interest. He would sometimes talk about "his boys" in the pulpit in a way that set the young aspirants to usefulness, and to weeping around him. Little children, too, he loved, and took a great interest in their schools. On this account, he was a welcome visitant in the various families whose hospitality he enjoyed. The little Indian children, even, would literally pluck his clothes, " to share the good man's smile." Nor did they fail in their object. He would often pursue these tawny little ones, and catching them would kiss them with all the fondness imaginable.

My next sight of him, after the occasion referred to, was two years later, when he and the REV. THOMAS MADDEN chanced to be together in the pulpit of the Old Framed Meeting-House—two of the strong men of that day. CASE preached on "Justification by Faith," the most doctrinal sermon I ever heard him deliver; and MADDEN followed with an address in further elucidation of the subject. I thought I had never heard anything so satisfactory. Madden was the clearer in exposition and more methodical in arrangement; but Case was more declamatory and persuasive. Up to this period he had been very popular as a *preacher;* he became less so after he got absorbed in the Indian work, and some brighter luminaries arose to transcend him. Case in the pulpit appeared to the greatest advantage *before* eighteen hundred and twenty-five. He did not excel in exposition, nor in doctrinal preaching, but in treating historical subjects—the destruction of Sodom and the case of Zaccheus, for instance—in preaching on relative duties and family religion; in portraying domestic scenes; and in a pathetic sort of declamation, to which his musical voice, his ready utterance, and tearful eyes, all lent their assistance. The intonations of his voice were not unlike those of the Indians, which we always thought gave his ADDRESS a peculiar persuasiveness to them.

Our subject was born in 1780—converted in 1803—received his first appointment to *Canada* in 1805. He continued in this Province till 1807, when he spent one year in the United States. He returned in 1808, and continued till 1810. Then, after five years spent on the other side of the lines, he returned and continued in Canada till the day of his death. He was *seventeen years* a Travelling Chairman, or Presiding Elder of various districts; four years the President of the Conference and Superintendent of the whole work; and the rest of his time till within a year or two of his death, exclusively devoted to the Indian work, as Missionary, Superintendent of Translations, and Principal of Alderville Industrial Institute.

In his relation as the "Father of the Indian Missions" it will become us particularly to speak of him. But before doing so, we must glance at the characteristics of his career among the *whites*. His early ministry, by the testimony of all who knew him at that time, was distinguished by activity, tenderness, and prudence. It is said that after preaching one of his persuasive sermons, he would sing one of those delightful *solos*, which he knew so well how to manage. Then when the young people were all enchained, he would walk around the room, take each by the hand, or, throwing his arms around the neck of the young men, he would beseech them to be reconciled to God. It was by such means he promoted the great revival in the West in 1808, when the voice of prayer and praise was heard by day and night in the houses and barns, in the fields and woods, all over the country. By his singing he found his way on some occasions into the families of genteel Romanists, to whose children (in one instance a young lady in dying circumstances) he, in that gentle way, communicated the knowledge of Christ. Music was his own solace, as well as the means of charming others. He told us, that in one of his long, solitary, bush rides, on a close, sultry day, when the feathered songsters were mute and all nature seemed to lie in a state of torpor, he was quite disposed to feel dejected; when he stopt, descended from his horse, selected the branch of a tree that would "peel," and made a whistle, with which he remounted and began to play: his own spirits were revived, his horse seemed livelier, all the birds began to sing, and he went on his way rejoicing. He was an early riser; and in later years, when greater refinement obtained, we have known him to rise before the genteel family with whom he was sojourning were astir, and call them to see the glories of a rising sun, and to inhale the balmy breath of morn, by stealing to the piano and thumbing slowly off some simple, plaintive air.

He was "instant in season, and out of season." Once when pursuing his way on the beach of one of our great Canadian Lakes, the only possible road at the early day when the event transpired, he met at a narrow pass a solitary man—stopped him, and spoke to him of salvation till he began to weep, then he proposed prayer—alighted from his horse, and wrestled in earnest intercession in his behalf till God in mercy set his soul at liberty. The two embraced each other, and went on their opposite ways rejoicing, perhaps never to meet till they met in heaven. Of his boldness and adroitness in causing his horse to swim the Niagara River, to avoid the embargo, when he wished to reach his circuit in the West, all our readers have learned from his JUBILEE SERMON.

Case, though he had none of the sternness and authority of Ryan, and perhaps was less methodical than he, was nevertheless a real general. The submission which others gained by awakening fear, he gained by exciting love. He was a shrewd, though silent observer of character; and knew how to put the right man in the right place. Many of these men were superior to himself in point of talent. When the battle for our public rights had to be fought, he did not draw the pen himself (although no contemptible writer) but put forth one of the youngest men in the connexion as its champion, because he knew he was the best qualified of any in the body for the task. At his Quarterly Meetings he sometimes employed the stationed minister to preach in his stead, when he thought he was qualified to make a better impression on the augmented congregation than himself. If he had circulars to write, he knew what good copyist to put his hand on to do it for him. We remember his coming into the school we were attending in 1828, and engaging our teacher to write out for each preacher in his district a draft of circular which he left; the decision of the American General Conference on our application to be separated from that body.

He was "wise as a serpent, while harmless as a dove." He never committed himself by a premature disclosure of his own views; but he had a quiet, unintentional sort of way of drawing out the views of others. He showed his self-control in his suppressed laughter. That rule of a "Helper," "Converse sparingly, and conduct yourself prudently with women," was exemplarily observed by him from early youth. This was a great achievement, in view of his youthful beauty, and constant exposure to company. He was near, or quite fifty, before he married. In fact, his long journeys and absences from home had nearly ceased before he asked any lady to share his joys and sorrows. Perhaps no person preserved a more prudent single life than he. Some pleasant things are told of his adroitness in disentangling himself from the attentions of fair candidates for the handsome young preacher's affections, but we shall not particularize them.

There can be no doubt but that his interest in the INDIAN WORK became a real passion. The aboriginal tribes which hung on the outskirts of civilization in this Province, especially the Chippewa Indians, were a most degraded and besotted race. Ignorant, indolent, improvident, filthy, drunken, and licentious to the last degree. No one hoped for their amelioration, or thought it possible. But CASE, in his frequent journeys through the land, had often anxiously revolved their condition in his mind. When, therefore, PETER JONES, a half-Indian youth, whose vernacular was Chippewa, and who knew something of English, was converted at a Camp-Meeting in *eighteen hundred and twenty-three*, he broke out with the exclamation—"Bless God! the door is now opened to the Indian tribes." And events transpiring in swift succession verified the prophetic character of the remark. There was a coincidence of three favoring circumstances which proved the work to be providentially commenced. A zealous young man, a local preacher, SETH CRAWFORD, by name, had come from the United States, unauthorized, except by what he thought to be a divine impulse, and commenced a school among the Indians of Grand River. Coincidently with that, the REV. A. TORRY had been appointed a Missionary to the scattered white settlers along that stream. Therefore, when Jones (who now resided with his father near where Crawford had commenced operations,) was converted, and his half sister also, who was a MOHAWK, there were experienced and pious men at hand to sympathize with him and to guide and assist him in his efforts for the salvation of his fellow-countrymen, which began at once. The first conversions took place among the Mohawks, among whom was an influential chief, THOMAS DAVIS; but soon the work broke out among the Chippewas of the Credit, to which tribe, or band, Peter Jones, by his mother, properly belonged. For a time the Indian brethren at the Grand River gave them a place among themselves, that they might be near the means of grace and of instruction. This was before their houses were erected on their own reservation at the Credit. And it would have been well if all the converted Indians could have permanently settled together in one place, and a community-ship if not a nationality given to them by which their efforts towards civilization and self-improvement might have been more effectually encouraged and brought to some good, productive issue. Even as it was, great and glorious things were achieved. The BELLVILLE, or KINGSTON Indians caught the flame; and it soon spread to RICE LAKE, MUD LAKE, LAKE SIMCOE, SCHOOGOG, MUNCEY-TOWN, and ST. CLAIR. No one can imagine, who did not witness it, how these wonders among the Indian tribes thrilled the souls and animated the zeal and faith of the old Methodists of the Province.

CASE specially became absorbed in it, so that his attention to the regular work ever after was only secondary. He labored, talked, and prayed for the Indians without weariness. A pleasant story is told of an interview between him and the renowned BISHOP GEORGE, in the United States, whither CASE had gone as was his wont frequently, to beg for his Indian Missions. GEORGE said CASE was called on to pray; and soon began to pray for the " poor Indians;" "but soon broke down with emotion—recovered himself, and began to pray for the Indians again, till he faltered again—praying for the Indians was alternated with weeping"—" till," said the BISHOP, " he forgot the *white-man* had a soul at all." Though still on a district till 1828, his spare time was spent at the missions, or in begging for them. The latter was certainly no sinecure. There were no funds and no organizations for raising them in those days. Missionary meetings such as we have now were not thought of for several years. The whole was left to fitful spontaneous effort. CASE, like DR. COKE, went from house to house and solicited aid, both here and in the United States, sometimes striving to enhance the interest by the singing and recitations of a few children from the mission schools. Many of the preachers imitated his efforts. We know that Ferguson, of precious memory did for one.

But after all that could be done, the support extended to the *laborers*—for they well deserved the name, working with their hands to teach the Indians agriculture and the mechanic arts, and to raise food for themselves and families, and to provide mission houses and chapels—was very slender. Happily they knew how to forage for themselves. A pack enclosed in a blanket, slung on the back by means of what was called a *tump-line* across the shoulders, and a gun with a small store of powder and shot, constituted an Indian preacher's outfit. I knew ELDER CASE to pull the socks off his feet to give to one of these extemporized evangelists, while my own good mother, (peace to her memory!) knit another pair with all posssible dispatch to replace them. He adapted himself to the *cuisine* of the Indians—no trifling achievement by the way—and maintained that no white woman could cook a fish like a squaw.

Case's calm, quiet, and yet cheerful manner was adapted to the Indian mind. A blustering, driving, direct man, could not succeed with them. But he had a method of administering the most effectual rebuke in a way that would not offend. The most defective part of the converted Indian's character is—their indolence and want of management. The good ELDER used to hold at ALDERVILLE what he called an "Inquiry Meeting." Some scripture character or piece of history was first discussed by the missionary. Then the natives were encouraged to ask questions concerning any point which they had not understood, or about which they wanted more information. This method was found entertaining and instructive. One evening the Patriarch Job was the subject. His case awakened a great deal of curiosity. He was put before them as an example of industry and economy. His great wealth astonished them much. They wished to know again how many *sheep* he had: and were told "seven thousand." "How many camels?" "Three thousand." "How many yoke of oxen?" "Five hundred." "How many she-asses?" And were told, "Five hundred." "Now," said Case in conclusion, "Suppose JOB should pay you a visit, and walk around among you; and look at the way you farm, and look at your cows, and oxen, and pigs: What do you think he would say?" "Don't know. What you think he say?" "Well, I think he would shake his head, and say, 'This catching *musk-rat* is a small business'!" The men all dropt their heads. They felt its force. They departed without saying a word, but they were not offended; for it passed into a proverb among them, which they applied to those who neglected agriculture for hunting—"Catching musk-rat is a small business."

Case's deep interest in the Missions appeared in his amassing a library of books almost wholly restricted to that subject.

Thus have we presumed to record a few of the incidents of his early career which came to our own knowledge. The rest will be best expressed in the words of the official obituary published in the Minutes of Conference for 1856 :—

"Question IV. *What preachers have died since last Conference?*

"Answer.

"WILLIAM CASE.

"From the autibiographical part of the venerable deceased Minister's valuable "Jubilee Sermon" we learn that he was born at Swansea, a town of Massachusetts, on the 27th of August. 1780; and he died, soon after a fall from his horse, at the Wesleyan Indian Mission of Alnwick, in Western Canada, October 19th, 1855,—his departure, which was expected by few persons, universally regretted by his brethren, friends, and the public, though a gracious Providence had permitted him to reach the honored age of seventy-five.

"The eventful period when he assumed the Christian profession is thus briefly stated by him : "After years of religious impressions, and a sinful course, I was converted in 1803." Under what circumstances this change took place he has not informed us; but of the fact, so necessary to ministerial fitness, satisfaction, and efficiency, there is no doubt; for in every subsequent year, and in all the vicissitudes of an itinerant life, his character was adorned with those features which bespeak a renewed mind, and entire consecration to God. He had not received the spirit of bondage again to fear, but the spirit of adoption, whereby he cried Abba, Father; and we believe that spirit was a permanent resident in his soul. At no time was there evidence that the peace he professed was fluctuating, and that the light of his heavenly Father's countenance had become dim. In his exhibition of the graces of the Holy Spirit there was neither uncertainty nor extravagance; and even to old age there was in his disposition and demeanor a child-like simplicity, affection, and uniformity, which elicited the willing testimony, " This is a man of God."

" His body was never robust, and his habits were always temperate. His presence was dignified and prepossessing. His mind, though never trained scholastically, was vigorous, searching, and tenacious, and by much reading, observation, and experience it became enriched with knowledge as practical as it was adapted for all the purposes which his diversified positions in the Methodist Church required. His acquaintance with Wesleyan doctrines, discipline, and usages was correct and comprehensive; his publication of those doctrines judicious, experimental, persuasive—often pathetic; his enforcement of that discipline in its integrity, while there was no lack of fidelity to our incomparable system, was invariably marked with moderation and caution ; his pastoral assiduities for adults and youth, parents and children, were spiritual, fatherly, and unremitting. He was a warm well-wisher of our Ministry, and Connexional Institutions; and in his entire intercourse with the Ministers he loved, especially at the sessions of Conference, there was a good sense, a prudence, and a heartiness, which made all revere and love him.

" A Divine hand led him into the Ministry, and his hallowed charity prompted him to volunteer his services for Canada; after which some remarkable answers to prayer, and much success confirmed him in his choice of this magnificent and favored Colony of the British Empire. And his selection of Canada at that time was expressive of a heroic intention, and a burning zeal; for the recesses of the wilderness had been little explored, and ruggedness, privation, and peril awaited his footsteps; while the scattered settlers were for the most part without stated Gospel ordinances, and the Aboriginal tribes were pagan and degraded : but he entered upon, and discharged with inflexibility of purpose his arduous duties; won the esteem of the people everywhere; and brought many souls to Siniai, and then to Calvary. In 1805 he was received on Trial by the New York Conference of the Methodist Episcopal Church,—a commanding and beloved branch of the great Wesleyan family; in 1807 was received into Full Connexion, and ordained Deacon; and the following year was ordained Elder,—when the apostolic Asbury was a bishop of that Church, and had the wide-spread States of the American Union, and Canada for the field of his evangelical and most effective superintendency. The Rev. Mr. Case commenced his itinerancy on the Bay of Quinte, and his first six years were spent under the direction of that Conference. In 1810 he was appointed a Presiding Elder, and for eighteen years he had charge of important districts,—the Cayuga, the Onedia, Chenango, Lower Canada, Upper Canada, and Bay of Quinte. In 1828 he was made Superintendent of Indian Missions and Schools. In 1830, and the two following years he was General Superintendent, *pro tem*, of the Methodist Societies in Canada. For several years he was a Missionary to the Indians, and Superintendent of Indian Translations. In 1837, and for fourteen years continuously he was Principal of the Wesleyan Native Industrial Institution at Alnwick, until ably succeeded by the Rev. James Musgrove. In 1852 he was permitted by the Conference to visit different parts of the work, as his health enabled him; and, without being superannuated, it was his wish—and his fine social spirit made it a pleasure—to pursue this course until his Master should bid his servant rest.

He rejoiced to see Canada greatly elevated socially, morally, and educationally. He rejoiced when the Canada Conference was constituted, and when the Missionary Society of our Church was organized, and the Indians were to be evangelized. He rejoiced when, on acccount of the wisdom and cordiality of the British Conference, and a congenial spirit in the Canada Conference, the Wesleyan Methodism of the Canadas and of the Hudson's Bay became one constitutionally and affectionately, and it is believed, indissolubly. He rejoiced to behold from his death-bed the jurisdiction of the Canada Conference comprehending 210 circuits and missions, 330 itinerants, and 38,000 members,—an extensive Book Room, and a popular University, and the Missionary Society, which once had a very limited support, cheered with an income of £9000. As an early pioneer, and untiring laborer of our Missionary Society, he was highly respected by his brethren, and by none more so than by the honored President of the Conference, the Rev. Enoch Wood, under whose very able General Superintendency of the Missions for the last eight years he was a faithful Missionary. In the language of our Missionary Notices we record the opinion of our lamented friend, that "however much to be valued in the offices he once filled," "and among his brothers and sons in Conference assembled, when he would rise with coolness and decision, and by his deliberate and prudent counsels carry many with him, it is thought that he was best known as our *apostle to the Indians ;* and for them he lived and died. Here we want space to set forth his early and manly dedication of himself to their interests, his acquaintanceship with their condition; the adaptation of his powers, and acquisitions, and means to their necessities; his influence over them; his sympathy, his vigilance, his shrewdness, his tenderness, his authoritativeness, his travels, labors, indefatigableness, success." The efficiency of a Native Agency was his prayer. He witnessed the conversion of a Native with exultation. Many Indians from the wilds of North America, once ready to perish, will be his glory and joy forever!

"At the unanimous request of his brethren he delivered a Sermon before the Conference last year in London, on the completion of the fiftieth year of his Itinerancy, which we heartily commend to our people and the public for its scriptural doctrine, and choice Methodistic reminiscences. And we have been gratified to receive intelligence of the testimonials of his character and labors published by the Wesleyan Missionary Committee in England, and by the Managers of the Missionary Society of the Methodist Episcopal Church in the United States, and of a Discourse on his death, delivered by a learned, and sincerely respected former fellow-laborer in Canada, the Rev. Dr. Bangs, of New York. He had many friends in Canada, and elsewhere on this continent, and his unsullied reputation had extended to other lands. He informs the reader in his Sermon, that he was prepared to state the names of two hundred Ministers who were converted in Canada; and of that number not a few, and some of them Indians, belonged to his own Church, and were allured by him to the Saviour, and into the Wesleyan Ministry,—whose recollections of their Father in the Gospel are vivid and imperishable. The Wesleyan Societies of Canada cannot forget his person, and his tender courtesies. They cannot forget his mature christian excellencies, his intelligence, sound judgment, and salutary counsels. They cannot forget his patriotism, his pure philanthrophy, and attractive catholicity. They cannot forget his works of faith, and abundant labors of love for half a century. He had to suffer hardship, but endured; he was in perils oft, but God was his preserver; he was assailed by the weapons of error and sin, but was triumphant through Christ.

"His Wesleyan survivors would emulate his great virtues, and follow in his path of distinguished usefulness; rendering to the all-wise Head of the Church thanks for perpetuating a scriptural Ministerial succession among them by an unusual accession of laborers this year, when He is calling some of the fathers home; rejoicing exceedingly, that the same adorable Being who gave a Swartz to India, an Eliot to America, and a Barnabas Shaw to Africa, gave also a WILLIAM CASE to this country,—whose name will ever be associated with the past progress, perpetuity, and glorious future of Methodism in Canada."

PART II.

THE CONFERENCE AND THE CRAYONS.

There is not a more genial, sociable, warm-hearted class of men in the world than Methodist preachers—whether found in the conventional society of Old England—the heartiness of Irish intercourse—the orential tendencies of European population in the East—amid the untrammeled sayings and doings of Yankeedom at large—or the *melange* of manners and habits which are exhibited in a British American Colony, where all is yet knew, crude, and in a state of transition, such as Canada, taken as a whole, has been, if not still, is a fair example. The theology they hold and teach, which asserts universal redemption, and "offers life to all"—the experience they have had of God's willingness to save the vilest of the vile, which enables them to sing—

> "Deeper than hell He plucked me thence,
> Deeper than imbred sin."

The perfect level on which they stand with each other in point of allowances and elegibility for offices—their rotation in the same fields of labor, bringing them acquainted with the same places and people—the training they have had and ever continue to have in christian sociality in the class-room, the fellowship meeting, and the lovefeast—a partnership in the same toils and trials, the same privations and sufferings, all tend to endear them to each other; and to place them on a footing of familiarity and fraternity not to be found among any other class of men. It is not to be wondered at, therefore, if the meeting of two or three hundred of these men in Conference is looked forward to, after the responsibilities and anxieties of a year, as a season of welcome relaxation and of pleasurable and profitable intercourse with those they love. Here brothers and sons of the same earthly parents meet, now doubly dear to each other, "both in the flesh and in the Lord"—here old school-fellows, class-mates, or college chums, re-unite—and here former colleagues,

> "Old soldiers of the cross,
> "Who have struggled long and hard for heaven,"

embrace each other, shed the tear of fond recollection on each others shoulders, or "fight their battles o'er again," in the cozy breakfast room of some indulgent Gaius, where the presiding genius at the tea-urn, looks as though she felt it to be her highest felicity to make the weather-beaten itinerant happy, and the strained and sparkling eyes of the little ones (God bless them!) betray the wonder they feel at the strange recitals, while some good little boy whispers in his mother's ear, as his lips quiver with emotion, "*Mama, I mean to be a minister!*"

The pleasure is augmented to the individual when the place of the Conference's meeting chances to be an old and favorite station, where, perchance, many of the now active members are his personal friends or his spiritual children: and this may be the case with several ministers in reference to that particular place. The scramble for these, and the loving altercation which shall have this or that one of them as a permanent lodger during the Conference, give no little perplexity to the current ministerial incumbents in their endeavors to make out a satisfactory "billet." Sometimes the parties take the matter into their own hands, the householders writing off, frequently three months before the Conference, to those ministers they wish to be their guests. If they consent, the matter is fixed. As all cannot have their choice, the disappointment must be compensated for by the preachers going out to tea, or dinner, whether to meet old parishoners, or former colleagues.

But while there is this feeling of equality and fraternity among the men who compose the Conference, there is a diversity which is to be found no where else. Methodism has won its trophies and enlisted into its ministry men from all the walks of life, from all professions and trades, and with every variety of early training, both secular and religious. There, is a young man whose parents were wealthy and yet pious, who brought him up in the fear of God and gave him a liberal education—all of which advantages of early culture, good habits, polished manners, and learned attainments he has brought with him into the ministry. Along side of him sits a brother, who perhaps takes his turn in the same circuits and offices, and who seems to sustain himself as well, and speaks with the same boldness in the deliberations of the body—only that there is an idiosyncracy about him not observable in the other—one who was born of poorer parents, perchance in the army, or on the mighty deep; one, who it may be, was schooled among rough men—in the barrack room, the sailor's mess, the backwoodsman's shanty, among lumbermen and raftsmen, who is self-taught (excepting that he has taken the "Conference Course" under the direction of his chairman) and who if he has not been classically trained, has by dint of reading and observing everything that came in his road, picked up a great deal of practical, and a great deal of an out-of-the-way sort of knowledge, which the grace of God makes available in the service of religion. The other knows more of books; this one knows more of men and things. The former has seen the smoother side of humanity; the latter has seen both sides of it, particularly the rougher.

In our Colonial Conferences are Englishmen, Irishmen, now a large infusion of Scotchmen, some Americans, now and then a

Dutchman, men of Welch extraction, a few Frenchmen, and native-born Colonists of all kinds. Our Canadian Conference exhibits these varieties in "glorious confusion." Nor have we merely natives of different countries, but men who have seen ministerial life in almost every part of the world and under almost every possible aspect. Men who have labored amid the matured institutions of English Methodism—others who have grappled with the disadvantages and privations which Methodist Ministers experience in Ireland—some who have known it in the presbyterio-prelatical form it has assumed in the United States—several who have labored in two or three other British Colonies besides this—some men who have traversed the frozen snow-banks of the far, far North—and those who have labored for their Master's cause under the enervating rays of a vertical sun within the tropics. These men have "seen life" in all its aspects. They have enjoyed the princely hospitality of the wealthy planter, and have sat down in the huts of his field hands; they have kept the polished society of foreign British officials, civil and military, and they have held daily intercourse with the peasantry and the poor of all grades and classes. One night they have slept in a bed of down in the mansion of the rich; another they have turned and shivered on a straw pallet in the cottage of the poor. To-day, they feast on roast beef and plum pudding; to-morrow it is well if they have a dinner at all. They hold frequent and delighted converse with the most gifted and cultivated minds; but they still more frequently commune with the lowly minds of the uneducated.

While, therefore, there is one thing which gives unity of aim and effort, and sympathy of feeling to this strangely constituted body; that is, while

"The love of Christ doth them constrain,
To seek the wandering souls of men,"

it is not to be wondered at if they should view an existing question in very different points of light; and discuss it as variously. Years ago, to us it was a source of amusement to sit in the Conference and watch this diversity. Sometimes we have been drawn out on this subject among our friends in the social circle; and always found that our description of its members excited interesting attention. Several years ago some of our ministerial brethren requested that we would prepare a volume of TAKINGS. This proposal we always refused to comply with, on the ground of its questionable utility, and because the doing of such a deed had once been formally condemned by very high authority. After that condemnation, however, sketches of living Ministers, Methodist as well as others, obtained in Europe and particularly in the United States, which publications were sold by our own Book-Room authorities, and eagerly read by both ministers and members. Seeing which, my conscientious scruples began to relax a little. I thought also, if they portray the outward man on canvass, why not the inward on the pages of a book? If the inner-man of the morally deformed be portrayed, as it is every day, why not paint the features of those who are renewed in heart? And if we read with interest the description of living ministers in Europe and the United States, why would not the description of Canadian Wesleyan ministers be equally, if not more interesting? Besides, this pictorial method may be made the medium of conveying information on the present phases of our Colonial Methodism, and of teaching many a grave moral lesson in this agreeable way to those who are young, both lay and clerical? These considerations had nearly converted me, when, on going to the Conference last summer (1859) I picked up at my boarding place, for the first time, Watson's "TALES AND TAKINGS," of the U. S. Conference. I had had some "TALES" by me for some years which now constitute the bulk of this volume. I thought I might hit off a few "TAKINGS," and thus produce a Canadian book of a similar character to that of Mr. Watson's. A few of those whom I knew best were briefly sketched—published in a paper for which I sometimes wrote, and handed around among those on whose judgment I could most rely, as a sort of *feeler*, when the verdict rather appearing to be in their favor, I went on and published a large number through the same medium. They have been freely criticised, as a consequence; some have been cancelled, and most have been revised, or retouched. As the name imports, they do not claim to be *finished pictures*, but CRAYONS, or *rough pencil sketches*. The author has drawn his subjects, not to caricature them, but to present the moral beauty comprised in the *contour* of each face. His discussing the peculiarities of his brethren and the distinctive attributes of their ministry must not be regarded as setting himself above them. Many a writer presumes to review a work which he owns he could not have produced. So with us, we feel the worst of these men to be superior to ourself. We have portrayed them as we would have done the beauties of inanimate nature. Yet all must be aware, that *light*s necessarily require *shades*, or else there can be no picture whatever. We have used as little shading as possible, except in the case of some particular friends, whom we knew to have sense to perceive the reason and to make the allowances. Some of those we have sketched with the boldest hand and made the deepest lines, are precisely the ones we have the greatest admiration of—the ED-ITOR of the *Guardian* and the CHAIRMAN of the Toronto District, for instance, not to mention any of the others referred to. Some really good and humble men may, on the other hand, object that theirs are too flattering. They must allow othe people to judge for them; and men who make such an objection, are not much in danger of being spoiled by flattery. *We have sketched none* we did not heartily approve of on the whole. There may be others we as ardently admire whom we did not sketch, simply because we could not describe every one, and did not "get the thought" of those particular ones in time. Some excellent men would have been gladly laid hold of, if we had not learned that they had decided objections to such freedoms with their names and doings. We freely own we have not said all the good of any one mentioned we might have done, but that would have made them too long. Some of the most superior men have the shortest description. If we have not placed any one in so good a light as he deserved, he must reflect that these claim to be but one person's opinion—and his, we frankly admit, of no great importance.

The very minuteness with which we try to stave off every possible objection is evidence that we feel that we, perhaps too recklessly, have ventured on very ticklish ground. If we have erred, or injured any brother's feelings, we humbly ask forgiveness. There are simply two things that encourage us a little—we are ministering to a great many living readers' gratification; and we shall have the thanks of posterity for our cotemporary descriptions of so many of the excellent ministers of this age. And it may be a salvo to others, if they think they have been made too free with, that the "poor author," is at the present moment the most thoroughly criticised man in the connexion. We leave the prefatory note to the EDITOR of the paper in which they were first published, as a farther explanation of our views.

CONFERENCE CRAYONS.

For the Hastings Chronicle.

HAMILTON, June 1st, 1859.

MR. EDITOR,—I have thought that a few Charcoal Sketches of members of the Wesleyan Methodist Conference now in session, might beguile the leisure moments of my sojourn in this city, and perhaps interest some of your readers, and I trust hurt nobody; for "naught shall be set down in malice." And if I take more liberty than some modest men would like, they must try to remember that much similar to what I *write*, is *said* about them every day, and that public men are public property; also, the consideration of personal characteristics may be useful in a great many ways.

Your's considerately,
* * * * *

CRAYON FIRST.

Having resolved to try and hit off, in an easy manner, a few of the more prominent members of the Canadian Wesleyan Conference, I begin with one of the oldest, one who was superannuated last year, but who still thinks himself effective, as he has applied for restoration to the active work. We have heard somewhere, that British soldiers never know when they are beaten. In this respect, as in all others, FATHER CORSON is a true Briton. He thinks he is as capable of circuit work as ever he was; and physically, I think he is nearly so. But, alas for the dear old man! he, as some others of us, is behind the times,—though, like most others in a similar predicament, he does not know it. He never was distinguished for very great intellectual power, although a shrewd man, and his early education was defective, a defect he never greatly remedied by private study, although he has been one of the most voluminous readers in the Conference. Even yet, he reads more books through in a year than almost any man we wot of. Furthermore, he has an excellent memory for the *historical* parts of what he reads. He is a sort of standing table of reference for *facts* and *dates* relating to American Methodism. Notwithstanding the drawbacks above mentioned, he has done good service for the Lord in the woods and wilds of Canada, during the last thirty-five or forty years. We remember our first sight of him at a camp-meeting thirty years ago, when his word was like electric fire among the people. And if he is not highly educated himself, he has raised up a family of educated sons, who are an honor to him, while they bear traces of the intellectual superiority of a good and dignified mother. Our hero never filled a City appointment, but he has traversed and re-traversed nearly all the rural parts of the Province, from Kingston to Sarnia, and from Lakes Ontario and Erie to Huron and Simcoe. For preaching *often*, and *visiting* he has no equal. He has been known to preach *forty* times in the month, and to visit a dozen families before breakfast. He has never filled any office in the connexion higher than that of Superintendent of a circuit, and has never received any particular mark of his brethren's appreciation, although he lives in the affections of every brother's heart. We know not that he ever published anything beyond a letter in a newspaper, but we once knew him to have written what we wish he had published.

No person ever bore toil and lack of honor better. He has sometimes made humorous allusion to his great abilities and high position. *Humor* is his forte. His is of the most broad and grotesque, yet genial and pious character. How he has "brought down the house" (for be it known, he is a celebrated Conference debater,) all acquainted with the deliberations of Conference very well know. In this respect he has answered a valuable purpose in our ecclesiastical discussions, often dissipating the acrimonious feelings engendered by a stormy debate, by one of his irresistibly ludicrous speeches. Though ludicrous, they are not trifling; he is often most laughable when most in earnest. Father C. holds very decided opinions on all questions, and is not afraid to express them either. He often does the latter by very sound arguments, which would be really weighty and convincing, if it were not for the odd and humorous way in which they were put. To see him rise in Conference is the signal for a titter of delight to run through the assembly, while significant nods, and winks, and smiles, amount to saying, "now for some innocent amusement." The make of his tawny, good natured face, is comical; and his nod, when he addresses "Mr. President," is formed on the most approved school-boy model of other days, when the urchin was expected to bring down his head to every passing stranger, in the use of the strictly enjoined "bow," with a jerk that was serious to the vertebræ of the neck. But if our hero's arguments are not telling in the ordinary sense, he often makes very lucky hits, which do good without hurting much. We have two of these in our rememberance, which were decidedly rich, but hesitate a little for the present in publishing them.

Still it must not be forgotten, that though Father Corson often provokes a laugh, he frequently beguiles the people of their tears, as he is by no means parsimonious of his own. Nor are they crocodile tears either; he has a warm, tender, and pious heart.

This old-fashioned itinerant, by an odd juxtaposition, has settled himself at Cobourg, where our rising Ministry are receiving the polish of a liberal education. They may very profitably take some leaves out of his book.

May God in mercy give him a serene old age, and the happy death of a "good soldier of Jesus Christ," such as he is! Amen.

CRAYON SECOND.

I am about to try my hand on a very different subject from the last. It is said, I believe, that an artist finds it harder to paint the face of a model beauty, than one who has some features a little out of proportion. It is true, I refer not in this to the *personal appearance* of my subject. He is no beauty, yet a personable, comfortable looking man,—healthy, florid, and bulky without obesity. An intelligent Scottish gentleman said he liked to see him on the platform, as one felt, from his appearance, "that there was no danger of his breaking down."

Our subject has a well balanced mind. He unites a very emotional nature, with a very sound and sagacious judgment. He is prudent and cautious almost to timidity, which sometimes leads him, I have thought, (though I may be mistaken,) to lose the most favorable opportunity of effecting some important object. He is not forward to take on himself responsibility which he thinks belongs to others; and yet we have sometimes known him to shoulder a great deal.

He must be a man of very successful management, or he would not have enjoyed the uninterrupted confidence of the British and Canadian Conferences so long continuously as he has: having been Chairman of a District in New Brunswick for several years,—Superintendent of Missions in Canada ever since the re-construction of the "Union,"—and President of the Conference no less than seven years in succession.

He began his itinerant labors in the West Indies, where he published an interesting little work, embracing some affecting matters of pastoral experience. Since then, we have not heard of his publishing anything, excepting his well written Missionary Reports. He seems to have had a thorough business education. As to matters of *learning*, it would be harder to tell what he don't know, than what he does. He has been offered, and declined, the degree of *Doctor in Divinity*. His general information is extensive; he has seen a great deal of what the world calls "good society," but seems to prefer the company of the pious to all others. He can be punctiliously polite when required, or very free and familiar among his friends; he can indulge in or take a joke when it is not out of character.

As to public engagements, he rather shrinks from notoriety than courts it. He is retiring and domestic almost to a fault;

yet capable of the most successful public effort when he tries, being a genial, able preacher, and an eloquent platform speaker.

He is English by birth and education, but a Colonist by adoption and feeling. He is Conservative, yet progressive. In a word, a great, good, kind, wise man is the Rev. ENOCH WOOD.

May he long hold his present honorable and useful position!

CRAYON THIRD.

I turn my eyes to another man of port and presence, who, if a good physique be a matter of so much consequence to mental healthfulness and activity, as some psycologists maintain, ought to be the greatest man in the Conference; for he is large, strong, and well proportioned; and all who know him must confess that he is no mean man.

First of all, he has evidently no ill opinion of himself, and this self-reliance has borne him up in many an emergency, always supposing also that he has had a proper reliance on God.

He is a Canadian—a Bay of Quinte man. Converted in early life, and faithful to the present—a period of over thirty years—a good part of which has been spent in the Wesleyan Ministry. He went out in 1832.

He received an excellent business education, and has a taste for secular and commercial matters. This may account for his being chosen to act so often on financial committees. Nor has any man in the connexion subserved the interests of the church's temporalities more than he. He seems to have a *penchant* for helping every one in the management of his business. I don't mean to say this disparagingly; it is not done with offensive obtrusiveness. Yet he has done a great deal of thankless drudgery for others; but sometimes he has earned and received the deepest gratitude from those whom he has thus served.

He is a good pathetic preacher, with a plaintive, tear-extorting delivery; and I think feels very much when he makes others feel; a correct speaker, and fair sermonizer. His singing makes him interesting in social meetings; his voice undulates and quavers.

He does not make so much impression in his Conference speeches as he would if he did not fidget about so much when he speaks, and were he a little more lucid in his arguments. We think he is rising above these defects.

He has had his share of honor and responsibility; has been Principal of Mount Elgin Industrial School; Chairman of two Districts; and is now the heir-apparent to the throne of the Book-steward, at some future day. His name is as fragrant as a ROSE.

CRAYON FOURTH.

I now sketch a twin-spirit of the last. He is not so stout, but he makes up in length what he wants in breadth. Tall, straight, strong, wiry, spry on foot, enduring. A fine person of a man is he; and a *man* every inch of him, too. Perhaps if there had been a little infusion of a softer metal, to modify the stern steel of which he is composed, it would have been better in the estimation of some.

Thoughtful and pains-taking, he has strong confidence in his own judgment. This gives him great advantages, with some drawback of unpopularity at times to one who is really a kind hearted as well as honorable man.

Pretension aside, he is really a very versatile, capable, yea, wonderful man. Few men are so clever in so many things as he.

He is a New Englander by birth—a New Brunswicker by education—and a Canadian by adoption. That is, he has adopted our cause and country, and we have adopted him. He is one of the first-fruit benefits of our re-union with the British Conference. He has done us good service—as City Preacher and Superintendent—Chairman—Church Builder—and Treasurer and Moral Governor of Victoria College.

I do not know that he is ambitious, I rather think not; but he is so buoyant, he will always keep on top. There is nothing in the way of effort in connexion with the Church's operation, he would not, if called to do it, undertake to do—even if she should confide to him the task of amputating a leg or an arm. He has any amount of physical nerve or courage, and has performed in his time prodigies of adventure—such as floating several miles on a strong-currented river on two inch boards, one laid on top of the other; driving his cutter a long distance through four feet of water; and swimming a river holding on to his horse's bridle.

He is clear-headed, logical; debates well, keeps his temper, and exerts a great influence. He will, however, be estimated for all he is worth. Without the grace of God, he would not have been so amiable and interesting as he is—a beautiful example of sanctified manliness. He is powerful in prayer, and a real revival preacher.

He may sometimes do a little harm, unwittingly—but will do a great deal of good on the whole—and will, there is little doubt, get to heaven at last. We want to get ready to meet him there. Amen. Need any one be told we speak of the REV. S. D. RICE?

CRAYON FIFTH.

If we are to have a picture gallery of Canadian Wesleyan Ministers, this one should have stood first in order,—not only by virtue of his office, but also by virtue of the *tout ensemble* which make up his well-balanced character, both as a man and a Minister. But the writer, for that very reason, as in another case already mentioned, has felt that diffidence to begin, which an artist would feel in attempting to sketch a faultless subject. But as we are now in for it, we must make a venture.

He is a native of England—fair and florid in complexion— medium sized, but symmetrical, compact, and heavy. He has the orator's full chest. We judge him possessed of great muscular strength. There are traditions of youthful feats of agility and strength, some of which he gave up at a very early age, as incompatible with his religious profession. Judging from his active habits and long-continued labours in different parts of the world, it is plain he must have great powers of endurance. Although he began his itinerant career at the age of nineteen, and has continued it in " summer's heat and winter's cold," by sea and land, for *thirty-five years*, at least, he would easily pass for one whose age was *only* thirty-five. He is the son, we are told, of an old Methodist Class-leader, (a good parentage); was made a Local Preacher when a mere boy,—and, as we have already hinted, began to labor in the full Ministry at the early age of *nineteen*. His first appointment was to Lower Canada, then Upper Canada, then England, then Gibraltar, and was then called home to England again. From England he came out to Canada as "Superintendent of Canada Missions," on the formation of the first "Union" with the Conference. That office he filled to satisfaction, and that also of President of Conference, for several years, performing some of the most toilsome journeys, on runners and wheels when he could, and on horseback when he could do it no other way. After the "dissolution" he was called home, where he still showed himself the friend of Canada, and exerted no small influence in bringing about a "re-union," when overtures were made for that purpose. In England he received offices and stations corresponding in importance to his previous position and usefulness—receiving in the meantime, the honorary degree of Doctor in Divinity from Victoria College, which he well deserves, although he says he has "perpetrated" but one piece of authorship. Two years ago he was the Representative from the British to the Canadian Conference, and one year ago was appointed its President. He presided in its last Session; has labored most indefatigably to advance its objects during the year, and is now conducting the business of the Conference with great propriety. He proves to be a much better President than we anticipated: serious, yet pleasant; good tempered and patient to a degree; fair and honorable.

He was originally well educated, and has acquired a great amount of various learning since, including the French and Spanish languages, which he speaks as well as reads. But there is no subject in which he is more complete than Theology. He is a great reader of his Bible, the words of which he quotes with beautiful propriety. His style in speaking and writing is chaste and elegant, but there are no prominences in it. It is "like the words of a pleasant song, of one who hath a pleasant voice, and can play skilfully upon the harp." To listen to him, is like a jaunt through a beautiful, flowery, odoriferous prairie, so slightly undulating that you cannot fix on any particular locality as beautiful above the rest, or as particularly memorable, or even as a way-mark by which you may trace your way over the same ground again.

Dr. Stinson's manners are those of a simple, humble, dignified Christian gentleman. His brisk, British-officer-like appearance, and fiery, restless eye, would make you think him a little haughty at first sight, but all that fades away on acquaintance. He is a true Methodist Minister, and God is giving him a son, "Joseph H. Stinson," to succeed him in the work.

CRAYON SIXTH.

Perhaps we are now in the midst of the most interesting service among all the prudential institutions of our wonderful

Methodism, not excepting the Class-meeting—the Love-feast—the Watch-night: What is it? It is the public reception of the young men into full connexion with the Conference, who have passed through their ministerial probation. Four young ministers have spoken with great propriety and good feeling, relating their christian experience and call to the ministry. The resolution for their reception has been moved by the Rev. Enoch Wood in an impressive manner. The motion is now being seconded by one who has never been called to perform the task before, although some *thirty-two* years in the itinerant field; a man very different in appearance from the preceding speaker, who is so rotound that his clothes sit smoothly upon him.

Our subject is somewhat tall, rather slight, haggard, and not very handsome, though interesting, whose arms hang loosely about him while speaking as though they were slightly articulated. He has notwithstanding good health, and seems wiry and enduring.

A man of a metaphysical, or rather logical, cast of mind is he; inclined to receive nothing but on the severest scrutiny, and thus disposed to suspicion of new measures, and by no means disposed to receive strangers at once into unlimited confidence. He is not, therefore, from the constitution of his mind, the man for prompt decision and energetic measures. A person of his temperament, however, in a deliberative body, which is both legislative and executive, may exert a good influence in restraining the intemperate ardor of the sanguine and impulsive. A drag chain may be as useful in its place as the motive power. Let no one understand us that he is sour and cynical. No man is more full of smiles than he, with sometimes a spice of humor; his attempts at the facetious, however, are not always successful. He is too good and religious to be a trifler.

He is wholly of Canadian growth—the son of a good old Methodist couple, who, though very plain and unpretending themselves, raised a large family of talented sons—not brilliant, but substantial; *five* ministers and *three* lawyers; with two farmers, one of whom is a highly respectable and useful *local* preacher. One of the legal gentlemen is a DOCTOR OF LAWS.

Our hero is a masterly preacher of his class, but not "popular" in the conventional sense of that term. He is a man to be appreciated by the reflecting and the thoughtful, who, alas! are not the many. For this reason, he occupied rather retired stations at the first, but has worked his way up into notice by dint of solidity and worth. He was once Secretary of the Conference, the highest office now in the gift of his brethren; also he has been Chairman of a District for a number of years. He is this year appointed to accompany the two highest officers of Conference as a Representative to the next General Conference of the Methodist Episcopal Church in the United States. He must be a man highly esteemed, or he would not so generally get the President's eye, when many others find a difficulty in catching it; and enjoy the patient respectful attention of the Conference to his not unfrequent and not very lively speeches. He is a good speaker; but better writer than speaker, having written some profound and elegant articles in his time. His clear, calm manner of treating questions reminds us of the productions of DOCTOR HODGSON of the M. E. Church in the United States. It is a pity but he would turn his attention to some work, which would leave a permanent example of his powers, and be a means of usefulness when he is gone from earth.

Although his pertinacity sometimes seems a little dogged, the REV. ASAHEL HURLBURT is a modest, pious, upright man, who might be trusted to any extent. We wish him all the happiness his merit deserves.

CRAYON SEVENTH.

Our present subject is a native of Ireland, but came to Lower Canada young. He was converted, when a youth, in Ireland, by reading Mr. Wesleys's works, but began to preach in Canada. He is a junior member of a family of respectability, which had met with some reverses. Although a man who claims to be respected, he can be very condescending and familiar when he likes. Nor is there any extra refinement about him, having never wholly unlearned his broad Irish accent. A high-minded honorable man is he. He married respectably, and was no loser in a pecuniary point of view by the alliance.

His personal appearance is good, being compact, strong, well proportioned and healthy—light complexioned and young looking. He has a changeable, expressive countenance, which ill conceals his constitutional mirthfulness. He has all the advantages of physique which phrenologists say should accompany a healthy and powerful mind,—unless, indeed, the rather disproportionate size of the head be against that conclusion.

His perceptions are quick and lively, which, with a spice of wit and humor, make him ready and good at repartee. His naturally good powers have been improved by a fair share of education and private study. He is a man of extensive reading, and has a retentive memory. His love of books is shown in the largeness of his library, the pains with which it has been assorted, and the care with which it is preserved. Few persons have a larger amount of, and more general and accurate information than he. This, with his constitutional quickness, makes him both instructive and entertaining in private conversation. A taste for Medicine and Architecture, to both of which he has paid some attention, is sometimes made use of for his friends and the Church. He is a voluble, ready instructive preacher; popular on the platform and very clever in doctrinal controversy.

His stations and connexional offices have scarcely corresponded with his general abilities, although he seems to have been more noticed of late, and is now in the fifth year of his District Chairmanship. He is not now a frequent speaker in Conference; nor is he one of the number of those who seem to sway that body and influence its decisions.

His sympathy for the poor, and his skill in settling difficulties, in which he combines authority and persuasion, counterbalance his want of pre-eminence in some other pastoral prerequisites. He is very *clerical* in his appearance; has high notions of ministerial dignity and the importance of the ministerial office; and thinks that ministerial functions should be performed in appropriate and distinctive vestments. Such vesments he thinks ought to be assumed by Wesleyan ministers; and has actually introduced the "gown and bands" into the pulpits of two of his stations.

Although the sun has its spots, it is still a glorious luminary; and although he may have some peculiarities, the Rev. JAMES BROCK is doubtless a wise and good man.

CRAYON EIGHTH.

I now turn my eyes to the oldest "effective" minister in the Conference; one who, though of the old school, might have merited attention before this. Although one of the original type of Canadian Methodist preachers, it by no means justifies the application to him of the epithet "*illiterate*," so liberally bestowed upon them in former days. He had more than ordinary advantages for the day when he commenced, and had been a popular school teacher in early life. That training, we are inclined to think, was received in the United States, where perhaps also he was born. If so, his early arrival in the country with the family to which he belonged, and his long continuance in it, have naturalized and acclimated him to all intents and purposes. He has been one of Canada's most laborious and self-sacrificing pioneer evangelists. Something like *twelve* out of the *thirty-eight* years of his public ministry have been spent in laboring among the Indian tribes, to whom he has a strong attachment. He is one of the few Missionaries to the Indians who have preference for this work. Others go to these heathen from a sense of duty; he from a sentiment of choice as well as duty.

The writer well remembers the first sight of this now veteran itinerant. He was then young, and being small of stature, round-faced, and light-complexioned, he looked still younger than he was. It was in our Upper Canadian capital, in the year 1825, as one of a troop of what the English peasantry call "riding preachers," among whom were the then distinguished names of Wilson, Wright, and Metcalf, on their way to the annual Conference. The experience of that young minister related in the Love-feast on the occasion, referred to it, while floods of tears channeled down his cheeks, deeply affected one boyish heart.

Our subject was never what is called a *great* preacher, but he was a lively, gifted, and soul-saving one. His ministry was characterized by pathos, zeal, and unction. Had a very musical voice, suited to the declamatory, hortatory sort of preaching which obtained at that time, and that seemed well adapted to reach the Canadian mind of that day—a style of preaching this, which seemed to be formed on the model of the Rev. Elder Case, who was considered a standard of perfection by young preachers at that period. Our hero was very pious, and would sing and pray in revival meetings the live-long night.

He holds his age well. He is still straight, active, and comparatively young looking, although he must be now over sixty. Several things have contributed to this: a good constitution originally; very temperate habits; plenty of out-door exercise; his not being a slavish student; the absence of disappointment, from his being un-ambitious and expecting little; and freedom from corroding irritation, being one of the best natured and most imperturbable men in the world. This last item is an element of character which a minister must have to succeed among the Indians.

Though not pre-eminently a bookish man, he has picked up a vast amount of practical knowledge. We know of no class of men whose conversation is more replete with intelligent remark than these old itinerants. The application of the *wise man's* name to him is, therefore, not wholly inappropriate; and the REV. SOLOMON WALDRON is a modest, sensible, and exceedingly companionable old gentleman, greatly beloved by all who know him. Our subject is on the outskirts of civilization labouring among the Indians of WALPOLE ISLAND.

CRAYON NINTH.

An affecting scene now presents itself to us, as we assemble in the last session of the last day of the Conference. It is the night season. The assembly is greatly reduced in numbers, many of the preachers having left since "the final reading of the Stations." The lamps shed their mellow light on the eager faces turned towards the platform, while business is being hurried to its completion. The galleries and much of the space below are full of respectable citizens, young and old, listening to the debates. After the reading of sundry Reports, and the passing of sundry Resolutions, it is announced by the President that "FATHER WRIGHT wishes to address some remarks to the Conference."

The occasion is this:—This aged Minister had been "superannuated" some years ago, and was subsequently returned "effective," that he might be sent to a particular Indian Mission, where they wanted their then Missionary to be removed, and Father Wright (an old friend) to be re-appointed among them. Now, after two years of sojourn among them, with the unreasonable capriciousness that sometimes characterizes even *white* people as well, " they wish a change."

There he stands, his ample locks blanched to the whiteness of snow with the frost of years, and pleads his former toils—his present health and ability to labor—the success he has had even on this Mission the last year,—with a pathos that draws tears from the eyes of preachers and people.

Though our hero is thus introduced under circumstances of tenderness,—and though he himself knew how to be tender, and in the palmy days of his Ministry to draw tears from the eyes of his auditors, yet you are not to associate the mournful and the melancholy with the name of jovial David Wright. His soul was naturally full of fun and frolic. Witty, humorous, and mischievous, he was in boyhood full of pranks and practical jokes. Through mercy he was converted young, and brought all his native vivacity into religion, which gave his piety an active, cheerful, and inviting character. He soon began to exhort and preach and after spending two years under the Presiding Elder, in what he used to call himself " stopping hog-holes," he was received on trial in 1821.

The early part of his Ministry was marked by great success. It was just of the character to suit the genius of most of the population of Canada in that day. His preaching was desultory, slap-dash, and discursive, though powerful. He was wonderfully great in exhortation. Furthermore, he was exactly the man to forage in a new country, and would live well where most other men would starve; he would get his support by hook or by crook, and not offend the people either. His beaming, handsome face, laughing eyes, and cordial shake-hands, soon won his way to every heart. He was once chairman of a District.

His former colleagues have a lively recollection of the pleasant hours spent in his company. He has stood by and comforted many a soul in " the swellings of Jordan ;"

and when the period may arrive when the Master whom He has loved and nobly served so long shall call for him, how it will delight his old companions who may linger a little longer, to learn that he was as happy in death as he has often been known to be in life, notwithstanding its cares and dangers. So prays an OLD COLLEAGUE.

CRAYON TENTH.

A little dark speck of humanity now crosses my mental vision, the original of which most Canadians have often seen; for though born in England, Canada is proud to claim him. But how shall I portray what is so unique? He stands some five feet six inches high, with width to correspond; very dark, and nearly as hard as an Egyptian mummy,—being little but a case of bones and sinews. His hair seems to have a decided objection to becoming grey; for though he is now on the shady side of fifty, its original raven gloss is not much impaired. I believe his eyes are black also, but I will not be sure; they are such a restless pair of little fiery orbs, that it is pretty hard to tell. To make some use of another man's figure, concerning another little man of talent and energy—Dr. Abel Stevens—he may be imagined to be composed of a piece of Canada's toughest blue-clay, wet up with lightning. Then, such an organization phrenologically! The disproportionate largeness of his combativeness, not to mention destructiveness, would render him dangerous, were it not for the very large amount of the grace of God which all give him credit for possessing. But, with this controlling influence, those mental peculiarities only add to his executive energy. Energetic he is.

He entered the itinerant field a *married* man, under many disadvantages, yet he sprang up into notice at once. The testimony of Father Prindle, his first Superintendent, was, "that he never knew a man who had so much preach in him." What a run of success and popularity he had from that time till the temporary failure of his health a few years ago! Long Point, Belleville, Chairman of the Augusta District,—Kingston, Toronto East, Toronto District, Hamilton, Toronto West, and London. During this period, he was first President, and then Secretary of Conference. He is a wonder of mental ability, seeing he is wholly self-educated. His sermons are studied with great diligence, and every argument and phrase carefully elaborated, and some of them re-written a dozen times; yet the matter comes out as liquid as lava from a volcano, and nearly as hot. When he is thoroughly excited with his theme, we can think of nothing but a man shoveling red-hot coals. His, however, is not a creative genius; but an acquiring, adapting, appropriating one. To use his own account playfully given, he "begs, borrows, and steals, from the living and the dead." But then, it is all fused over again, and run into one homogeneous mass.

Though he is a man whom his brethren "delight to honor," he does not take a very conspicuous part in the deliberations, or doings, of Conference, besides serving on most of its important Committees. He is more of an Executive officer, than Legislator. Two things seem to prevent his being an effective debater: first, his unfeigned modesty; second, we opine, his inability to command himself in the midst of so much confusion and excitement. He does best at a set speech.

Several slight productions, such as Sermons, Lectures, Reviews, &c., have emanated from his pen; and like everything else about him, they are all *sui generis*. With returning health, his activity and influence are returning. But his greatest praise is that he is a holy man—a faithful, laborious pastor—and very successful in promoting conversions and revivals of religion. Who will not recognize in the above sketch the features of our own HENRY WILKINSON?

CRAYON ELEVENTH.

Our present subject is an older Minister than some placed before him, having gone out into the itinerant field in 1826. He was born where more than one Methodist preacher first breathed the vital air, in the British army. I have always thought there was a moral heroism in such men, not always found in others. His conversion was one of the fruits of a great Revival in the Military Settlement in the Townships of Drummond and Bathurst, brought about by the instrumentality of the sainted Metcalf and colleagues. He is a strong-built, portly, and not unhandsome man. As he has been one of the hardest workers, so he has proved himself one of the most enduring men in the Conference. Has scarcely been a week laid up from his work in thirty-three years, excepting once from a broken leg. Though fifty-four or five, he looks young, and scarcely uses an eye-glass at all.

He has not been often a City preacher, but has been mostly on large rural circuits, and (under the old *regimen*) on districts. Has been more years a Chairman of a District than perhaps any man now in the active work. Is one of the ex-Presidents, and has for many years sat on the platform till this year, and now is likely to go on to it again, as the Conference, by a vast majority of ballot votes, have asked his appointment as the President's Co-Delegate.

It is somewhat hard to account for this man's high position. His natural abilities, though good, are not great; he makes no pretensions to *learning*, in the highest sense of that term; and his preaching is not of what is called the "popular" kind. Furthermore, being rather stiff and sturdy, he is not so much *beloved* by preachers or people, as some others. Yet there is something about him that commands *respect*. He early took a respectable position, and he keeps it. It perhaps arises from fair abilities, good character and conduct, hard labor, prudence, and a reputation for being a safe man, acquired by never venturing beyond his disciplinary "record."

In preaching he begins deliberately, feeling his way along—drawing out his words a little—till he gets self-command and the mastery of his subject; he then becomes heated with his theme, when his powerful voice makes the house literally jar, and the sinner's heart to tremble. He preached an excellent sermon on Christian Perfection, in Hamilton, on the Sabbath preceding the Conference, which was attended with a heavenly influence. He is evidently ripening in holiness as he gets older. To all appearance there are still many years of ministerial toil before him. May he be eminently successful!

From what has been said, all will be able to identify the REV. RICHARD JONES.

CRAYON TWELFTH.

Circumstances having thrown me for several days of late into the company of some of the more junior members of the Conference, I am induced to sketch one, if not more, of these. A painter, though he may be able to paint from memory, nevertheless requires to have his memory refreshed by a sight of the original from time to time; and the more recent his contact with the object to be portrayed, the more lively the recollection, or the more distinct the impression which the lineaments of that object have left on the mind. Besides, painters, like poets, are "maggoty;" as the one cannot write without "getting the thought," so neither can the other sketch without it.

I have before my mind's eye at the present time, a model young Minister; he is a native of England, but owes his spiritual birth to Canada, and is a decided Canadian in his sympathies. He has always had tolerable opportunities of improvement, of which he has most faithfully availed himself. He was a beautiful example of filial piety when at home with his parents, and a pattern Local preacher. His leisure hours were given to private study; the hours of school (for he was a teacher) were devoted to the acquirement of the means of placing his aged parents in the possession of a home when he should leave them— and his nights and Sabbaths spent in travelling far and near to preach Christ and to promote the salvation of souls, by holding protracted meetings, in which he has always been singularly successful. In view of so many engagements, the wonder is that he has become so well read and informed on all subjects. His Ministerial standing is six years, and his age is a little over thirty.

As a preacher, he excels in dealing with the conscience, especially with the consciences of professors of religion. His topics are not hacknied, nor his matter common-place. His sermons are original, and masterly in their conception and structure; and if his personal appearance and voice were as commanding as some men's, he would be one of the most impressive preachers amongst us. "Popular," perhaps he would not be; there is too much searching, disagreeable truth in his discourses for that. His voice is small and plaintive, but well managed, and his utterance distinct. His elocution is not so free and graceful as some, which gives the several parts of his sermons a somewhat angular and interrupted appearance. But continued practice will contribute to wear off the points, and make the variousparts of his discourses flow into each other in a more pleasing way.

He is now in the third year of his Superintendency on one circuit, and that a very important one; and he is proving himself a sound-hearted Methodist, and a thorough disciplinarian. He is industrious and exact—modest, but bold—mild, but firm and faithful; and, although his fidelity makes him to be thought punctilious by some, he is evidently winning golden opinions from all the right-minded and reflecting.

Should he keep in his present course, and God spare his life, he is destined to render great service to the Church of God. May Infinite Mercy uphold and direct modest, faithful WILLIAM TOMLIN!

Should any person who has not seen him, wish to know *how he looks*, we have to say, he stands about five feet nine or ten inches high. He is muscular, but lean, being, like Wesley, "without an ounce of superfluous flesh." He is straight, active, and wiry. His skin and eyes are dark, his features sharp, and face almost beardless. The hair comes far down on his forehead, which, however, is counteracted by a sort of "cow-lick," causing it to stand upright. Such is our hero in mind and body.

CRAYON THIRTEENTH.

In writing of the last mentioned brother, we were reminded of his last year's colleague, a younger Minister, though he is a somewhat older man. He was born in Scotland, and though brought up mostly in Canada, has a considerable tinge of the Scottish accent, which is rather in his favor than otherwise. His voice is good and well managed; and his manner, though plain and unpretending, is very agreeable and winning.

His conversion was rather late in life, and early opportunities for mental improvement were neglected; but he has made a good use of his time since he came under the influence of religion, and being possessed of active, facile powers of mind, his profiting has been great. We scarcely know a Minister of his years more desiderated, as a companion, pastor, preacher, and platform speaker. He is amiable—has good sense—and is not without *poetical* genius.

He is going the present year where he will not find his responsibilities "all poetry." He is the apostle of Methodism on the Opeongo Road. A more suitable man for that pioneering enterprise perhaps could not have been selected—being pre-possessing, laborious, self-denying, versatile, and capable. He should enlist the prayers of the Church. May God prosper him!

His career having been short, we dismiss him with this brief notice, believing that, if spared, the friends of Methodism will hear another day of JAMES MASSON.

CRAYON FOURTEENTH.

Now comes a lump of good nature from the Emerald Isle, longer in the Ministry than either of the two last. His *status* is fourteen years. He owes a good deal to our College, where he was one of the first probationary students. His age is unknown to us; he may be forty, and he may be a great deal less. He is strong, stout, and fresh-colored, with curly locks. He is voluble, and rather oratorical as a speaker,—but we should think not very profound, and not a very hard student. [Since writing this, we learn he studies more than we gave him credit for.] He loves and serves the people, and they love him. He will get on as pleasantly through life as any one we know, and after doing very considerable good, will get to heaven at last. There are not many, the prospect of meeting whom affords us more pleasure, than that of ROBERT ROBINSON.

CRAYON FIFTEENTH.

A tall, dark, lank figure now stands up before us. His face is flattened, nose prominent, teeth projecting, eyes large, full, and black; and there is a slight natural deformity in his hands. But still, he is so attentive to his person, and so genteel, that he is rather interesting than otherwise. Though newly ordained, he is not young; and may thank the "sliding scale" for coming into the connexion at his time of life. But he is an illustration of the usefulness of that *scale*, in allowing us to employ matured talent without too much jeopardizing our funds. Our hero was a studious, popular, and practical Local preacher for more than twenty years in England. This makes him the profound, well-furnished, deliberate, impressive preacher now; and his former commercial experience makes him the judicious manager and skilful engineer in church-building, and all the temporalities of the Church. He is SWEET in name, and by no means *sour* in disposition. There is perhaps *one* person in the world, at the present moment, a little anxious to know that this is the case. That person has decided favorably.

CRAYON SIXTEENTH.

We turn to the greater lights again. The subject we now propose to consider, we find rather hard to sketch. We know not that we appreciate his character truly. The difficulty arises from some apparent contrarieties.

He is a native Canadian, of a pious, respectable parentage. Converted to God in youth, at a Methodist Seminary, while prosecuting his preparatory studies for a learned profession. Being full of zeal for God and souls, he almost immediately entered the itinerant ranks, as a probationer, in 1831, when about nineteen years of age, and continues to this day. He was one of the last batch of what has been called "Old Dispensation" men.

He has the advantage of a fine personal appearance. He stands about five feet ten inches high; but being rather stout and heavy, he may not seem quite so tall. He is by no means unwieldly, however; but straight, full-chested, and trim built. His hair is dark and abundant, skin clear, head good, and face massive, with Grecian nose and features—and to crown all, a genteel hand and foot.

His voice is strong, clear, musical, and manageable, but sometimes perhaps raised too high. His elocution is easy and elegant, and if he had as many advantages of mind as body, he would have few superiors as a public speaker. His mind was originally good enough, but we suspect he has not worked it so hard as he might have done. He has been rather practical than studious and literary. Thus, while he has not the reputation of being very intellectual, he has the satisfaction to reflect that he has been one of the Church's most enthusiastic pioneers. For many years he was a sort of "Missionary Bishop," and performed wonders in the "Huron World." One who was privy to his labors there says, that "He was the right man in the right place." He travelled extensively, revived camp-meetings, was the instrument of forming thirty new circuits, promoted the erection of thirty new churches, and nearly as many parsonages. For fear I may not have ranked him high enough, I will insert the description of him given by an American minister who shared his labors at an Indian camp-meeting on the shore of Lake Huron, and published in a New York paper:—" The Rev. Mr. —— is a gentleman of a large, robust frame, a broad and full English face, the very picture of perfect health. From the cast of his cranium a stranger would accord to him a high degree of intellectual power. There is in his carriage an air of haughtiness; but this is only in appearance. If the discourses he preached while amongst us were a fair specimen, he ranks considerably above mediocracy as a preacher. They were excellent, not as specimens of pulpit orations, in the popular sense, but as clear, full, scriptural exhibitions of Gospel truth, practically applied to the hearers, and accompanied with the power of the Holy Ghost. Blest with uncommon strength of lungs, he made the encampments resound with his thundering appeals to the hearts of sinners. Nor was he anywhere more at home, or more active than in the prayer-meeting. While in his sermons he cast into the deep the Gospel net, by the fervency of his prayers he helped to draw it ashore and gather up the fishes."

Although our friend has served the Church long and well, as he is now comparatively young, and particularly young with regard to health and stamina, we expect he will be permitted to serve it for many years to come. God grant that he may!

Most of our readers will recognize in this portrait the features of our genial, good natured friend WARNER.

CRAYON SEVENTEENTH.

We turn to a very opposite character. One not possessed of the same advantages of personal appearance; one not so tall, graceful, and dashing; but shorter, meek looking, and less attractive. True, he is fair, fat, and comely, and that is enough. But he has superior advantages of *mind*. Not that it is original, philosophic, or marked by strength of genius. Our subject is rather characterized by the *power* of, and *desire* for, mental acquisition. For this he has had great facilities; and when he had them not, he made them. First, he was favored with a very liberal *classical* training in boyhood,—then, several years *commercial* experience was to his advantage, as teaching him business and accounts, and, what a boy can learn no where so well as in a shop, *politeness*. During this period he was converted, and, being very pious, he improved it in reading much in Theology, reading up his classics, and acquiring the French language. His early call to the itinerant field, and his appointment, for several years to bush circuits, seemed not to hinder his systematic progress in every branch of knowledge. He availed himself of his long sojourn in the two Toronto circuits to study in the Provincial University, where he successively bore off the prizes in Hebrew, Chaldee, Arabic, and Syriac. He reads twelve languages.

His learning has not marred his piety. He is the same humble, lowly Methodist preacher as at first. Indeed, he is naturally modest and retiring,—had to be thrust against his will into his first City appointments, Kingston and Toronto—and instinctively shrinks from office. Still, it is forced upon him. He is not only a Chairman, but holds the highest office in the gift of the Canadian Conference, and fills it well. In one matter, he is a little stiff: *time* to *study*, he *will have;* will not be at the mercy of every invitation to tea ; will not go to see the people any oftener than he thinks necessary; and believes his subordinate may serve the " out places," in general, quite well enough. This is the true way to gain *respect ;* for though the people will grumble a little, they will always do more for such a man than for one who slavishly serves them night and day.

In one respect Mr. HARPER excels all men we wot of,—in his desire for, and skill in amassing a Library. Perhaps no person in Canada has a better knowledge of books than he. For the number of volumes, their rarity, choice of edition, beauty of execution, order of arrangement, and careful preservation, his Library is a sight to be seen.

Mr. H. is just such a preacher as you might expect from the description given above of his personal physique, mental calibre, scholarly habits, and pious disposition. Not oratorical and showy—not loud and boisterous; but evangelical, spiritual, expository, rich in matter, and always opportune and appropriate. A workman he is " who needeth not to be ashamed, rightly dividing the word of truth." Is about forty years of age, and has been in the Ministry *eighteen* years. Will some day be no mean author. An Irish-Canadian is he.

CRAYON EIGHTEENTH.

And now my noble hearted friend POLLARD, bare thy neck and shoulders for a sketch. Though thy person is small there are beauties in thy mind; though thy body is diminutive, the heart of a christian hero glows in thy breast; though thy face be plain and beardless, thy high expansive forehead shows intellectual power; and thy large expressive eyes, prominent nose, and wide mouth, show thee to be a man of character and eloquence. The soul of eloquence is in thee.

Here is one of the best pieces of stuff we ever saw done up in so small a quantity. Our subject was born and converted in England, but had the discernment, on coming to Canada, which some old countrymen have not, to perceive the true genius and character of the Anglo-Canadian mind, and to adapt himself to it. He is acute and discriminating, polite, flexible, and versatile, with good business talents. Unites great sociality and pleasantness with lively, fervent piety. He is a shrewd observer of men and things, and has a lively, piquant manner in describing them; excels in personating others. This makes him very entertaining in company. His opportunities for intellectual improvement in youth were wasted in gaiety and folly, but since his transformation by the grace of God, he has read extensively, and what is more, *thoroughly;* and has kept the company of none but the best standards of style. He excels in *verbal* memory—only needs to read a brilliant passage or paragraph *twice*, to make it his own. This he has done with all that suited his taste and genius. So much so, that it is hard now to tell what is *original* in him, and what is not. Nor do we think he very well knows himself. To *scholarship* he makes small pretensions, but of general intelligence he has a large amount; has a legal turn of mind, and would have made a successful lawyer; but that would have spoiled a soul-saving preacher. He is not ambitious, but has been lately preferred to the Chairmanship of an important district,—an office for which he has been long qualified. He knows well how to manage both men and matters. His practical turn of mind is shown in his acquiring the French language.

He has been in the Ministry about seventeen years, and has filled our most important City appointments,—Toronto, Hamilton, London, and Quebec. He is generally beloved, and many hearts pray for his prosperity.

CRAYON NINETEENTH.

Canadian Methodism has had the honor of bringing up from " the dark and unfathomable caves" of human corruption, "full many a gem of purest ray serene;" and though she may not have had all the facilities for cutting, polishing, and setting them that could have been desired, she has rubbed off some of the rough exterior, and placed them in a position in which coruscations of superior light have flashed on the astonished gaze of beholders. One of these occupies a place in my mind's eye at the present. A great overgrown, white-headed youth, uncouth in his appearance, and shambling in his walk, and imperfectly educated, some forty years ago, came under the power of the Gospel as preached by the warm-hearted itinerants of that day, and cast in his lot among the Methodists. True, he was not so much of a "green-horn" as our first description might have led the reader to suppose. He was the son of a U. E. Loyalist, born in New Brunswick, who had borne a commission in the Revolutionary War, and probably had the best advantages of schooling, and seeing the best society, which a country neighborhood in that day afforded. Furthermore, he had the schooling—for better for worse—of the British army during the late American war; in which, though the merest boy, he was thought worthy to carry a standard, and wear a sword and his Majesty's uniform; and on assuming the Christian profession, he proved himself a "good soldier of Jesus Christ," sacrificing his father's house and friendship sooner than give up his religion: an instance of fidelity which was crowned with the conversion of a family of brothers.

Having married early to provide himself a home, he was not the first of the brothers who entered the itinerant field; but the necessities of the Church, and the fame of his increasing abilities as a Local preacher, drew him from his seclusion in the woods of Oxford, into the ranks of the regular Ministry. His first efforts proved him naturally eloquent, and earned for him the name of the "Canadian Orator." A more loveable man than he was in the early part of his Ministry could not be found. He was humble and condescending, good-natured and affable,—pious and zealous to a degree,—and one of the most earnest, winning, voluble, pathetic, and persuasive preachers that one could wish to hear.

Eloquent he has been and still is, and no mistake. We can remember masses of people moved by his word, like forest trees swayed to and fro by the wind. And even now, there are few localities in Canada where the news that the "old man eloquent" is to be the speaker, will not bring out multitudes to hear. The elements of his power were a plaintive, agreeable voice, when not unduly strained; though weak—abundant command of language—vast stores of information—good reasoning powers—strong feeling on his own part—and power to make other people feel and realize the truth and importance of what he was saying. But if he excelled in anything it was in *sarcasm* and ridicule; and these, in his more serious moods, he made to bear with withering effect against vice and villany. Of these also he made a very frequent, and sometimes efficient, use in the Conference debates, in which he took for many years a very prominent part, in overthrowing the argument of an opponent; this, many a hapless junior or weakling in that body knows to his heart's content. He and the present Bishop of Huron were antagonists to each other in the celebrated discussion on the Clergy Reserve question and Voluntaryism, held in Simcoe some years ago. Several other talented Ministers too took part in the debate, each characterized by some particular kind of ability; but the now Right Rev. Prelate said that Mr. Ryerson's sarcasm was unequalled, and that it was worth the journey from London to Simcoe to hear it. Sometimes he has exercised his conscious power in this particular too severely, and made an enemy of many a one who would have been a friend, or planted a pang in many a bosom which would nevertheless " earnestly consider him still." True, in course of time, those who knew, learned to make allowances, and to join in the laugh which the good cynic was raising at their expense. This peculiarity of his orations, is now rather a source of amusement than otherwise.

He never did anything by halves; as when he castigated it was with a vengeance; so also when he would commend, he eulogised. No person could pay a compliment more neatly and flatteringly than he. But no person must suppose from the extremes into which he was sometimes hurried in the heat of debate, or of public speaking, that he was deficient in *judgment*. Few men had more solidity of judgment than he; and at this hour I know of no person whose advice I would feel safer in taking on any matter that did not concern his feelings or prejudices, than his.

He is a man of some little learning—of most universal general information—and of a rare order of genius. He has devoured books with perfect voracity. Plan of study he has never had; but, like the ox, he has gulped every kind of edible that came in his way into his capacious reservoir, and ruminated on it at his leisure. He has a mind unceasingly active; hence, if he is not in conversation with a friend, or with book in hand, he is usually pacing backwards and forwards, like a chained bear, (he will pardon the figure) working out some of those huge masses of thought which are ever laboring through his intellectual laboratory.

His conversational powers are extraordinarily good, having such stores of information, such accurate recollection, and such a sprightly conception.

He has a great *penchant* for *public* questions; and is perhaps too much of a *politician*, conversing on such topics sometimes when others more sacred would suit the occasion better. But then we must remember that these tastes have been formed during a long, *consistent,* (*on his individual part*) and successful campaign in the warfare for Canada's civil and religious rights.

On reviewing what we have written, I cannot forbear remarking how much we have spoken of our friend as relating to the *past* tense. But he is still alive; and his brethren would still be glad to see him in their midst. That respect which once placed him in the Presidential Chair, and that sent him a a Delegate to England and the United States, still fondly lingers in their hearts for WILLIAM RYERSON.

May his heart be replenished by every grace and consolation of God's Holy Spirit. May his last days be his best! And may "his sun in smiles decline, and bring a pleasant night." So prays one who has been his parishioner, his subordinate in the Ministry, and his fellow-Chairman.

CRAYONS TWENTIETH AND TWENTY-FIRST.

This is a portrait of two brothers, who are so "lovely and pleasant in their lives," that they ought not to be "divided," even in a picture. Being tidy little men, they can easily go into one case. They are not twins, but very nearly of an age— perhaps *forty-five* and *forty-seven*. The *elder* looks full as young as the *younger*. He is the younger Minister, though he is the older man. These two brothers are pretty nearly balanced, the one excelling in little matters, the one who exceeds him in greater. They say "comparisons are odious," but I can't help it in this case.

They are natives of England, and though born into the world in different years, they were born again in the same revival of religion. *Samuel* knows the more, but *William* can make the better use of what he knows. *Samuel* is the younger man, but *William* is the handsomer man. The first has a drooping, diminutive appearance; the second is straight, and elegant in his movements. His face is fair and florid, which his abundant hair and beard, prematurely but beautifully white, adorn. Samuel has perhaps the best acquaintance with the *original languages* of any man in the Conference, without academic training. William knows no language but his mother tongue. Samuel has the better intellectual and theological furniture for a preacher,—William, the better delivery. We have often regretted that the elaborate, excellent sermons of the former were shorn of part of their effect by a mouthing manner of delivery, which, though it is now natural to the speaker, seems unnatural to the hearers. Again, Samuel, though just as pious as William, his piety is not so apparent; and though he is quite as amiable, perhaps more so, by a certain sneering manner and habit of banter, is thought not to be so amiable. The result is, although William would own himself the inferior, he has had the better stations, if any thing, and higher offices, having filled the Chairmanship in an important District. They are now, however, both Financial Secretaries.

Two more sensible, pious, laborious, estimable men, it would be hard to find in the Ministry of any Church. Their personal labors have been a blessing to Canada; and they are likely to leave sons in the Ministry after them who will more than supply their places. They will pardon the liberty taken by one who loves them dearly. May the Lord bless the "TWO PHILPS'!"

CRAYONS TWENTY-SECOND AND TWENTY-THIRD.

These are brothers too—Cornishmen also—converted in the same revival as the two last. It is well that *Lost*-withel was ever *found* again after its submergence, for Canada owes much to it. We may have to sketch more Lost-withelians before we have done. Our present heroes are no *pigmies*, nor "babes in the woods," but a pair of strong, strapping, stalwart men, some five feet ten or eleven, and stout in proportion.

They are very pious and laborious, and Methodists in heart and soul. Their minds, too, are naturally good, which they have labored assiduously to cultivate. *William* has the more sense; *Francis*, perhaps, the more learning, and probably is the smoother preacher,—William's preaching has the more pith in it. The preaching of the former would be the more *admired*, the latter the more *felt*. The one knows more of books, the other more of nature.

Being modest and retiring, they have neither had a very great run of the more prominent positions. Each has been a Chairman for a short time; and Francis is one now, by the ballot choice of his brethren.

Their highest praise is, their eminent sanctity and holiness. If there are any examples of Christian perfection on earth, they are doubtless among them.

The current of these men's lives has been so even and quiet, that we find little of incident to lengthen out our notice. They have been in the Ministry severally, *twenty-two* and *nineteen* years. The older man is also the older Minister. Like the two brothers sketched before, they are distinguished for attachment to each other. They will doubtless meet in heaven. A blessing on "THE TWO COLEMANS!"

CRAYON TWENTY-FOURTH.

Here comes another *Lostwithelian*,—one converted in the

same revival, some older than either of the other four, and longer in the ministry. His standing is twenty-eight years; he is not near so large as the smallest of the others; a sprightly, wiry little man is he. His voice is clear, and his delivery, despite a " pretty lisp," is good. Little men have often the best stuff in their composition; this is an example.

He is clear-headed, sound in judgment, well informed, bold as a lion, studious, active, adroit, managing (could have made a fortune if he liked, and is not wholly indifferent to what the world calls " the main chance,") and preserving.

He has had good appointments, though he has generally shrunk from those where there was frequent preaching in the same pulpit,—and has filled almost every situation of trust in the connexion, excepting that of President and co-Delegate; has been a Chairman of District a very long time; was "Journal Secretary" many years, for which his bold, copy hand, and accuracy, qualified him well; then, " Secretary" proper. He has been Principal of both our Missionary Industrial Schools, an office he holds at Mount Elgin at present.

He is an effective debater in Conference deliberations, when he chooses to take a part, which, however, he is not overforward to do. He is more active on Committees, to which he is usually " nominated by the chair." He is just radical enough to be backed by all the *juniors*, and to ensure the deference of all the *authorities*.

An upright, reliable, faithful, good man is he, who commands more influence than many a man of more calibre. We wish him well. JAMES MUSGROVE is the man.

CRAYON TWENTY-FIFTH.

The perusal of our pen-and-ink sketch of the Rev. Wm. Ryerson (Crayon nineteenth) since publication, reminds us of another personage, who, in some respects, bears a strong resemblance to him,—though in other particulars there is a great dissimilarity between them.

Our present subject is at least fourteen or fifteen years younger than the other, and was more systematically educated than he. But they resemble each other in being both large men, with massive heads. The younger has much the larger head, though, in other respects he is not quite so large. They have both giant intellects, and the soul of eloquence is in them. Both are distinguished for breadth of thought, and a philosophic manner of viewing questions; and they are desultory, both in study and business matters, disdaining the plodding, punctilious process by which ordinary men bring things about.

Our hero has great power of keeping one subject before his mind for a long time; or rather, perhaps, he is characterized by the want of power to divest his mind from an enticing subject of thought. Though his aversion to the details of business is one reason why he is not oftener put on business committees, yet, like some others, who have the name of *not* being "business men," for a similar reason, is capable of the most efficient transaction of business, when he chooses to direct his attention to it, leaving fussy pretenders far in the distance. Hence, though several years left out of that office, when he ought to have been in it, he is a wise and successful Superintendent of a circuit. Nor, great as he confessedly is, does he think our Rules too small to be kept. He is a sound-hearted Methodist, who has stood up for its vital principles when they were in danger. He is a penetrating man; but I think his habit of reading others, when unduly exercised, is liable to degenerate into suspiciousness.

As he is not much employed in the labor of committees, as his mind is active and his tongue is voluble, and as he has a good deal of nerve withal, it is not surprising that he should be drawn out to take an active part in Conference discussions, in which he is very effective, speaking very often. He is evidently a favorite with the Conference, for he always gets a hearing when even older men cannot squeeze in a word edgewise. He has the requisites for commanding attention—such as a fine person, ready utterance,—heavy, commanding, and musical voice, &c. He is also deferential to his brethren, genial, and polite. His eloquence is senatorial and forensic.

As a preacher he is evangelical, earnest, powerful. He showers down on his hearers a torrent of exposition, argumentation. and exhortation. He is not common-place, but rather involved and beyond the reach of ordinary minds.

He is eminently pure and good, and has of late years become very dignified and polite; but he can be playful and even very droll, when he likes. These matters, however, principally develop themselves in private, where he is a very engaging companion. He is willing to talk by the hour with any friend, however lowly, so companionable is he. He has been *eighteen* or *twenty* years in the work, and for that length of time he has had no undue proportion of conspicuous positions, considering his eminent abilities. He has been stationed in the cities of Toronto and Montreal,—is now a Chairman for the second time,—and was once the Secretary of the Conference.

Incessant thought, or something else, had nearly divested his head of its hair at an early age—which is now not more than 43. A severe indisposition had unfitted him for mental effort for a couple of years, but we are happy to observe that he is rising above it. Such a man ought to give to the world some permanent fruits of his thought; but, like his prototype, I fear he will not turn out a *writer*. Some ephemeral pieces show that he can write if he will.

One of his peculiarities is, if I mistake not, he is averse to personal scrutiny and criticism,—on which account, I pray that he may not visit with his wrath the luckless wight who has presumed to steal the likeness of WELLINGTON JEFFERS.

We must not omit to say that he is an Irish-Canadian of talented paternity, and respectable connexions.

CRAYON TWENTY-SIXTH.

As we have initiated the practice in some cases of putting relatives together, the last mentioned gentleman having a brother in the Conference, he might feel entitled to come next. And yet perhaps it is scarcely fair to dwarf this respectable mediocre Minister by putting him in juxta-position with his gigantic relative. Although THOMAS is a little sensative with others, he seems in no wise jealous of WELLINGTON'S reputation, but is rather proud of him than otherwise. Nor is any person more willing to concede his superiority than he. Thomas is the younger preacher, though a little older man. His personal appearance is good, being younger looking than his brother. We have not heard him often enough to pronounce on the character of his preaching,—it is respectable; but we should judge that his sermons are got up with as much hardship as the acquirement of the other's is with ease. Diligence distinguishes the lesser preacher; and by his laboriousness, he effects perhaps more for the salvation of souls than the other. He is sincerely pious. May they both shine resplendent in glory everlasting!

CRAYON TWENTY-SEVENTH.

Next to the brothers perhaps should come the brother-in-law, the husband of the talented and pious sister of these worthy men. He is a man dissimilar from both, somewhat younger, stout and strong, fair, florid, and the picture of health. He is a native of old England, if *Yorkshire* is in England, which some deny. His spiritual nativity originated in Canada. His spiritual father was the Rev. W. Ryerson, who, if he had been the means of no other good, by this paternity becomes a benefactor to his country.

Our hero in cast and calibre is just the man to be unboundedly popular with the great mass of our Methodist people, and to get on swimmingly in the large, rich, rural circuits which he usually travels. He is good natured to a degree, which renders it almost impossible to put him out of humor,—pleasant and amusing in private intercourse,—with an ability to describe all the queer scenes and to personate all the odd people which an itinerant meets with in his checkered career; gifted and lively in preaching, without any profundities to bother any one, and the very life and soul of social religious meetings,—ready to pray, sing, or shout, as the case may require. No wonder that honest MICHAEL FAWCETT turns his circuits all topsy-turvy, and makes it hard work to any one to come after him. This difficulty arises from two sources,—his great favoritism with the people, and his peculiar mode of doing business, which, while it is perfectly orderly to him, does not always suit other people's notions of order.

By rule, or not, he succeeds in doing a great deal of good; and will continue to do it, till he overtakes his much loved Bro. THOMAS, "where the wicked cease from troubling, and the weary are at rest."

In one respect, he is a genuine Yorkshire-man: he keeps a good horse and knows how to handle him too. His Ministerial status is *eighteen* years, to which it is not unlikely God may add *eighteen* more.

CRAYON TWENTY-EIGTH.

In the year 1841, a precious waif fell into the hands of our Church authorities, in the person of a youth who looked like the merest boy,—a military local preacher, who had been born and educated in the army, and converted to God in the West Indies (in Antigua), through the instrumentality of Wesleyan Methodism. An opportune improvement of a favorable occasion, which might not have occurred again for years, transferred him from the service of her Majesty to our itinerant ranks; and a more worthy and true-hearted recruit never enlisted among us. He has proved himself a prize worth possessing.

He is another instance of a clever *little* man. His form and appearance are almost femenine,—being slight and smooth-faceed. He is, however, healthy, active, and enduring.

The *inner* man corresponds to the *outer*. He is naturally amiable, genteel, tasteful, and clever,. Though his rank was not high, he was respectably connected, had influential friends, was educated beyond his situation in life, having received the basis of a classical one, and, had he remained in the army, would doubtless have been promoted. These prospects, and more congenial offers of the Ministry in a Government Church, he relinquished for a place in the Wesleyan itinerancy. Since his entrance among us he has been very studious,—accomplishing his "Conference course" in a highly creditable manner, and performing a very liberal curriculum of learned and scientific study, of his own accord.

He is what is usually called a "popular" preacher—pronounced eloquent by the many, and sought after by the more aspiring places as an attractive pulpit man. The secret of this attractiveness, we never could exactly make out—unless it is that his personal appearance and manner are good in the pulpit; his voice is pleasant; his utterance is ready; his spirit fervent; and his style what may be called ornate and elevated. With regard to this last—his style—both in writing and speaking, we, for our individual part, have thought it faulty; but as the great majority approve it, we must acknowledge ourselves heterodox in our tastes and opinions. One reason for Mr. Gemley's great success is no doubt his prudence, amiable considerateness, and indefatigable attention to all the members of his flock, both rich and poor.

No minister of his years amongst us, has had more good appointments than he. He has run up the scale after this fashion: Prescott, Port Hope, Belleville, Dundas, Peterborough, Toronto, Montreal Centre. Last year he was Chairman of this important District (the Montreal), and performed the duties of his office well; but the adoption of the *ballot* vote displaced him, at the late Conference, by a very small majority. The one elected in his place is everything that is good, but it seemed ungracious to turn a brother out at the end of a year, who had done his best. This case is a proof that the ballot system will sometimes show the majority of the Conference to differ from a unanimous District. He has, however, an elastic mind, which rises to the level of every emergency.

We have been much pleased to see our hero take so active and efficient a part in the deliberations of the Conference during its last two or three sessions. He is likely to make himself respected in that body. Being yet young he has by no means reached his culminating point. We wish him abundant prosperity.

We had almost forgotten to say that our subject is one of that class of Ministers, not very numerous, who have the good or ill fortune, (just as you are pleased to view it), to be lauded in the papers—to be donated, *feted*, and testimonialed—and who are summoned a long distance to open churches, to marry friends, &c., &c.; and he is one of the very few of the class who has the good sense and piety not to be spoiled by it.

CRAYON TWENTY-NINTH.

We pass from one of the "highfalutins," to one *still higher*, perhaps the most so of any one in the Conference,—if indeed he can be said to be of that body,—who " by permission of the Conference," spends his time in the service of a public charity, and in travelling for his personal pleasure and profit. He is an unique man, and altogether *sui generis*. He first breathed the vital air amid the " bonny hills o' Scotland," " that land of rock and glen." His mother tongue is Gaelic, which, with all Highlanders, he thinks the most beautiful and expressive language spoken. He can and does preach in it when occasion serves, and it is when he has a congregation of Highlanders before him that he truly fires up. He speaks English rather with the rich accent of the educated Lowlander, than that of the Gael. He early got so much of a knowledge of Latin as would have enabled him to matriculate, but he never went through College. He has, however, been very studious and observing, and his attainments on all subjects are very respectable; has studied Greek and Hebrew.

But a superior genius done for him what a University education has failed to do for many who have been favored with it. His imagination is gorgeously poetical—delights in towering flights and bold imagery. His descriptive powers are good, and there is a great deal of the historical in his sermons. These qualities of mind, joined to fervent piety and the most large-hearted benevolence, have earned for his addresses the universal mode of *eloquent;* although his is rather the eloquence of poetry, than force of diction; yet his diction is forcible enough.

His exuberant good nature, ready wit and humor, render him a universal favorite on the platform, where (if in any one particular above another) he excels.

His fine personal appearance and stentorian yet musical voice, and free and easy movements, greatly add to his ascendancy over an audience. Imagine to yourself a noble person of a man six feet high, straight as a rush, well-proportioned, yet lithe and supple, with a mass of coal black hair, coarse and a little inclined to curl, combed back, revealing a fine though not very spacious forehead, while an equal mass in the form of beard, (his head on the whole is very long), embellishes the lower part of his well-proportioned face. Imagine him coming forward to the front of the platform with a light and sprightly tread; hear him accost "Mr. Chairman, Ladies and Gentlemen," in a full, round, musical tone of voice; wait but a little while till he kindles with his theme and begins to use his arms, those levers of eloquence and argument, till the audience become enwrapt, excited, and moved to thunders of applause, and you have some conception of our Scotch-Canadian Wesleyan Orator, LACHLIN TAYLOR, Agent of the Upper Canada Bible Society, and now travelling in the lands of the Bible.

Mr. T. is a good Theologian and Expositor of Scripture, but no better than scores of his brethren who do not possess his other advantages. He gets at things rather by a stride of his genius, than the slower process of induction or ratiocination. He excels in pathos—not without a little bathos at times.

He was brought up in the bosom of the Established Kirk of Scotland, of which his father was long an Elder and Parochial School Teacher. But being brought to God in Lower Canada through the instrumentality of Wesleyanism, while he is one of the most catholic-spirited men in the world, he is a decided Methodist. Arminianism seems to suit his large heart and expansive soul.

He has been in our Ministry *twenty* years; and has been always in demand for the best stations, when he was willing to go, or stop in them, when there—which he never has in any one more than a *year* at a time. In one thing, he resembles the Rev. Robert Hall—he is too fastidious about his composition to write much for publication. The reader will be surprised to hear, after learning that he has so fine an imagination and such good extemporaneous powers, that all his sermons and addresses are painfully elaborated, and that he is foolish enough to trammel himself with *notes.* An over carefulness of his reputation has led to this. We are persuaded, if he were to throw away these buoys, and strike out fearlessly into the deep, he would effect even more than he now does, much as that is. He should be more independent of the opinions of his hearers—he could afford to be. He will take this well from an "old crony."

The most wonderful thing about this most wonderful man is, that, with the most captivating sociality of spirits, the truest politeness, and the greatest gallantry towards the softer sex, which make him a universal favorite with the Ladies, he is yet *unmarried*, though already on the shady side of forty. His public reason, playfully given, is, "he loves them *all* too well to love *any one* of them in particular." Our hero, along with his general affability, is one of the most prudent and purest of mankind. A lot among the blessed and holy society of heaven awaits our friend. May we meet him there!

CRAYON THIRTIETH.

Well on to forty years ago, two or three young men came over in company from the United States to try their fortunes in Canada. One of them, a large inexperienced youth of about twenty-one years of age, was a Methodist, and bore an "Exhorter's Licence," as they phrased it then. He was sincerely pious, and had better advantages of education than most young men in his position in Canada at that day. It was soon discovered that he had good gifts for public speaking, and was encouraged by his Presiding Elder, the now sainted CASE, to give himself to the itinerant work; he consented, and appeared at the *first* session of the Canada Conference, held in Hallowell, August, 1824, accoutred in the usual paraphernalia of a travelling preacher, with horse saddled and bridled, valise and over-alls. And though not regularly received on trial till the next year, was appointed to the Smith's-Creek Circuit, which extended from the Carrying-Place on the East, to Darlington on the West; and from the Lake shore on the South, to the remotest settlements (beyond where Peterborough now stands) on the North.

He began at once to attract attention as a *preacher*. His preaching was a little unusual, being declamatory and florid in its style. It had its defects no doubt, not being equal, or equable in all its parts—the young orator, as it is said, sometimes "going up like a rocket, and coming down like a pole." Yet even his failures showed a noble aspiration. And, ere long, he certainly became very respectable as an Expository and Hortatory Preacher; and, being lively, pathetic, and ornate in his style, he was soon very popular. He was a favorite in the pulpit so long as his voice, which was never very strong, (though well managed) allowed of frequent preaching.

He went up in all other respects as well. He was the favorite *protege* of the then ruling mind in Canadian Methodism, ELDER CASE, by whom he was highly valued till the old man's death. He got the best circuits—was elected Secretary of the Conference—chosen to preach Missionary Sermons—placed on "Stations" (the preachers on which were beginning to constitute a sort of *elite* amongst us, when a salutary return to the good old circuit system discouraged the formation of that kind of aristocracy)—made a District Chairman in the *eighth* year of his ministry—which led a punster, in allusion to his *youth* and his name, to say that "we had *a green* [A. GREEN] Presiding Elder." His good nature will pass over the indignity of relating this.

Such were the antecedents of the famous DOCTOR GREEN, many years Chairman of the most important Districts in the Province—once President of the Conference—for many years, as he is now again, our Connexional Book Steward, Treasurer, or Bursar, of the College—thrice our Representative to the British Conference—and thrice to the American General Conference. He married respectably—acquired some wealth than which nothing could show good financiering more, as his itineracy was confined to the early days, when salaries were small—and has taken a genteel social position. Some years ago, he received the degree of DOCTOR IN DIVINITY, from one of the most respectable Methodist Universities in the United States.

It may be asked, How has he so wonderfully out-stripped most of his compeers in the matter of honors, offices, and distinctions of all kinds? This is a question which it may not be very delicate for us to answer; but we venture to say, by more than ordinary good abilities, and by unusual skill in management. Very *learned*, in the highest sense of that word, he does not profess to be; for though he is worthy of his degree, many of his brethren, on the ground of *attainments*, would be equally deserving. He is distinguished by an assemblage of fair qualifications of all kinds. He has a good practical judgment; and possesses a native sagacity on most subjects, that amounts to genius: and he is so cool and self-possessed as not to betray his designs prematurely. These qualifications have made him the successful diplomatist, in the management of several difficult matters. Such as the defeat of certain *pseudo* claimants to recognition, as legal and standard Methodists, before the American General Conference in 1844; the negotiation of the advantageous arrangement with the Methodist Book-Concern in New York, in 1848; and in the active and successful part he took in the restoration of the Union with the British Conference, which has since worked so harmoniously.

He is very kind as an administrative officer, and yet has a good degree of boldness and firmness. There never was a more satisfactory presiding officer in a Quarterly or District meeting, or in the Presidential Chair of the Conference, than he; he has that peculiar combination of talents that qualifies a man for conducting routine business. He was never so ambitious of talking as to interfere with the debates; and he would treat all with fairness and yet keep them to the point. His coolness and weight of character always paved the way for successful *debating*, when not in the chair.

He has ever showed a lively interest in the financial affairs of the connexion. His brethren have gladly, and almost necessarily, availed themselves of his abilities and bent of mind in this direction, to do what many ministers are not qualified to manage; and he has proved himself a safe and successful business man. He is one of those to whom we are indebted for the origination and maturity of our connexional funds—the father of the Ministers' Annuitant Fund is he; and, like most fathers, right fond of his offspring. His financial talents alone are sufficient to account for his position.

But, besides what we have mentioned, his self-reliance, composure in the presence of the great, and observance of conventional proprieties, have all contributed to give him position. His complacency with the ceremonies—his ability to pay a compliment, and to act as master of ceremonies, point him out as a fitting man to wait on civil authorities, to lay the foundation of public buildings, and to take a part in that most intolerable of all bores, to all but the very dignified—ceremonious speaking on what may be called "state occasions." But "every man in his own order;" some must do these things, and his talents for doing them have subserved the cause and contributed to strengthen his position.

We should mention, both to make our description complete, and to account for his respectable standing, that he is a man of "port and presence," and attentive to his person. He is large, but even now not ungainly. In youth, he would have been pronounced handsome, being well proportioned, blue-eyed, dark-haired, and well-skinned. His face is large; his head is wide, but not so high proportionately; and his once glossy hair is now "silvered over with age." He cannot be far from *sixty*—fifty-six, or seven, at the least.

He was "superannuated" for a time, but has come to the rescue, at a juncture when on account of the monetary circumstances of the country, his presence is needed in our Book and Printing Establishment: in which, if he succeed, he will confer a lasting blessing on the connexion and deserve the grateful acknowledgements of the ministers of the church. Our friend has the rare satisfaction of remembering that he has been undeviatingly identified with the Conference "in weal and woe," from the year of its organization to the present day.

We must not omit to say, he is catholic-spirited, and enjoys a good share of respect beyond the pale of Methodism. Being a good natured, liberally minded man, we presume on his forgiveness for bringing him unauthorized before the public.

CRAYON THIRT-FIRST.

As I have sketched our excellent Book-steward, his Colleague, seated in the Editorial chair, may feel slighted if I do not honor him in a similar manner. It is a task of which the poor artist is somewhat afraid; for, any way you take him, he is a difficult subject to "handle." An unusual genius is SPENCER. I sharpen my *stylus* afresh, and address myself to the work with strong trepidition.

He is an Upper Canadian, and born, if I mistake not, near the celebrated battle field called Lundy's Lane. Whether this has made him bellicose, I will not presume to say; but he is composed of pretty stern material. He is medium-sized, strong, and healthy. I should pronounce his face decidedly Grecian, but not handsome. His head is large, high, and poised on a pretty stiff neck. He is not ill formed, but has a certain careless manner of walking—slapping the ground with his feet—which certainly was not acquired in a school for the study of calisthenics. His manner of dressing, I should think, to be a little on the Dr. Abernethy order. His style of wearing his hair (if that may be called a "style" which is left pretty much to nature) is what might be called *porcupinish*,—it stands fiercely up in front. His whole appearance is of a don't-care-what-the-world-thinks character.

He is of a respectable Methodist parentage—at least we have been told his mother was a sterling old christian of that denomination. That was a good thing to begin with. His plain manners, industrious habits, and healthy constitution, were formed and nurtured on a *farm*. Subsequently, he became a very ingenious *ameteur* mechanic; and early showed taste and skill in that mechanical inventiveness for which his name is likely to be handed down with those of Hutton, Watt, and Arkwright, to future generations.

Mr. S. was very respectably educated—receiving first a good schooling at home; and then attending Academies and Colleges both in the United States and Canada. He was regarded as a good student in his College days. And though he never regularly graduated, we regard him as far in advance of some who have. He is well and extensively read in Latin and Greek; and his excellence in the natural sciences, particularly as a chemist, is known and appreciated by all his acquaintances who are capable of judging. No University would be wasteful of its favors, though it made him *Doctor of Laws*.

He was early converted, and became a sober, steady, pious youth. We remember well that he used to be called "the Bishop" many years ago, when a student at "old Vic"; and his usefulness in that Institution in promoting revival meetings, was one reason why his friends recommended him for the travelling Ministry, and thrust him into it, rather against his will. The writer knows a person against whom our hero seemed to have a decided pique for several years, for his share in this business.

His itinerant career was marked by considerable success in some circuits; and he seemed to effect the most, and to be the best beloved, where he remained the longest. His first appearance as a preacher is not captivating. An apparent want of energy, and a certain monotonous sing-song in his voice, detract sometimes from the power of his truly eloquent sermons. These peculiarities of voice and manner cease to offend after the hearer becomes familiar with them. The characteristics we have mentioned, kept him from taking the first appointments, where many vastly his inferiors were received with *eclat*.

He had been thought of for years, by those who would call themselves the "liberal party" in the Conference, as Editor of our connexional organ, and unsuccessfully run him for it two or three years before his election to that position in 1851. But no sooner was he in than he began to win golden opinions,—and it seems now as difficult to get him out as it was to get him in, at the first. Take him for all in all, no Editor has given so much satisfaction. This is saying a great deal, when we consider the respectable character of all who went before him, and the transcendant abilities of some. We need not dwell on the qualities of his style, which is classical,—his controversial powers, in which wariness and self-command, and a fondness for the *argumentum ad hominum* conspicuously appear—or his industry and research in his selections, which would sometimes appear to more advantage if he had not too many "Addressors" and other machines in his head. But we spare him, as we observe an improvement of late. Like all *liberals* out of office, he is a little stern *in office*. But with all his sternness, and impracticable unmanageableness in any position he has taken, in which he doubtless thinks himself right, he is a very good natured man, possessed of a large vein of quaint, quiet humor, and is, by consequence, a very engaging private companion;

and a very reliable friend is he, who would risk any thing in defence of those he loves.

With an occasional feeling of displeasure at him, "we do earnestly consider him still."

We recollect ourselves, and must not omit to say, that of late years he has become conspicuous as a debater and legislator in the Conference, exerting more influence than any man of his years. He is 46 years of age, and 21 in the Ministry. The characteristics of his debating are nerved and dogged perseverance. His legislation has introduced some sweeping changes, which we must wait for the fruits of, before we with too much confidence pronounce them *reforms*. His doings in the Conference, however, answer a valuable end. And here we end our remarks.

CRAYON THIRTY-SECOND.

Whatever deficiency there may be in the Methodist system with regard to the standard of Ministerial qualification, as it respects science and scholarship, it must be confessed to have the praise of not only securing a converted Ministry, but of securing the *best class of minds* in the ministry. In other communities, where a liberal education is made the *sine qua non* to an exercise of the Ministerial functions, many men are set apart to the sacred calling, who but for that training, would never have been able to speak at all with any tolerable degree of acceptability and effectiveness. Now we are bold to affirm that, while no knowledge comes amiss to a minister, and while he is all the better for the addition of learning to grace and natural gifts, yet he whose qualification for preaching has been wholly created by schooling, is scarcely fit for the work after all. We rejoice in the facilities now afforded for giving the Wesleyan Ministry the advantages of a more liberal education, yet it is to be hoped it will be restricted to those whose natural gifts would have made way for them irrespective of such training; and that connexional money will not be squandered in imparting *learning* to supply the place of *mind*, instead of directing and polishing minds of native force and vigor.

The person's mind whom I now essay to sketch, was no doubt of the highest order of intellect naturally, and although he never had a regular Collegiate curriculum, he has so far improved upon his Grammar-school education as to become a man of extensive erudition and boundless general attainments. So completely out of the common order is our subject, that our attempt to measure the proportions of his giant mind is, we fear, like the attempts of a fly to scan the dimensions of the dome of St. Paul's. Another thing embarrasses us: our subject has had an eventful, checkered public history. Still we have presumed to "show an opinion."

We can well remember when we heard in boyhood that another and a *third* son of old Col. R. had embraced religion, and had become a Methodist preacher. It was our good fortune to see and hear him after that. It was at a camp-meeting. We remember his text, " O, Israel, thou hast destroyed thyself, but in me is thine help." He was then, perhaps, twenty years of age—fat, and boyish-looking, like Spurgeon, only with a far more intellectual looking face. The physique and physiognomy of our hero, whether in youth or riper years, has been such as became our notions of a great man. Rather over than under the medium size—well proportioned—fair complexioned—with large, speaking blue eyes—large nose, more Jewish than either Grecian or Roman—and then such a head! large, full, well-balanced, without any sharp prominences, but gently embossed all over like a shield. The mass of brain before the ears is greater in him than any other man we wot of. The height, and breadth, and fulness of that forehead is remarked by all observers.

He is benevolent and generous to a fault; has a very emotional nature, and we are safe in saying, a very *devotional* one also. He was converted in early life, and "nourished up in the words of faith and holiness" by pious maternal influence and care. No wonder that he should have early decided in favor of the *Gospel* against the *Law*. With all his versatility, it seems a pity that his attention should have been divided and distracted between sacred and secular subjects. Had he devoted all his attention to law and politics, for which his statesman-like views, his extensive knowledge of history, and his powers of debate, if not of special pleading, so eminently qualified him, he would likely have passed through all the gradations to the highest pinacle of secular eminence attainable to a subject in a colony. And had his thoughts and studies been confined to the Bible, and Theology, and to the various accomplishments desirable in a minister, he would have attained even greater eminence in ministerial ability and usefulness than he has, high as has been his excellence in those particulars. But the peculiar circumstances of the country and of all denominations excepting the then dominant Church, rendered it necessary that some one should step forth in vindication of their rights, while the anonymous review of Dr. Strachan's defamatory Sermon and Report pointed him out to the leaders of the Connexion as a champion, at the early age of *twenty-two*. Right boldly did he draw the sword of controversy, and right skilfully and successfully did he wield it also. But to write the doings of his public life, would be, to a great extent, to write the history of Upper Canada; and his Life and Times, it is to be hoped, he will find time to record with his own hand.

In point of ability, it is not too much to say that he has proved himself a great *preacher*, a great *writer*—this is perhaps his forte—and a great *debater*. As a preacher, when he does himself justice in the matter of preparing, he is able in exposition, and pointed and powerful in application. His, we should judge, is the true style and method of preaching—he steers clear of "random rant" on the one hand, and of slavish memorising on the other. He uses so much of previous meditation as is necessary to master the outlines of his theme, and then draws on his general resources to fill it up and illustrate it, as he passes along. His characteristics as a *writer* are well known to the reading public—perhaps strength, and clearness, and forcibleness of illustration may be said to be its prominent attributes. The figures he most uses are antithesis, climax, and irony. He can be keenly sarcastic when he likes. Both in writing and debate he is not very choice of the means by which he demolishes an opponent, so long as it is done. When scientific missiles are not at hand he extemporises others which answer his purpose. His onslaughts are like an avalanche of snow and ice from a mountain's brow, which brings every destructive thing along with it—trees and rocks, and, it may be, a deluge of muddy water if it stand in the way.

He has been charged with mystifying an unacceptable subject—with inconsistency in his public career—and with frequently deserting from one side to another. That he knows how to conceal the objectionable parts of his projects, is no doubt true, but that he does more of it than his opponents would *if they could*, is doubtful. As to his inconsistency, he maintains that he has never changed his great leading views and principles; and that it is only when others have abandoned these, that he has seemed to change sides. One thing is true, that in nearly every apparent change, he has gone from the *strong* side to the *weak* one. It was so when he sacrificed his old Tory friends, who were then in the ascendancy, in 1826, when he took scot and lot with those who were moving for equal rights. So when he published his "Impressions" in '33, and was accused of changing, the Reform party were the vast majority; but when he took up his pen in favor of Bidwell, in '37-8, that party was prostrate in the dust, and its leaders expatriated. Again, Reform was in the ascendancy when he took up his pen in favor Lord Metcalf. We simply refer to these facts of history, and leave them to speak for themselves.

We do not pretend to say that he has been without his faults,—we ourselves have often been offended with him,—and it is said that the faults of great men are generally *great* faults. Their errors and deviations are more palpable than those whose talents and errors are not so conspicuous.

His greatest mistakes, in the eyes of Methodists, have been, when he has showed an indifference to their public religious sentiments on the subject of certain fashionable amusements, and relative to the preservation intact of those institutions by which the life of religion in the heart can alone be preserved. But we ascribe the peculiarity of his views in these particulars to the particular stand-point to which his position, that of Superintendent of Education, has for several years restricted him. Notwithstanding the peculiarity of his views in these respects, we regard him as the well-intentioned and ardent friend of Methodism, who, while he is distinguished by an enlightened catholicity, has shown the most decided preferences for the church of his choice.

Perhaps we have erred in discussing a subject so generally known, but we could hardly pass so prominent a member of the Conference as Dr. Egerton Ryerson.

We must not omit the after thought, that he is very pleasing in his private manners, being very condescending, affable, and polite. His conversational powers are great.

CRAYON THITY-THIRD.

"Train up a child in the way he should go and when he is old he will not depart from it." The truth of this declaration is illustrated and confirmed by the conversion of the subjet of the present sketch, and that of his now sainted brother. Two little brothers some forty or fifty years ago used to accompany their pious mother (the wife of the Captain and owner of a merchant ship,) to the Wesleyan chapel in the seaport town of Hull, in Yorkshire, England. In its Sabbath School, and under the Ministry of the Apostolic itinerants, who spake the word of life within its walls, as well as by maternal instruction, they were "trained up in the way they should go."

While yet in youth, commercial disaster and reverses of fortune happened to the father,—the family was reduced in circumstances,—and parents and children sought a home in the woods of Lower Canada. Now the superior commercial education of these young men began to stand them instead of other means of support. They betook themselves to teaching, in which they were very successful; and they found their way into Upper Canada. Unhappily their religious training was defeated for a time by intercourse with a degenerate world. They lived for some years an irreligious life, and even tried to be sceptical. They endeavored to satisfy the cravings of their immortal minds with literary pursuits; and they had each a Novel in course of preparation, when their conversion occurred. That of *James*, the elder, took place first; *Ephraim's* soon followed. The honored instruments were the never-to-be-forgotten Metcalf and his then youthful colleague, our prospective Co-Delegate, who were the Circuit preachers. This occurred in the Township of Bastard. We speak of the two EVANSES.

James's talent for preaching, though afterwards he became so eminent as a Missionary to the Indian tribes, did not develop itself so fast; but *Ephraim*, our present hero, was perhaps the soonest called out on a Circuit after his conversion, of any man amongst us—that is, as soon as his probation for membership was completed. Yes, and after a few weeks' trial in the country, he was sent to the second station in importance in the Province, the town of Kingston, and to take the place of a rejected preacher too. He told them at his first *debut*, that, though he was from the *country*, " he knew no difference between *town* and *country* sinners, excepting this, that *town sinners* were generally a great deal worse."

Let no person say that his introduction to the work of preaching was premature. He was a man for age, being twenty-five years old; he was an educated man, and possessed of great *natural* endowments, and one who had drank in the purest theology in early life. It was only directing his extraordinary abilities in another and the proper channel, and he was the accomplished preacher at once. Like Bunting, to whom, we should think, he bears a strong moral and intellectual resemblance, he seemed to preach as well at the first as he does now. And having then the fire and vivacity of youth, with the zeal of a new convert, he was much more popular than he has been of late years. He was always deliberate, argumentative, and prolix. These, since he has lost his youthful sprightliness, cause his long, correctly expressed, and profoundly argumentative sermons, notwithstanding his beautiful language and musical voice, to be regarded as *heavy* by many hearers.

Canada during the early part of his Ministry was full of *isms*, some of which were heretical. Methodism had to club its way through much opposition. In the work of controversy he was a champion, and a host in himself,—fearless, cool, and ready to debate by the day with all comers. This he often did *literally*. He went out in 1827.

A person so gifted and so constituted, would soon become a man of mark in the Conference, and take a very decided part in its deliberations, which he did. At first he was a great admirer of E. R., who, though his *junior* by a year, was his *senior* in the ministry. The anxious discussions of following years, sometimes placed him in antagonism to his early friend. And now that F. M. had retired, he perhaps was the only man in the body who was likely to do it, that could fairly cope with him. Still in our humble opinion, he was never quite his match. Evans was clear, direct, honest, and able; but the other could place a subject in that plausible light that would carry the majority with him.

DOCTOR EVANS has stood in immediate relationship to the English as well as Canadian Conference; and held two very responsible situations in Nova Scotia under its immediate direction. In Canada, he has been Secretary of Conference, Chairman of District, and Editor of the *Guardian*. He is a strong, clear, correct, and forcible writer who, however, was not quite provident and plodding enough for an Editor. He has a lawyer-like mind. He is very versatile, and exceedingly well informed on all subjects; he has a good share of what is called *learning*, and is, therefore, worthy of his Degree, but he does not seem inclined to incumber himself with the lumbering part of it.

He has a strong will, and a little tendency to arbitrariness, although he designs to be fair and honorable. Such men, however, crowd less tenacious spirits out of the arena of discussion, and preserve the floor pretty much to themselves when present.

It is somewhat singular that just such a man as we have described should have offered and been sent to his present position in New Columbia. He seems, however, to be displaying his characteristic resolution, and will doubtless do much good. Though pretty impracticable with equals, we opine that he is bland and indulgent towards juniors and inferiors in general, though there is an air of *hauteur* about him. He is tall, well made, and graceful; and when young, was decidedly handsome. His age must be about 57.

His private manners are characterized by dignified and simple politeness. A very composed and self-possessed man is he, whether in the pulpit or parlour. We deeply sympathize with him in the bereavment he has suffered in the death of his virtuous only son; a and circumstance which will add to his loneliness in that distant land whither he has gone. God be gracious to him and his, and support them!

CRAYON THIRTY-FOURTH.

Our present subject is a sort of *cynic philosopher*, rather disposed to view things in a morose and gloomy light, not wholly free from severity on erring individuals. He is, however, possessed of good nature at bottom, as we can easily see when his grim and wrinkled features are lighted up with a smile, which we are glad is not seldom.

His looks, in their *prima facie* aspect, are against him; and he *seems* more cynical than he is, by the grum and oracular manner in which utterances are made from his deep bass voice. Imagine a man of medium size, rather stoutly built, light complexioned, and freckled, and you have some idea of the person. His head is of large dimensions and taurine shape, covered with a light coating of very peculiar hair.

He is one of a family of preaching brothers already referred to in these sketches—Canadians. He was the *third* introduced to the Conference, although the eldest of *four*. He had been several years employed as a local preacher and missionary school teacher among the Indians, before his name appeared on the "Minutes." The way in which he began the account of himself at his "public reception" was characteristic of the man: he said, "It is with peculiar feelings, I come before this assembly as a candidate for reception into the body, as it must be evident to you all, that I am not a *young* man."

He is a man of excellent sense and judgement—of good intellectual powers, rather strong and weighty than brilliant—sincere piety—and of great probity and worth. He views matters in a very sober light; and would be far more likely to under-value, than over-value anything he was doing for the cause.

Although he seems to have a distaste to it, by some means or other, he has been a large part of his time connected with the Indian department of the work. This is the more remarkable as he has been very acceptable in his appointments among the whites; he was Treasurer of the College, but has not attained his brother Thomas's proficiency in the Indian languages. He has, however, the elements of character to earn the confidence of the observant and reflecting Indian mind, and to maintain an ascendancy over it. His gravity, integrity, and consistency are a tower of strength to him among this peculiar race. He has been for several years the very successful Principal of the Alderville Industrial School.

His dress and manners are plain and farmer-like, and he is very practical in his views and habits. He stood high in the esteem of the late venerable William Case, "the father of Canadian Missions," to whom he was a sort of " right hand man,"

Our friend must be well on towards *sixty*—although his compact frame, sound health, and simple habits, would at present seem to insure a longer continuance in the work, than some who are *twenty years* his juniors. We pray the church may long enjoy the benefit of his self-denying labors.

There are few in the Wesleyan body, who will not be able to recognize the features of the REVEREND SYLVESTER HURLBURT.

CRAYON THIRTY-FIFTH.

I am inclined to think I had better *dispatch* all the HURLBURTS, while my hand is in. THOMAS now by order of seniority falls into our hands.

A remarkable man is he. He stands out by himself from all the members of the Conference—we have but one THOMAS HURLBURT. He is a strong, stout, farmer-looking man of just about fifty years of age. As we usually phrase it, "he holds his age well," notwithstanding the many hardships through which he has passed. But he makes himself very patriarchal-looking by wearing the whole of his stout, coarse beard, now a little sprinkled with grey, while the hair on the crown of his head begins to wear thin. He is rather light complexioned.

He began at the age of twenty, and has been consequently thirty years in the work, the whole of which time has been spent among the Indian tribes of this continent. After spending a few weeks at Grape Island in 1829, he was sent on as Missionary School Teacher to Muncy-town, where he got the first insight into the Chippewa language. Thence, he was sent, after being ordained, to Saugeen, on the shores of Lake Huron. There he remained two years. Then he spent a year at St. Clair and Walpole Island. The next three years he was in the Lake Superior country. The next two, namely 1841, and '42, at the Pic, in the Hudson Bay Territory. The next year he returned to Canada and was appointed to Lake Simcoe. From thence, obeying what he thought to be the call of God, he went in 1844, to the assistance of our brethren in the United States, where he was a member and Presiding Elder, in their Indian Mission Conference, stretching, I believe, from North to South through all the States West of the Mississippi. While there, he extended his acquaintance with the Indian dialects. There he continued till 1851, when he returned to assist his first friends in Canada, and was stationed at Alderville. The next two or three years he supplied the Rice Lake Mission. In 1855, the Hudson Bay Missions having been transferred from the direction of the British Wesleyan to the Canadian Conference, Mr. H. was entrusted with the Superintendency of the whole work in that Territory. His own station was Norway House, Lake Winnepeg. Here he performed progidies of labor in preaching, school-teaching, board-sawing and house-building, type-founding, printing, translating, and studying languages. While there he added the Cree to his previous stock of Indian dialects.

We regret to have to say, that he was forced from this very useful position by the failing health of his devoted wife, who found herself unable to endure the rigors of the climate. He came down to Garden River, where he had the charge of Lake Superior District in 1857. In 1858, he was transferred to the old and important mission of St. Clair, where he now resides.

Besides discharging the ordinary duties of a missionary, he is likely to serve the cause of missions as a Professor of the Indian languages. The Conference made a commencement the present year to train missionaries for the Indian work expressly, instead of leaving the matter to accident. It was decided to place two young men at once under the tution of Mr. H. with a view to their spending their lives in that department of the work.

Our hero, (for *hero* he has proved himself) is altogether a a very remarkable man. He has been too long among the Indians to be a very captivating preacher in *English*. He has learned the Indian so thoroughly, and has spoken it so much, that he speaks English with an Indian idiom and intonation. He can *think* in Indian, and says that at one time, he used to *dream* in it also. The Indians themselves give him credit for great expertness in their language, one of them pronouncing him "an Indian in a white man's skin." In their language he is very voluble and persuasive.

Besides expertness in learning and systematizing barbarous tongues, in which he has showed a philosophic perception of the essential structure of language and linguistic affinities, he has shown a philosophic turn of thought in general matters. His knowledge of natural science, particularly of Geology, is very considerable. He has amused himself and imposed obligations on scientific discovery by his careful observance and public record of natural phenomena of various kinds.

He is a kind, equable tempered man, with a quiet vein of Indian sort of humor running through his conversation. Although he represents himself as behind the conventional usages of civilized society, his stores of information being of a character so very unique, render his company very agreeable and much to be desired by the best informed persons who have formed his acquaintance. He is healthy and may serve the church another twenty years. Long may he live!

CRAYON THIRTY-SIXTH.

ERASTUS, though the younger of the four HURLBURTS, was perhaps the best educated originally of either. But although a sound and excellent preacher, it is doubtful whether he will ever attain to the eminence of his brothers. That is, RELATIVE eminence; for it may be questioned whether he is not held back relatively by the rapid augmentation of talent and energy among those who are nearer his own age in the ministry. It requires more learning and more ability to be distinguished now, among increasing numbers and increasing talent, than in former years when ministers were few and their talents small.

Our brother has received a new religious impulse of late years, and in his last circuit before the present, he was made the instrument of a great and glorious revival. May his present one be similarly blessed!

He is about thirty-eight years of age, but as he is very light complexioned and healthy he looks much younger. He is very attentive to his person, equipage and parsonage premises. He has any amount of good nature; and, whatever may be the number of his admirers, we should think he has no enemies.

He is one of that sort of men who will wear a long time,

and who often wake up in middle life and make their influence felt for good during the rest of their days. We shall rather expect this of him. We have some special reasons for feeling interested in his success. God bless him!

CRAYON THIRTY-SEVENTH.

Seven years ago the Methodists in Montreal, experienced somewhat of a trial. Their principal minister in the city, and the newly appointed chairman of the Lower Canada District, a man of rare accomplishments and unbounded popularity, whom the people had almost idolized, suddenly announced his acceptance of a call to a popular and wealthy Presbyterian church in the city of Philadelphia, where his salary was to be vastly in advance of the very liberal allowance of the Montreal Stewards.

The officials very politely and properly declined his services for the balance of his time among them; and sent to the Missionary Secrataries in London, to whose jurisdiction they were then amenable, for a supply. The person sent was regarded as one of the best students and preachers in one of the Branches of their Theological Institute, where he had been about three years. He had been an acceptable local preacher for several years before going there and must have had very respectable attainments. But they were much greater, when he left the Institution. If his qualifications are a fair specimen of the sort of training received in those Institutions, a sojourn at either of them must be an incalculable blessing to a junior preacher who may be favored to attend it. Our friend's knowledge of Theology, Latin, Greek, Hebrew, and Bibical criticism, was very considerable.

So thoroughly trained a young man we have perhaps never had in our Canadian connexion. He has systematically built on the foundation so broadly and deeply laid at the Institution. He seems to have little desire for any kind of study, excepting what has a *direct* reference to his sacred profession. This would appear to be the true method in general. It is undoubtedly so for him; for it is in accordance with his *tastes* as well as his convictions. But where a minister's tastes and opportunities lead him to more general and miscellaneous reading and study he may safely imitate the example of John Wesley, who read everything which came in his way, and of Adam Clarke, who "intermeddled with all wisdom." For divinity, and the means of illustrating divine truth, may be drawn from every branch of knowledge, by an ingenious and pious mind. Preachers who pursue such a course are among the most interesting and useful to the mass of hearers. They may not please accurate theologians so well.

Our subject is a neat, clear, sound preacher, with a distinct and deliberate utterance, much esteemed for his preaching ability in the circuits in which he has been stationed, which, with the exception of one year, have all been *city* appointments—Montreal and Toronto. He has excellent qualifications to make an able Minister, pleasing in his address; pointed, and earnest; and attends to all his work with regularity and fidelity.

He is rather short of the medium height, but stout-built and healthy. Being very light complexioned, with a round, rosy face, he looks almost boyish, although he is perhaps 34 or 35 years of age. He is a good natured person, with risibles easily excited. He has, however, a just perception of clerical propriety, which he always preserves.

He begins to occupy a useful place in the doings of the Conference. His report as Secretary of the Sabbath School Committee last June was ably drawn up, and impressively read to the Conference. He has been honored the present year with the Financial Secretaryship of the district to which he now belongs—a post for which he is well qualified. A rising man is he. His *office* is suggestive of his *name;* for by all who hold Presbyterian views, he will be regarded as a true and scriptural BISHOP.

CRAYON THIRTY-EIGHT.

One year after the first UNION with the British Conference, (that is 1834) there being then a deficiency of laborers in the Province, the Canada Conference requested of the Parent body to send out six young preachers from their list of reserve for that year, which Dr. Alder pronounced "the best batch" that had gone out for several years. In due time, the brethren arrived. They were not very young, although they were "young men" technically. But if there was a want of the sprightliness of youth about them, they possessed what was of vastly more importance—experience and maturity of preaching ability, the result of having exercised the local preacher's office for several years. They were also men of some learned attainments, and much general information. They all, excepting the lamented GLADWIN and PRICE, who died after a few years labor, rendered considerable service to the cause. The now sainted SLIGHT labored successfully in Upper and Lower Canada among *Indians* and whites, for the space of *twenty-three* years—proving himself the accomplished preacher, the faithful, judicious pastor, and an author of no mean ability. Among the three that survive, *one* (eminent for his piety) is a *superannuate;* one has filled some of the highest offices of the connexion, and is one of its best financial minds; and one remains to be described in this paper.

He is plain in his appearance, portly and grave-looking, and now begins to look elderly. He is a man of sincere piety—of very industrious habits—decidedly Wesleyan in all respects—well-educated—extensively read, with literary tastes and talents. He is also a sound theologian; and nothing but a slight occasional hesitancy (a nervous affection, much influenced by circumstances,) in his speech, prevents his being considered the eloquent preacher. Eloquent he is in thought and language, if those " thoughts that breathe and words that burn," could but find a readier utterance. He is both imaginative and pathetic. His addresses excel in originality, in ingenuity and fancy, and in variety. An address of his at a public reception of young Preachers, delivered before the Conference held in the town of St. Catherines in 1845, is often referred to by his brethren as a most successful effort, and a model for such occasions. While in the active itinerancy his prominent features were his great partiality for pastoral visitations and revivals; dogged adherence to old Methodism; enthusiastic love of Britain, but firmly attached to Canada, and Canadian Methodism. His conscientiousness and high sense of honor would lead him to distrust ungrateful, vascillating, or jesuitical men. As a Missionary spirit brought him from England, this noble institution shares largely in his aspirations and sympathies.

But perhaps our subject is more known and celebrated as a *writer*, than in any other department. His first appointments were Indian Mission Stations, in which work he was very acceptable; but some pungent articles from his pen on public questions which affected the interests of religion, brought him into notice as a writer, and led to his election to the Editorial chair of the Connexion, of which he was an incumbent *four years*. The characteristics of the paper in his time were *religiousness* and *non-political*. His style is perhaps rather too diffuse, and his articles sometimes slightly prolix. These are his only defects. He was once elected Secretary of Conference, but declined the honor.

The indisposition of an excellent wife, who cannot endure the fatigue of moving, obliges him to hold a *supernumerary* relation, who otherwise would be very *effective*. He is, however, exceedingly useful to the connexion, as the Secretary of the General Superintendent of our Missions, and by his preaching far and near on the Lord's day.

With all the capabilities above described, the voice of our friend is never heard in the deliberations of the Conference. Yet, when its decisions are promulgated, he is ever ready to expound and defend them with his pen. Still his services to that venerable body are known and appreciated in the almost unanimous adoption of several important addresses to the British Conference, a number of Pastoral Addresses, and of the longest Obituary found in the Minutes,—that of the Apostolic Case. A thorough Colonist is he in his sympathies and views. Who that knows him does love and revere the Reverend JONATHAN SCOTT?

CRAYON THIRTY-NINE.

It is strange that we should have overlooked our present subject till now. His sizeable person, bustling habits, and very respectable abilities, cause him to fill a considerable space in the public eye.

He is the son of a worthy Irish Methodist, and was himself born in Ireland. He was classically educated at Victoria College; and before his entering the ministry, was for some years a popular and efficient teacher of a higher school.

His ministerial life and labors have been marked by great success. And no wonder—he pays the price which can alone ensure it. He is fervently pious,—serious in his conversation,—impassioned in his sermons, exhortations, and prayers—abundant in labors, and pastoral in his habits. His preaching talents may be pronounced very good; but his advantages of voice and manner, the one being strong and the other fervent, may cause him to rank higher with the masses than his actual level.

Although he does not show it, by participation in the debates of Conference, he is public spirited, and has done a great deal of connexional work—not to say drudgery. He was for two years the successful Agent of the Victoria College. His stations have been very respectable; and he is now (1859-60) the pastor of our Collegiate Church at Cobourg.

Being of a pushing disposition, laggards may perhaps consider him pertinacious and intolerant, a conclusion not uncommon in such cases.

He is a very good defender of our connexional proceedings, whether "on the stump," or with the "grey goose quill." In both he is practical, and comes down to the popular level.

He is now in the *fourteenth* year of his ministry. Although one of the most serviceable men to the body of his standing, he is a little too conservative and deferential to existing authorities to receive the suffrages of that numerous class whose management in caucuses influence all appointments to connexional offices. He will, however make his mark on the body, if he live long enough. And as to living, his robust health, renders this probable for many years to come. His age must be *thirty-six* or *eight*.

It is almost a superfluity to say we are writing of the REV. WILLIAM HENRY POOLE.

CRAYON FORTY.

When a person has symmetry and beauty of body—vigor of intellect—amiableness of temper—great educational attainments—manners polished by good society—and real, evangelical piety into the bargain, they make the possessor a very loveable object. Such is the one we are now about to sketch.

He had his birth (and spent his childhood under the roof of pious, Methodist parents,) in an interesting rural part of Upper Canada—Mount Pleasant. He was brought up on a *farm*, where many of our best public men occupied their boyish days. There they acquired simple habits and good constitutions. We rather suspect our subject never labored more than enough to harden his muscles a little.

The first place we ever heard of him was at Victoria College. But we are told by himself that he was converted at the Genesee Wesleyan Seminary, N. Y., before going there. He was, however, licensed to preach as a local preacher at Victoria; and while there, decided in favor of the full work of the Christian Ministry. This is one of the many instances in which that too much undervalued Institution has been the means of sequestering the highest class of minds to the cause of sacred truth.

He finished his collegiate course at Middletown University where he received his degree—first A. B., and then of A. M. He entered the full work of the ministry in 1847, and was stationed in the Port Hope circuit. His highest ambition seems, to have been, to be a faithful, laborious Wesleyan Minister. Nor did he aspire to the *cities*, as do some young men of far less ability to go into them. From these he seemed to shrink, but wished to begin, where that man of iron powers, Dr. Dixon, told our Conference he began—" at the fag end." He wished to work his way up. This would be wise in every young man.

His second appointment, however, was the city of Toronto. His third, the city of London circuit, which embraced at that time a great deal of country work. Here he was not suffered to complete the year; but was urged, against his preferences, into the Principalship of Victoria College, where he has ever since remained.

For some time after his admission to "full connexion," he seemed to act in the Conference as though he had not much right to speak, excepting on such matters as related to *Education*; he now, however, takes a pretty active part in its general deliberations—much to the general good, and much to the satisfaction of his brethren, among all grades of whom he is a favorite.

He showed his talent for eloquent speaking, first in the debates of the Philalœthic Society at College; and he now proves himself the masterly preacher, by his unhackneyed manner, his probing the conscience, and his bursts of eloquence; the eloquent declaimer on the platform; and the effective debater on Conference floor. His style is unencumbered and lucid, but he sometimes takes the boldest flights of oratory.

He is handsome in person—medium-sized, but so straight, as to appear taller than he really is. His full chest, we suspect, is partly the result of a wise and vigorous system of gymnastics. His hair and beard are black, coarse and curly. His head widens from the base of the brain upwards. His face is well proportioned, and his lips curved. He would do for the "tall, dark young man" of the novelist—for he is yet *young*, probably not more than thirty-five or six; and he does not look so old as that even. His voice is pleasant and well managed; and his gestures have become very beautiful and easy, yet quick and energetic.

We do not know whether other senior members of the Conference have noticed the resemblance, but there is much about President Nelles, which reminds ourselves of the late lamented Metcalf. The resemblances are in their very *personal appearance*, (although Metcalf was the taller, and his hair was chesnut and straight,) in the purity of their character—the ease of their manners—the gracefulness, and even similarity of their gestures in the pulpit—and in the playfulness of their conversation among familiar friends. Mr. M. was characterized by *innocent wit*: so is Mr. N. And, to us, there appears a resemblance in the kind of it. An example from each may be given :—In the second Conference after the first Union, an eminent minister, who was not always distinguished by his suavity of temper, moved " That the Rev. Ezra Adams and the Rev. T. Turner, *as being two of the best natured men in the Conference*, be a Committee to wait on the Trustees of the American Presbyterian Church, and thank them for their kindness in proffering their Meeting House for the use of the Conference, and to respectfully decline the offer,"—on the ground that it was not needed. Metcalf immediately suggested " the addition of the mover, as being the stationed minister of the town, and also for the purpose of *adding to the quantity of good nature!*" In the last session of our Conference, two strong men, leading members of the body, got into a pretty earnest altercation on the sacred and somewhat difficult subject of *entire sanctification*—in the midst of which Mr. NELLES stepped forward from a retired seat to the end of the platform, and expressed " a hope that there might be no quarrel between these two brethren on the subject of *sanctification*, for he was sure in such a case they could not be *justified*." The first half of the sentence produced a shade of seriousness on the countenances of all, which soon turned into a laugh, when they discovered the *pun* in the latter half. It was a piece of pleasantry, however, which dissipated a rising cloud. Nelles is an incorrigable, yet innocent punster.

One might think that such playful sallies were incompatible with the dignity of his position, and adverse to his ascendancy among the students in the College; but no man knows better how to maintain true dignity when the assumption of it is required; and as to his college government, that is a decided success. He is almost idolized by all under his care. Men of extra dignity do not always succeed so well.

His *scholarship* comports well with his opportunities and duties; but, if one so much inferior to him in that respect might express an opinion, he is as much distinguished by his literary and speaking talents, and by natural genius, as he is by filling his head with a great amount of learned lumber. There is no pedantry about him whatever.

We are glad to write that he is a sound-hearted Wesleyan, who has a scrupulous respect for our distinctive principles, while he has the largest catholicity of feeling towards " all who love our Lord Jesus Christ in sincerity."

CRAYON FORTY-FIRST.

It is said that "comparisons are odious." Or, as that mythical personage, Mrs. Partington, affirmeth, they are "odorous"—a pretended mistake which contains a great amount of truth, and tends to illustrate the legitimacy of the maxim as litterally expressed. All such maxims are more or less founded in truth, and may be very useful as guides to our conduct, and this one among the rest. Yet there are some things we can only illustrate by comparison, indeed all illustrations imply comparison. Plutarch resorts to this method in bringing out the peculiarities of the great men of antiquity. We have been led to use it to some extent in illustrating the individuality of some of the men of God whom we have sketched, as well as to diversify our mode of treating the subjects. We have not meant our comparisons to be individious. And we are about to resort to it once more.

In the years 1834, 5, and 6, our present President was stationed in the city of Kingston. During the early part of his pastoral sojourn in that place, a modest, steady youth, who had been trained in the Sabbath school, became converted to God and joined the church. He had a fair English education, and soon gave promise of usefulness, and was made a local preacher.

Next, he entered as one of the first students in Upper Canada Academy, which has grown up to our present Victoria College. In a year's time, however, he was withdrawn from its sacred shade, and sent into the work on the then laborious THAMES circuit, in which work he has continued to this day, a period of 22 years.

Immediately on beginning to preach, he showed points of resemblance to his spiritual father, which some thought might be that *imitation* so common to young men of those they admire; but to the present, although they have not been much together, that resemblance continues, which we are sure is only *accidental*, as it is but *partial*. First, they are very much of a size, being compact, rotound, handsome men, and light complexioned. The younger, (who is about *forty-four*) not appearing so much so as to make any material difference. Their voices are very much the same in tone and compass. The elder, however, speaks fluently, the younger with more hesitancy, and always with some, till he warms with his theme. Both are chaste and elevated in their language and illustrations. One is perhaps textual, the other more seemingly argumentative. Our subject is practical and evangelical, and rises sometimes to eloquence. He is not, however, so great a preacher, perhaps, as he gave promise to be when young. Two things may have retarded him. He is, we suspect, a little sluggish constitutionally, which may have prevented laborious preparation; and he has been entrusted with connexional engagements adverse to study and practice pulpit-ward.

He was appointed *Editor* in 1846, in which position he maintained himself no less than *five years*. His style *we* find ourselves unable to characterize, and leave it undescribed. His taste, however, we may say was choice and delicate. After serving what might be called our *collegiate* church and the Cobourg district three years, he became the connexional *Book Steward* several years, comprehending the period of the late *monetary crisis*. And whatever the knowing ones may say, by way of criticizing his commercial management, he is no doubt one of our best financial men. He has been the Treasurer of our Church Relief Fund.

He does not speak often in the Conference, but when he does his is usually a set speech of considerable importance. Though courteous and possessed of self-control, he goes through with his measures with great determination. He generally returns left-handed compliments with great punctuality, when a suitable occasion offers. He has some learning, and is possessed of good literary talents, although, as yet, he has published no book.

Though a little inclined to quiz and tease his familiar friends, he is a serious good christian, and sound in all Wesleyan matters. Notwithstanding he is at present somewhat retired, from observation, his position is respectable, and he will come into notice again one of these days, by some revolution of the connexional wheel. We are proud to say that the Rev. G. R. SANDERSON is a native of Canada.

CRAYON FORTY-SECOND.

The consideration of Mr. S. reminds us of one to whom he stands officially related as his *Superintendent* and *Chairman*, but one very dissimilar from himself in many respects.

Our present subject is a native of that "Green Isle of the sea," so justly celebrated in story and in song. He is a true representative *Irishman*. A *Celt* by origin, on his father's side at least, as his name indicates, and with all the wit, vivacity, warm-heartedness, eloquence, and, we may add, amusing oddity, which are characteristic of the genuine specimens of that race. His looks also are unmistakably *Hibernian*. He is low of stature, and particularly short in the pedestals on which the column rests. His strong features make up the *tout ensemble* of a real old country face. We take a little liberty with him as he often refers with playful irony to his great personal beauty. His appearance has, however, some redeeming qualities—he has a finely developed head, partially bald, skirted, as is his face, with a margin of luxuriant hair, venerably white. He is extra neat and clerical in his dress and person, and though vivacious, very genteel in his manners.

He is a trophy won from the Church of Rome, to which Crayon No. II, largely contributed when on the Miramichi Mission, within the pale of which he was brought up, and for the priesthood of which he was educated, being before his conversion, actually in its ecclesiastical *noviciate*. This transition began in New Brunswick, and was consummated in Nova Scotia. Being brought to the saving knowledge of the truth, through the instrumentality of Wesleyan Missionaries, he naturally cast in his lot with that section of the Protestant church, and was soon in the ranks of its ministry. This took place about 28 years ago. Since then, he has filled some of the best stations in the four provinces—New Bruswick, Novia Scotia, Upper and Lower Canada.

He received a good classical education, and obtained *first*, the degree of *Master of Arts*, we believe, from Middletown University; and subsequently, that of *Doctor in Divinity*, from Newton University. He placed in its archives, we have been told, one of the best " Latin Theses" the Senate avered, they had ever received.

He frequently quotes Latin, and makes a liberal use of classic allusions; though all his allusions are *not* classical. No one can be more droll and familiar when he likes; and indeed, he is necessarily often so, whether he likes or not. He can hardly open his mouth without saying very unusual things. And by the amount of laughter he provokes, a stranger might suspect him wanting in proper consideration. He is one of that class of men who will receive credit for less piety than they possess.

He is, however, undoubtedly pious, and of late years, it is evident, he is increasingly so.

As a speaker, we may remark, his volubility is without let or hindrance, and his imagination is of the most gorgeous and discursive character. The boldness of its flights and the oddity of its gyrations, are beyond description—they must be witnessed to be appreciated. These are allowed their utmost latitude on the *platform*, but more restrained in the *pulpit*. He is, however, rather brilliant than powerful as a preacher.

Specimens of his style and the topics he delights to dwell on, with his mode of treating them, may be seen in the "Autobiography of a Wesleyan Missionary," a book which, from the variety of its matter, the strangeness of its incidents, and the liveliness of their treatment, will amply repay perusal. Let it be bought and read. He wrote also the "History of Miramichi," a work referred to by subsequent historians as a standard. Part of his pre-ministerial life was *editorial*, he has, therefore written a great deal, as he writes with facility. He is an unique and popular *lecturer*, having in former years done a great deal of that sort of work in the several cities where he has been stationed.

He is a sound-hearted Wesleyan, and only needs to be known to be loved. Though literary and oratorical, he is more of a business man than he seems to be; we suspect however, he has no love for its details. With the asssistance of an excellent conjugal co-adjutor, he does not neglect his pastoral obligations.

The REV. ROBERT COONEY, D. D., is probably about *sixty years* of age.

CRAYON FORTY-THIRD.

Our present subject is very much to our notion, as a Wesleyan minister. He is a native of Canada, with an admixture of

Anglo-Saxon and Teutonic blood in his veins. He is rather tall, straight, slender, and handsome, having a clear skin with dark hair. Age has not yet impaired his beauty, although he is *forty-one* or *two*. He has been 19 years in the itinerant work, having gone out into the *Canadian* ministry at the memorable " Special Conference." He egressed from the halls of the " Upper Canada Academy," where he was respectably educated. All his pre-ministerial life was spent in study and teaching.

He is somewhat scholarly, but not pedantic—studious, but not slavishly devoted to books—genteel, but plain and condescending—cheerful, without levity—serious, without moroseness—devout, without fanaticism—and earnest, without rant. He excels in his ability and tact for working up his circuits—which he always does—or straightening them when needed. We scarcely know his equal for nerve and thoroughness in cleansing an Augean stable. He can differ with a man without quarreling with him—he is mild, but unflinching—almost to stubborness.

He preaches good, thorough, practical, appropriate sermons, but none for show or effect. He is laborious and pastoral and unusually successful in promoting revivals. We have often wondered how he brought them about. With no extra eloquence, passion or sanctimoniousness—with a voice not very strong or commanding—and with a peculiar manner of utterance resembling a stammerer, arising from rapidity and hesitancy combined, yet he will fix attention, produce conviction, and keep the people all at work, till the tide of prosperity sets in, and sinners by scores are brought to God. And he is just as useful in building up as he is in gathering in. He carries his religion into everything, and has a family ordered as a christian minister's should be.

Our hero has received good appointments, but has had more *work* than *honors*. His beautiful chirography and exactness in copying have entailed on him the drudgery of "Journal Secretaryship," for a number of years—long enough to have earned the post of principal Secretary before it did. He is in the largest city of the two Provinces, and is now the Chairman of that District—the first year of his Episcopate.

His Conference speeches do not produce a very profound impression, owing to want of weight in his voice—distinctness in his manner of coming at a question—and his usually appearing after the minds of members are wearied with the discussion. He has too much work on hand to take an early and effective part in the debates, although he sits in a conspicuous place.

His baptismal name is after the hero of Queenston Heights, and ISAAC BROCK HOWARD is a real *Christian* hero.

CRAYON FORTY-FOURTH.

The most of the troubles we experience from others in this world are of our own procuring, as they arise from our want of discretion, litigiousness, pertinacity, or ambition. If any man tells you that all men are leagued against him; and that, go where he will, they are determined to annoy him, you may rest assured "there is a screw loose" in his own machinery somewhere. On the contrary there are others, who always seem to be sailing in smooth water, just because they so placidly adjust their sails and helm to the varying winds and currents. Such a one we conceive to be the subject of our pencil just now.

Without any very large pretentions or attainments—or without any extra zeal or bustle, he has taken circuits of great respectability, and has continued to stay in them, with only one or two exceptions, during the longest period possible consistent with our connexional law. The people are not disposed to part with the *man*, any more than the preacher.

He is a native of old Ireland; and his name is not only

Celtic, but rejoices in one of those honorary prefixes, which indicates that the first who bore it, was the *son* of some person of distinction. He accompanied his father's family to Canada at the early age of *twelve years;* and like many of the public men of the country, got his only academic training in learning to wield the axe and flourish the handspike. Farming and shantying occupied the most of his time till early manhood. Then the voice of God, through the pioneer itinerant aroused him from the sleep of sin, and gave a new stimulus to his powers. He began to be useful in his own vicinity. And it was no ill augury that the sagacious *Madden* (the elder) predicted that he would " make a preacher." He did, soon after; and began his labors on the circuit on which he was brought up.

A new and higher course of study was adopted at the time he commenced his probation (26 years ago.) The satisfactory manner in which he accomplished that course, showed that he had a mind for acquisition at least. Indeed, we regard him as having the power to learn with great ease. We opine that no man amongst us has prepared his sermons with more facility than he. They are methodical, plain, and evangelical, and to a certain class of minds very grateful.

He would have become a greater man than he is, if he had not good-naturedly bestowed so much talk on the people, and allowed every "chatterbox" to obtrude on his time for study. His accessibleness, affability, and communicativeness, however, have made him popular. But the people, ought not to require too high a price from their ministers for the favor they accord—the price of *most sacred time.*

Our friend, though he has an easy way of doing it, has been instrumental in promoting several extensive revivals.

He is not now "the tall dark young man" he was *twenty-six* years ago, when we first made his acquaintance. Returning years, though they may not have much enfeebled his strength as they have not yet bowed his manly form, have rendered it more venerable, in turning his once auburn locks to *iron gray*. He is now in the *fifth* year of his *Chairmanship*.

We need not wish him *happiness;* for we do not know that it is in the power of any one to take it away, from the mild and pleasant WILLIAM MCFADDEN.

CRAYON FORTY-FIFTH.

We have in our mind's eye at the present moment, a strongly marked character—one who is no other man's imitator—but one with a decided idiosyncracy of his own. His name is of *German* origin (or "*Dutch*," as the people call it) at both ends, but we believe there is an infusion of *Scotch* blood in his veins, perhaps from his mother's side: our new countries are the places by an admixture of races, for new and unusual types of human kind. This has given the vital current in him a little more warmth and a more rapid circulation, counteracting the proverbial phlegm of the Teutonic race. *Religion* has been known to give vivacity to the Dutchman; and his nature is a soil in which religion in the form of *Methodism* luxuriates. But our subject, who is of Canadian growth, was known to be of a mercurial temperament before his conversion. A more vivacious, droll, and sport-loving and sport-making, young man than he, before he was subdued by the grace of God, is seldom seen. And though then heir to a considerable estate, and educated quite beyond most of his compeers in the "*Fifth Town*" and neighbourhood, yet he was distinguished for the use of *cant* or *slang* phrases, which he has since sometimes pressed into religion.

He would, at that time, have been just the man to relish the "sayings and doings of Sam Slick," or to have written such a work himself. *Humorist* he is, by nature, no doubt. But in saying that, it amounts to a declaration, which is true in his case, that he is possessed of a warm, generous, and affectionate heart. Aye, and a more *honorable* one never throbbed in human breast. True, there may be persons who think otherwise, and think so sincerely, but we think they are mistaken. He may have enemies, but if so he has made them unwittingly; or in striving to befriend some unfortunate acquaintance in difficulty. A sympathizing man, by the very strength of his compassion, is liable to be drawn into offices of friendship for others, against his own private convictions of fitness, by which he is unjustly charged with want of judgment and discretion.

Every part of our friend's history has been unusual. He was married earlier than usual; and lived without religion till he was *twenty-seven*. Then he goes to a camp meeting, where little or nothing is accomplished—excepting his own conversion. With a joyful heart he heighs him home, " warns out" his neighbors, and holds a meeting with them the following Sabbath. A revival, I believe, ensues. He speaks in public ever after. Is made first, an exhorter, and then a local preacher, just so soon as ecclesiastical routine will allow. In less than two years after his conversion, he is out on a circuit. A most unusual preacher, at that day, he was. Were we to tell a tithe of his sayings and doings during the early years of his ministry, we should move the risibles of the most grave: yet, though we think there are many worse things than a smile produced by the contemplation of such honest and original efforts in the cause of Christ, we shall forbear, least we " offend against some of the generation of *his* people."

Our hero " went out" in *twenty-nine*, and, as he has possessed a vigorous constitution and much zeal, he has labored far and wide, and accomplished much for the Church. He has had his full share of large, laborious country circuits—has been once or twice a " stationed" preacher—Treasurer and Governor of the College, when he devised the important " Scholarship Scheme"—Chairman of a District—and Missionary to the Indians. This unpretending man is a beautiful pensman, and was once the Secretary of the Conference. We are sorry to add, he is now among the "Superannuated," but as he is yet young in appearance at least, and his affection is only *local*, we hope he will soon return to the *effective* ranks. It must be affecting to a mind so active and so evidently social as his, to be secluded and "laid on the shelf."

He was noble in person when in the zenith of his strength and there is yet very little appearance of age, or decrepitude, about him. He stands about five feet eleven inches high; light-complexioned, but with that bilious shade seen also in Germans from the "Fader Land." He is straight, strong, and well-proportioned; and though not lean and haggard, he has no superfluous flesh—very wiry and muscular, is he. Some feats of personal strength and courage, performed in days of yore, when these accomplishments stood the itinerant preachers in greater stead than they do at the present day, I will not relate. His loyalty and activity during the late Rebellion were conspicuous.

He has met with some strange adventures in his day, and we know of nothing more interesting than to hear him relate them. Whoever dislikes him, which we know the great majority do not, *we* shall ever feel a strong affection for dear CONRAD VAN-DUSEN.

CRAYON FORTY-SIXTH.

We are now about to bring forward the moral portrait of a person the contemplation of which, if we can succeed in presenting it correctly, ought to do us good, such is its beautiful symmetry.

True, our present subject may not possess a mind of the first order, though we persist in thinking his a good substantial mind of ordinary power. Not that he has been favored with large educational advantages—" chill penury" and the exigencies of the work, which required his services at the very time he was anxiously desirous of entering on an academical course, cut him off from a collegiate training, although none of the young preachers of his day ever more thoroughly prosecuted and accomplished the "Conference course," than he. What his habits of study, of late years, have been we know not; but if he has kept on as he was proceeding for several years, he must have made no inconsiderable attainments by this time. We know he does not rank high as a preacher with those who are ever craving after the brilliant and the novel; but if a quiet, pleasing manner in the pulpit—if a very happy command of language—if very just notions of exposition—if an easy, intelligible, and just method of sermonizing—and if a yearning compassion for souls, be of any consequence in pulpit ministrations, then is our brother a *good* and *effective*, if not a *great* preacher. We confess our notions of preaching ability differ from some persons, who think it consists in the power of rummaging up something to make people stare and gape; but he, in our opinion, is the preacher, who has ever something on hand wherewith to feed the flock of Christ. One who does not shine in borrowed plumes, but who has the ability of framing a sermon for each emergency, such as the necessities of the people demand; and such is the case with our friend.

He is remarkably successful in winning souls to Christ and in building them up in the most holy faith of the Gospel. How does he do it? Not by making any very confident professions of high attainments himself—not by any vociferous demonstrations of zeal: but by evincing the purest love for souls and concern for his flock, and by incessant labor all the year round. He is never absent from his circuit; never seeks what is called "recreation"; and is unremitting in his exertions. His pastoral visitations, for system, extent, and thoroughnesss, exceed anything we have met in most others. He rather over taxes himself: hence, though he is naturally a stout, strong man, he has several times given alarming indications that he might soon have to give over.

His *abilities* as well as *labors* begin to be appreciated, and he is now for the third year in a very important station. If some of those pertinacious circuits which insist on choosing their own preachers would sometimes make choice of such a man, it would be no worse for them in any one particular.

Our subject is of Scottish parentage, though he himself was born in Canada. Scotch Methodists are rare, but his father was a Methodist and a Class-leader, and must have been favorably affected to our church before the birth of his son, as he gave him the family name of the founder of Methodism.

I hope I have not shocked the modesty of a very retiring brother in thus dragging him before the public; but we have little fear of spoiling one who evidently knows his own heart so well. A good man is he. And despite a little thickness of articulation, and absence of a great *many* flowers of rhetoric, we shall persist in pronouncing JOSEPH WESLEY MCCOLLUM a *good preacher*, as well as a *good man*. May both one and the other continue to be increasingly true of him! Amen! His ministerial age is *eighteen* years—his natural age, perhaps *forty*.

CRAYON FORTY-SEVENTH.

Here is a brother whose history and antecedents seem to promise much. He is "an Hebrew of the Hebrews," or a *Methodist of the Methodists*. The son of an aged Class-leader, always steady from childhood—gave evidence of conversion while yet a boy—naturally gifted as a speaker—possessed of a good capacity for acquiring knowledge—studious and ambitious to excel—and favored with excellent educational advantages, being a long while at Cobourg, "where he stood high as a student and his profiting appeared unto all." His attainments in the Greek and Latin Classics and in Mathematics, are far in advance of most Wesleyan Ministers. His studies in Theology were commenced well, and thoroughly prosecuted. He furnished himself with a library of the best standard authors when he entered the work, and studied them systematically. We know of none who in this respect has been more exact.

He has been a serious exemplary christian from the first; and though perhaps *personally*, not so cordial an approver of some of the peculiarities of Methodism as he might be, yet he has never betrayed his trust officially.

His attention to his work has been most exemplary. If he has not declined of late years, we know of few who excel him in the systematic and faithful manner in which he performs his pastoral work, doing everything by rule, and always doing it.

He went off a ready, able preacher at the first blush. And we have reason to believe he has made proportionate improvement since. We heard him preach a sermon some years ago—about midway between his commencement and the present time—on a very hackneyed, though very important text: namely, "What is a man profited if he should gain the whole world and lose his own soul? Or what shall a man give in exchange for his soul?" And we must pronounce it by far the most just and forcible exposition and enforcement of those solemn words that we ever heard or read.

While a junior, he took good appointments—such as Hamilton and Toronto; and sustained himself well. Some of his stations, too, since he became a Superintendent, have been very respectable, such as *Brockville*, *Bytown*, and *Brantford;* nor were *Chatham* and *St. Thomas*, perhaps exceptions to this remark.

Our subject is medium-sized, light-complexioned, genteel in

dress and manners, and so straight, that, like the old Indian's tree, "he leans over a little the other way." (He must pardon our playfulness.) This is owing partly to his make—and partly to defective sight, which obliges him to wear spectacles constantly: looking through glasses in the street causes a man to carry his head very erect. This minister's *status* is *fourteen years*, and his age perhaps *thirty-six*. NOBLE FRANKLIN ENGLISH is a formidable name; and its wearer is no contemptible man.

CRAYON FORTY-EIGHTH.

We turn our attention to one of the "Lower Canada District"—of yore; one born in Lower Canada, and who still continues to labor there, though the district aforesaid has now for some years stood connected with Upper Canada Methodism. If we have sketched few of the excellent men who once composed that body, it has not been because we have thought them unworthy of such a distinction, but because we feared we did not know them well enough to do them justice. But, though we may not be able to do justly by the one now in hand, we are fairly committed to say something.

He is a native, we believe, of the Eastern Townships, a portion of country not to be surpassed for natural advantages or the character of its population by any part of United Canada; but a portion, the excellencies of which, secularly or religiously, are little known in Upper Canada. His *name* imports that his forefathers may have been foreigners to England at one time. He looks, too, as though he might have some other as well as Caucasian, or at least, Anglo-Saxon, blood in his veins. He is magnificent in person. More than six feet high—large-boned—muscular and athletic; his general appearance, especially his strong, dark, crisp, and abundant hair and beard, indicate a strong constitution and great powers of endurance. He is one of that sort of men, like John Hampson, who single-handed, awed a whole multitude of men who had come to maltreat John Wesley, by threatening to "strike the first man dead," who ventured to molest him; and who, when Mr. W. expressed his surprise at his conduct, said, "Sir, if God has not given you an arm to quell this mob, he has me!" Which led Dr. Clark, to say that the Creator had formed these men of great physical strength as specimens of his own unlimited power. And yet he is no belligerent, but a truly peaceful follower of Him who did not "strive nor cry." He will pardon us for glancing at some of his early adventures.

He is, however, a pushing man, who will go through with his laudable projects, if the thing is possible; and he generally finds it so. He is said to be a strong, able, lively preacher. He is an excellent financier and business man in general (a District Financial Secretary) and very active and laborious. He must be very well received in his several circuits, which are quite respectable, remaining in them no less than *two*, *three*, and FOUR years at a time, and then has been parted with reluctantly.

He received a liberal education, as he was once a disciple of Esculapius. He turned his phials and pill-boxes bottom upwards, and went to prescribe for the moral maladies of men. He never speaks in Conference, except on business with which he is personally, or officially connected, but then he speaks to the point, and shows a good degree of determination. He is, however, elected to represent the interest of his district on most financial committees, on which he serves efficiently. His active habits, we opine, have often conflicted with the extensive prosecution of his early classical studies. He has been *seventeen* or *eighteen* years in the ministry, and must be at least *forty-years* of age. God has given him a large and lovely family. A sensible, resolute, modest, worthy man is RUFUS A. FLANDERS. May the blessing of the Most High rest upon him! Amen.

CRAYON FORTY-NINE.

With this Crayon we shall cease our sketching, for a time at least; although we may take the privilege of re-touching and re-producing some of the portraits we have published through another medium. But with whom shall we finish? This is a puzzling question. There are many men of learning, eminent piety, great business talents, and eloquent, effective preachers, among the three hundred and fifty who remain unsketched, that deserve attention as much as any of those we have described. As, however, we have shut ourselves up to *one*, we shall take a person who has a great assemblage of opposite excellencies concentrated in himself.

His outer man has not the advantage of towering stature and herculean strength of the brother last described. This one is what you might pronounce *petite*. He is some five feet seven inches, well made, and well proportioned in all respects. His hair and beard are dark; but he is well-skinned and roseate. He is graceful and easy in his movements; these with his natural quickness and vivaciousness of mind and amiableness of temper, give him a very sprightly air and carriage. A handsome little man is he. He excels for tact or ready resources—whatever way he may be jostled or thrown, he is sure to alight on his feet.

Our subject is a fine exemplification of the advantages of the Wesleyan system to give impulse and direction to powers that would otherwise remain dormant, or misemployed; and to sequester them to the promotion of God's glory and the happiness of human kind. He is a native of Cornwall, England, that garden (or rather *hot-bed*) of Methodism; and one of a blessed coterie in the Canada Conference, several of whom have been already described. Religion found him a playful lad, with an ordinary English education, learning a mechanic art, in a country village or small sized town. A thirst for knowledge and zeal of usefulness were the immediate results. His gifts are exercised and his time improved in study. Soon is he "put on the PLAN," as a local preacher. Now a call comes across the broad Atlantic, to come and help on the work of God in Canada. He comes and finds immediate employment. His labors are made instrumental to the Salvation of souls; and he performs his "Conference course of study" satisfactorily. No sooner is he ordained, than he is put in charge of a circuit, in which he has been ever since; and he has succeeded to admiration. He has worked his way up into such appointments as St. Thomas, Brockville, and Port Hope. He proves himself the clever, varied, poetically eloquent, and yet soul-saving preacher; excels as a pastor and manager, and raise his circuits numerically, financially, and religiously. Is firm and unflinching in the exercise of discipline. He maintains, very justly his pastoral prerogative: and the John Bull sturdiness with which it is done, is the only feature about it that ever lays his administration open to exception. "Take him all for all" there are few more valuable ministers than he. His surname is identical with that of another member of the Conference—an elderly man, a preacher of Canadian growth, strong and compact in physical structure, very laborious, and successful too, like our present subject: but very dissimilar to this one in other respects. By this time it will be discovered we are writing of RICHARD WHITING.

How rapidly does time fly! On looking for his *status*, we find that this brother, whom we have always thought of as one of our *young* men, has entered the *fifteenth* year of his itinerancy. His age, therefore, though he does not look so old, must be about *thirty-seven*. The church of Christ may yet expect much from his labors. May continued prosperity attend one for whom we have ever felt a great partiality.

www.ingramcontent.com/pod-product-compliance
Lightning Source LLC
Chambersburg PA
CBHW021157230426
43667CB00006B/431